LOONS

OF NEW HAMPSHIRE

Preserving a Natural Treasure

GLENN A. KNOBLOCK

Foreword by Harry S. Vogel

Senior Biologist & Director, Loon Preservation Committee

THE
History
PRESS

Published by The History Press
Charleston, SC
www.historypress.com

First published 2024

Manufactured in the United States

ISBN 9781467155434

Library of Congress Control Number: 2024931453

Courtesy of Nancy Masterson.

This book is dedicated to Cathy Butman Eastburn (1967–2023) of Orford. She is sorely missed by her family and friends, but her spirit lives on in all the loons that she has monitored, nurtured, protected and helped rescue on the Bakers. She was a true friend to her local loon population, as well as all wild birds. The accompanying photo shows Cathy, a "hardy soul," holding a loon for the first time after helping to rescue it from the ice in December 2021. When next you hear the beautiful call of the loons on the Bakers, please offer Cathy a silent word of thanks for helping to preserve this natural legacy.

CONTENTS

Foreword, by Harry S. Vogel, Senior Biologist and Director,
    Loon Preservation Committee   7
Acknowledgements   11
Introduction   15

PART I. GETTING TO KNOW *GAVIA IMMER*   19
  1. Physical Traits of the Loon   23
  2. Sight, Hearing and the Mind of the Loon   33
  3. The Calls of the Loon   41
  4. The Loon Habitat and Feeding and Maintenance Activities   45
  5. The Loon's Place in Nature's Food Chain   52
  6. Loon Territorial and Social Interactions   56
  7. Starting a Loon Family   66
  8. Raising Loon Chicks   80
  9. The Mysterious Lives of Immature Loons   87
  10. Loon Longevity   90

PART II. SAVING OUR NEW HAMPSHIRE LOONS   95
  1. The Loon and Its Slow Decline   97
  2. Rawson Wood and the Loon Preservation Committee
    to the Rescue, 1975–81   121
  3. Setting the Groundwork for the Long Term, 1981–97   136
  4. The Loon Preservation Committee Expands Its Mission,
    1997–Present   157

CONTENTS

5. Keepers of the Loons: The Men and Women of Today's LPC
   and Working Partnerships   190
6. Loon Threats Now and Hopes for the Future   211
7. Unraveling the Secrets of the Loon   232

PART III. NEW HAMPSHIRE LAKE ACCOUNTS   243
   1. Adventures with the Loons of Barnstead   245
   2. A Loon Pond Which Shall Remain Nameless   252
   3. The Loons of Upper and Lower Baker Ponds   256
   4. The Big-City Loons of Lake Massabesic   262
   5. A Curious Case on Wolfeboro's Back Bay   266
   6. A Little Gem in the Monadnock Region   275

About the Organization   281
Bibliography and Further Reading   283
About the Author   288

FOREWORD

I f you are fascinated by loons—and I will guess that you are if you are reading this—you are in good company. Native Americans listened to loons calling on brand-new lakes at the edge of retreating glaciers in what is now New Hampshire 13,000 years ago. The connection then was practical: loons were food, clothing and ornamentation—but also something more. Some tribes considered the haunting calls of loons as exactly that: the voices of slain warriors calling back to the living. The rich mythology that has surrounded these birds for millennia demonstrates our long-standing captivation with them.

The arrival of European settlers changed everything, of course, including our relationship with loons. Now they were seen as competitors for fish as well as prizes for collectors of skins, feathers and eggs. The life history characteristics of loons (see Glenn's first few chapters) made them particularly sensitive to these insults, and over decades and centuries, these practices and other unhelpful human activities took their toll. By 1975, loons were absent from Massachusetts and in danger of disappearing from New Hampshire. Our lakes were unnaturally quiet places then.

The Loon Preservation Committee (LPC) was a response to the dramatic and ongoing decline of loons in New Hampshire. Our founders reasoned that if human activities had played a role in those declines, then our activities, if they were thoughtful and coordinated, could reverse them. It was a daunting undertaking with no assurance of success and maybe even some expectation of failure; no one had tried anything remotely like it before. At least one prominent New Hampshire wildlife biologist gave LPC all of three years before it was relegated to the dust heap of good intentions.

The things we didn't know about loons in those days could fill a book—they still could today—but with many missteps and setbacks, LPC's stubbornly persistent staff and a growing corps of dedicated members and volunteers began to make a dent in the issues facing loons. We floated nesting rafts made of wood and mud to mimic loon nesting habitat, and loons took to our rickety rafts and began to hatch chicks from them. We put signs around nesting loons to protect them from the close approach of people and researched other threats and ways to counter them. We talked to anyone who would listen about loons and their challenges. Those were simpler times in many ways, with simpler problems; flame retardants, stain-repellant chemicals, wake boats and climate change still lay far in our future. Today, our research represents the longest and most complete study of any loon population, a record that becomes more valuable with each passing year. Our management is recognized as the most comprehensive, innovative and successful of loon conservation efforts anywhere, and our educational activities have helped to fundamentally change the way people view loons and their place in our world. We have plenty of loons in our freezers or under glass at the Loon Center as proof of our failures to save them from their various and increasing trials. But we also have a growing number of loons on our lakes—more than four times as many as when we started—as evidence of our successes.

As we learned about loons and their challenges, we discovered that they are uniquely able to illuminate threats to other wildlife and to the aquatic environments on which we all depend. So, we expanded LPC's mission to monitor the health and productivity of loon populations as sentinels of environmental quality. Today we are working on projects, and with partners, that we could hardly have imagined at the start of our work to help loons.

Despite our efforts and our progress in recovering New Hampshire's loon population, the loon remains a threatened species in our state and faces many challenges. Our growing human population will continue to make wild places and quiet spaces harder to find, and we will need to find creative solutions to help loons survive. The world has shrunk in the past five decades; today we are aware of the smallness of our planet and the interconnectedness of all things. New perils like climate change are providing compelling evidence of our effects on our world, with potentially grave consequences for humans and wildlife.

It's hard to imagine that one small organization protecting one species of bird in one of these United States could have much of an impact on that vast challenge. But over the past 50 or so years we have shown that we can change the fortunes of loons. And our work extends far beyond loons and far beyond New Hampshire. When the Loon Preservation Committee was formed, it was a voice in the wilderness for a voice in the wilderness. Since then, our success has inspired the creation of statewide, regional and even international organizations to help loons, and our efforts continue to benefit other species that depend on functioning ecosystems.

This book celebrates loons and our relationship with them, with all of its ups and downs. It's a twisting and turning and unfinished story, and I hope it will have a worthy ending. Their challenges continue to grow in number and scope, but the unlikely and welcome result of our work is that our loons are persisting, with the chance to thrive. Our goals remain the same as when we began our work in 1975: a bright future for loons and other wildlife that need clean water and quiet places, and a real and substantive renewal of the spirit of these northern lakes. Thank you to all those who had the vision and resolve to spark and nurture that improbable dream and give it a chance to be realized.

Harry S. Vogel, Senior Biologist and Director
Loon Preservation Committee
Moultonborough, New Hampshire
April 30, 2023

ACKNOWLEDGEMENTS

First and foremost, many thanks to Senior Biologist Harry Vogel and his staff at the Loon Preservation Committee for seeing the merit in this book project and agreeing to participate and offer their loon expertise during my research. While any errors that may have crept into this work are solely of my own making, LPC biologists Tiffany Grade, Caroline Hughes and Vogel did signal work in reviewing all the loon facts in the book and keeping me on the straight and narrow, with Grade providing in addition her expertise on Squam in detailed fashion. Biologists Betsy McCoy and Linda Egli Johnson were especially helpful in reviewing my account of the LPC's early years, with Johnson being a very helpful, kind and enthusiastic go-to person for other varying matters. Senior biologist John Cooley Jr. was an excellent source of information during our many loon conversations, and it was exciting to see him at work during a routine (to him!) rescue. Additional thanks go to Caroline Hughes for letting me take part in the ocean release of a rescued loon. I can easily see how that experience never grows old! Data technician Joan Plevich was a huge help. Once John Cooley put me in touch with her at the very beginning of my research at the LPC, she promptly and happily answered my every query and request for loon data, which information adds immeasurably to this book. Kirsten Knell was quite efficient in digging out some archival materials in the form of photos and news articles. Finally, a big thanks to Trustee David Govatski, with whom I consulted on my history of the Kancamagus Highway, for encouraging Harry Vogel to hear my proposal on this project, thereby getting him onboard and making this book a reality.

My thanks to many LPC alumni and partners who agreed to be interviewed for this book and provided valuable insights, as well as several other key contributors: Jeff Fair, Palmer, Alaska, an enthusiastic supporter, and loon spiritual guide of sorts, encouraged me to interview many of the folks below and reviewed the manuscript; his encouragement has made this project much less daunting than I first thought it might be. Scott Sutcliffe, Trumansburg, New York, for his excellent information and insights into the LPC's formative years, its work and early personnel; Jack Noon, Sutton, New Hampshire, for details about his work on Lake Umbagog and his unique perspective; Ralph Kirshner, Meredith, New Hampshire, for the details of his work in the LPC's early years and his candid and forthright comments; Connie Manville Johnson, Center Harbor, New Hampshire, for details of her early career with the LPC; Dr. Mark Pokras, Scarborough, Maine, for details of his veterinary career and loon expertise in conjunction with the LPC, as well as allowing me to attend one of his necropsies. Having heard Mark was working on his own loon book, I was somewhat hesitant to seek his input, but he quickly dispelled that notion and was a most friendly resource; Kate Taylor, Portland, Maine, for details of her career and insights into the LPC's operations during her tenure; Kappy Sprenger, Bridgeton, Maine, for a highly interesting and entertaining talk about her career as a wildlife rehabilitator. I now know more about loon defecation than I ever thought possible and am somehow the better for it; Maria Colby, Henniker, New Hampshire, Wings Wildlife Rehabilitation, for details of her interesting career as a wildlife rehabilitator and LPC collaboration; Ellen Barth, San Francisco, California, the daughter of LPC founder Rawson Wood, for details and insights of her father's career and character, as well as his early loon activities; Bill Gassman, Moultonborough, New Hampshire, for a very illuminating and interesting talk about his work with the LPC's LoonCam operations from the very beginning; Lin O'Bara, Laconia, New Hampshire, for details of her career with the NALF and LPC, as well as insights into Rawson Wood; Rebecca Suomala, senior biologist, New Hampshire Audubon, Concord, New Hampshire, for her help during my visit to their archives at the McLane Center; Matthew Thomas, Fremont town historian and friend, who reminded me of his town's Loon Pond.

Big thanks go out to the individuals who have contributed photographs—some of the best loon photos you will ever see—for this work. Some of these individuals are far more than wildlife photographers—many of them work, or have done so in the past, as LPC volunteers or field biologists on their lakes and are true citizen scientists who watch over their loons. Each of these contributors provided their stunning photographs enthusiastically and without compensation, doing so in the cause of the LPC and its continued conservation work; Brian J. Reilly, Keene, New Hampshire, former LPC board member and trustee who also gave insights into the ponds he has frequented; Nordell and Beth Gagnon, Madison, New Hampshire; Cathy Eastburn, Orford, New Hampshire, who provided many excellent accounts of her loons and is a kindred spirit with whom I look forward to further loon discussions; Catherine Holland, Hanover, New Hampshire, who also put me in touch with Cathy Eastburn; Rick and Libby Libbey (yes, really!) of MooseMan Nature Photography (https://www.moosemannaturephotos.com), who offered great details and insights into their favorite loon haunts and whose photos are also available for purchase both online and at the LPC's Loon's Feather Gift Shop; John Wilson, New London, New Hampshire, whose late wife, Kittie Wilson, took many spectacular pictures of loons over the years, many of which have been reproduced in the LPC's newsletters and in calendars that were sold to benefit the LPC's work. She was a beloved LPC volunteer, a kind soul and a true friend to New Hampshire's loon population; Jon Winslow, Dover, New Hampshire, who also gave his interesting account of an eagle versus loon confrontation on Bow Lake; Emily Turteltaub Nelson, Ipswich, Massachusetts; Brett Hillman, wildlife biologist, USFS, White Mountain National Forest, Campton, New Hampshire; Brooks Campbell, Wolfeboro, New Hampshire, who not only provided me with many photos but also offered his own loon experiences in Wolfeboro's Back Bay. It's because of Brooks that we now know more about the far-ranging loon that has resided there of late.

I'd also like to thank those countless people with whom I've come into contact during the course of writing and researching this book, as well as tracking my Back Bay loon here in Wolfeboro. I appreciate their enthusiasm and support for an obviously popular topic. Knowing that there many people out there eagerly awaiting this book is a nice inspiration for an author! I also thank my co-workers for putting up with my loon obsession at times. I'm the boss, so I guess they have to listen, but I was surprised that several of them were also loon observers in their outside activities, and so our loon talk has been a much-needed distraction from everyday work matters.

Once again, acquisition editor Mike Kinsella at The History Press was a vital partner in making this book happen. Not only did he enthusiastically support the project from the outset and recognize its worth, but he also championed it at every turn, even when it grew in size and scope beyond what was originally planned. I thank him for that!

Finally, I must thank my family for their support: my brother-in-law and best friend, Dave Wemmer, who has accompanied me on many kayak outings on the Suncooks and, as usual, lent his photography expertise and some outstanding pictures of his own; my grandson Gordon Knoblock, who accompanied me on many loon spotting expeditions throughout 2022 (he calls the Wolfeboro Back Bay loon "Diver") and, at eight years old, has become a birder like his grandpa, with his good ear probably a better one soon enough; and, saving the best for last, my wife, Terry Knoblock, who has always supported me in my every endeavor, not just in my career as an author and historian but in every phase of our 42 years together, raising a family and supporting our daughter, Anna. None of this could be done without her.

Glenn A. Knoblock
Wolfeboro Falls, New Hampshire
May 10, 2023

INTRODUCTION

The common loon, simply put, is one of New Hampshire's most iconic wildlife symbols, ranking, perhaps, only second to the moose. Whether you're a kayaker or canoeist, boater or angler, a shorefront or beachfront observer, chances are you've heard or seen one or more loons while out on the waters of one of New Hampshire's hundreds of ponds or lakes or somewhere nearby. No matter what your encounter, whether by sight or sound, this magnificent bird is a marvel to behold. And yet, it's a bird of mystery in a way, one that relatively few know a great deal about and one, frankly, that is often taken for granted. There are two sides to our knowledge of the common loon, the first being that of the physical traits of the bird itself, its habits and life-cycle events, the more scientific stuff if you will. The loon has been studied in New Hampshire since the mid-1970s, as you shall discover in these pages, and what has been learned from field observations, conservation efforts and actual handling has been fascinating and has increased our overall store of knowledge exponentially. Still, there is yet much to know about this bird, and the loon does not always reveal its secrets quickly or easily. This book, whether you're an avid birder, boater or shoreside observer, offers up some of the lesser-known aspects of the loon and even busts a few myths along the way. As this was written with the general reader in mind, what you discover in these pages will enhance your knowledge of our loons and their population in New Hampshire and, accompanied by stunning pictures by contributors from all over the state, will make you appreciate this wildlife icon even more.

The second part of our loon knowledge in New Hampshire concerns the presence, and numbers, of the bird itself, from pre-colonial times down to the present, and how our attitudes toward the common loon have changed. Sure, it's a beloved symbol of the wild in the Granite State for many today, but it wasn't always that way, and many may be surprised to learn how the common loon progressed in our state from an abundant bird to its current status as a threatened species. Indeed, we should understand that the loon's history here is also a cautionary tale, for it is one of our "sentinel" species in New Hampshire: its rise or fall is a predictor of things happening and of things to come, the proverbial "canary in a coal mine." Like it or not, what humankind does has an impact on our planet, and some of these effects have come at the expense of our loon population. It's an interesting story, and a sad one in many aspects, but in New Hampshire it's also a story of guarded hope and optimism. With the formation of the Loon Preservation Committee—the first organization of its kind in the world devoted to the conservation of this bird species—in 1975 by a man named Rawson Wood, the common loon has now been a restored presence in many bodies of water in our state. The story of this grassroots nonprofit organization, which will receive half of the net proceeds from the sale of this book, is one that is not well known by many, but it should be, for its formation has had wide-ranging consequences, spurring on loon conservation efforts far beyond New Hampshire's borders. Without the efforts of this organization, I believe it is fair to state that our loon population in New Hampshire might now be nearly extinct.

As to the genesis for this book, it came from my desire to know more about New Hampshire's loon population and its history. I first became acquainted with loons when I moved to Wolfeboro many years ago. Little did I realize that I would encounter loons close up and personal on the water. With these increasing encounters, I wanted to know more about this amazing bird and its presence in our state. Searching quickly proved there wasn't much to be found in book form. Biologists Judith McIntyre (a pioneer in the field of loon studies) and James Paruk have published detailed books on the subject, the first a classic, but their experiences mostly covered Minnesota and Canada (where there are many more loons) and give New Hampshire only brief mention. Of course, there are a number of loon picture books available, many with stunning photographs, but these are not the sources for the full story of our state. As both a historian and a birder, I decided to rectify this situation, and in close cooperation with the Loon Preservation Committee, as well as many contributing photographers, the book you now hold in your hands is the end result. The key emphasis in this book is the New Hampshire experience, and to that end, I've included many eyewitness observations of loon activity, both normal and on the unusual side, that have taken place on our lakes and ponds. Perhaps even your own favorite body of water is given mention! Many of these observations come from experienced Loon Preservation Committee biologists, who have been loon-watching for the past 47 years, but also normal folks like you and I who just love loons and have happened to be in the right place at the right (or wrong) time. While it was not feasible for this book to cover all the hundreds of lakes and ponds in the state that have had loon activity, the wide range of those mentioned herein gives an accurate portrayal of the state of the loon, so to speak, in the Granite State as of early 2023.

If you're already a loon-lover, I hope this work enhances your enjoyment of this incredible species. If you're just starting out, whether with loons or as a birder at large, I hope it serves as an inspiration to make your own loon memories and, perhaps, to even get involved with conservation efforts on their behalf. Whether by our actions or our contributions (which you do by purchasing this book!), the loons in New Hampshire, and the Loon Preservation Committee by extension, continue to need our help in conserving this Granite State treasure. Please visit the LPC's website for further information and details at https://loon.org/supportlpc/.

A Note to the Reader

Because this work is published in the United States and will be largely read by an American general audience, all weights and measures figures are stated in U.S. customary units (pounds, miles and so forth) rather than the metric system used by the scientific community in America and the entire rest of the world.

All New Hampshire–specific loon information comes from unpublished Loon Preservation Committee (LPC) gathered data sources or from interviews with LPC biologists unless otherwise cited. All other published sources may be found listed in the bibliography.

All photos in this book are of loons sighted in New Hampshire waters— the lake is identified in most cases, and when no location is given, it is in deference to the sensitivity of the nesting sites on that body of water.

In order to avoid needless repetition, the Loon Preservation Committee is referenced by its initials, LPC, throughout this work.

Unless otherwise indicated, the term *loon* in this book refers to the common loon, one of five loon species and the only one that makes New Hampshire its home.

Details for the published sources cited in this work may be found at the end of the book. All quoted information from the following individuals is based on personal interviews and correspondence conducted between the fall of 2022 and summer of 2023, unless otherwise noted: Jeff Fair, Scott Sutcliffe, Ralph Kirshner, Ellen Barth, Connie Manville Johnson, Kate Taylor, Mark Pokras, Lin O'Bara, Bill Gassman, Kappy Sprenger, Maria Colby, Jack Noon, Cathy Eastburn, Rick Libbey and Brian Reilly. Quoted material from current LPC staff members, including Harry Vogel, John Cooley Jr., Linda Egli Johnson, Caroline Hughes, Tiffany Grade and Betsy McCoy, is from our personal communications unless otherwise noted.

PART I

GETTING TO KNOW *GAVIA IMMER*

The loon is easily recognizable in its breeding plumage when seen on New Hampshire's lakes and ponds, but it is also an elusive bird, here one moment and gone the next. Some of its daily activities take place close to the shoreline, but many others take place either underwater, farther offshore or even at night. Because these aspects of its life are less commonly witnessed by the general public, the loon is ofttimes viewed as a mysterious creature. In this section, we'll take a simple look at the physiology of the loon and offer up some details and examples about its daily and seasonal behaviors. Once you know more about this bird, that sense of mystery is replaced with one of wonder or awe.

The loon has a long history as a species, although it is not as old or ancient as is commonly thought. Though bird-like dinosaurs existed well over 150 million years ago, the loon doesn't date back this far, and there are a number of birds today that are much older than the loon, including the kiwis of New Zealand and the southern cassowary of Australia. However, the loon is no spring chicken, so to speak, and fossil remnants (none found in New Hampshire) indicate that its lineage dates back at least 1 million years ago and possibly as far back as close to 4 million years. Today, loons are in a family (Gaviidae) of diving birds all on their own. There are five species of loons, only two of which appear frequently in New Hampshire waters or off its coastline. The arctic loon (*Gavia arctica*) is found in northern European or Asian waters and has only been rarely found as a vagrant here, one being sighted on January 6, 1985, just south of Odiorne Point in Rye, a loon hot spot. The yellow-billed loon (*Gavia adamsii*) breeds in northern Canada and Russia and winters in the United States off the Pacific Northwest coast up to Alaska, as well as the western coast of Norway and north coast of Japan. It has never

A loon pair on a northern New Hampshire lake. *Courtesy Nordel Gagnon.*

been reported in New Hampshire and, in general, is the largest of the five loon species. However, though it is the largest in terms of length, this loon and the common loons of New Hampshire are very close in terms of weight to each other. This loon is known for its yellow beak, which is the longest of all the loon species.

Two other loon species can be found along the New Hampshire coast, one as a stray and one as a regular migrant. The small Pacific loon (*Gavia pacifica*) is primarily found on the West Coast of the United States, as well as northern Canada and into Siberia. However, single migrants blown off course have made their appearance in our state from time to time. The first mention of this loon is found in the ornithological journal *The Auk*, which mentions a specimen that was shot at Hampton Beach in May 1910. In recent times, *New Hampshire Bird Records*, compiled by the New Hampshire Audubon Society, noted a stray Pacific loon that was sighted off the Rye Ledges on June 14, 1986, while another lingered for several days off the New Hampshire coast at Pulpit Rocks in Rye beginning on July 10, 2004. Another of this species was seen off Rye on October 31, 2005, and again off Pulpit Rocks on May 15, 2007, a rarity as it was in breeding plumage. Additional single sightings have been made in 2009 (Rye), 2012 (Hampton Harbor), 2013 (Rye, Odiorne Point), 2014 (New Castle) and one in breeding plumage in May 2019 (Rye). Perhaps due to climate change, the Pacific loon has become an "increasing visitor," even if the numbers are small. It should be noted that it's no coincidence that the town of Rye is a place where many unusual bird sightings, loons included, occur. It is New Hampshire's easternmost town, and its coastal location is along major bird migration routes, making it a birding hot spot.

The red-throated loon (*Gavia stellata*) is a regular migrant that appears off the New Hampshire coast in numbers while on the move and, occasionally, on inland waters in very small numbers. It is the smallest of the loon species, weighing no more than about six pounds, and is known for its red throat patch when in its breeding plumage, though when spotted in New Hampshire waters it is usually seen in its non-breeding plumage, which more resembles that of a common loon in winter plumage. These loons breed in the Arctic but spend their winters in northern coastal waters on both the American Atlantic and Pacific coasts, as well as in Europe and Asia. *New Hampshire Bird Records* mentions many fall migration sightings of this diminutive beauty off the New Hampshire coast, including over 1,000 during a three-day period in late October 2008 and a record count of 1,625 off Great Boar's Head in Rye on November 10, 2013. Inland sightings are much rarer, usually migrants that have gone off course in the western part of the state, and almost always occur in the fall. Summer sightings are rare— one lone example was spotted twice on Squam Lake from late June to late July in 2017, a first since one spent nine days on Squam in July 1967. Single example sightings in the fall include one on the Connecticut River at Hinsdale in November 1987; on Gile Pond in Sutton and Mascoma Lake in Enfield in 1994; Mascoma, Sunapee and Newfound Lakes in 2012; and an unusual vagrant in March 2018 that was found at the city of Rochester's wastewater treatment plant, a popular birding site. These sightings of the red-throated loon are brief, as New Hampshire is not its migration destination, but they are an impressive sight, whether viewed in large numbers from afar or single birds close up and personal.

Finally, there is the common loon (*Gavia immer*), which counts the lakes and ponds of New Hampshire among its many (yet shrinking) breeding summer homes in the United States and is the subject of this book from here on out. Its breeding range is large,

Red-throated loon in winter plumage, off Hampton Beach State Park, Hampton, November 2022. *Courtesy Emily Turteltaub Nelson.*

ranging from the northern United States and most of Canada to even farther north into Greenland. So, let's take a closer look at this bird and its physical traits and characteristics, many detailed by the biologists at the LPC based on their expertise and New Hampshire field studies from 1975 down to the present, as well as Cornell University's Ornithology Lab's authoritative publication, *Birds of the World.*

1

PHYSICAL TRAITS OF THE LOON

BODY SIZE

The size and weight of our New Hampshire loons are basic aspects of their appearance that can be hard to determine at first sight. When viewing from afar, it is difficult to gain a sense of their size. However, even when seen close up, say from a kayak or canoe, a true gauge of these measurements can also be challenging depending on the bird's activities. Loons in the United States can weigh anywhere from just under 5 pounds to over 16.5 pounds, with males being larger than females by about 20 to 25 percent, and measure anywhere from 26 to 36 inches long. However, those found in New England, especially Maine and New Hampshire, are on the far end of this spectrum. Thus, it is that, though otherwise equal to their relatives in such midwestern states as Minnesota and Michigan, New Hampshire loons are distinguished by their "very large" size compared to other loons. The reason for this is quite simple—evolution. Loons in the upper Midwest, for example, migrate to wintering grounds in the southern states or in the Gulf of Mexico and often have to fly over 1,000 miles to get to their winter destinations. Their lower body mass means they require less energy to successfully make that grueling trip than would be required of a larger loon. On the other hand, New Hampshire loons typically migrate to New England coastal waters to spend their winters, a much shorter distance. For example, the trip from Lake Winnipesaukee to the New Hampshire coast is less than 70 miles, while from Lake Umbagog in Errol to the Gulf of Maine is a slightly longer trip of about 100 miles. Less time, effort and energy are required to make these journeys, nature thereby allowing these birds to maintain a larger mass. The size of our New Hampshire loons, indeed, is impressive when fully realized, especially when compared to our other familiar waterfowl birds. For example, a well-fed juvenile male loon rescued on Partridge Lake in Littleton in December 2022 by the LPC measured in at 10.19 pounds. In contrast, a full-grown male mallard or common merganser duck (the latter sometimes mistaken for a loon from a distance) each weighs about 4 pounds on average.

PLUMAGE

The loon's summer plumage is its most distinguishing physical aspect and the one most familiar to casual observers. And for good reasons, for it is a strikingly beautiful bird. However, the loon is a bird of several seasons, and its look changes over the course of a year's time. At birth, loon chicks are covered with a blackish-gray down that quickly dries after hatching, with white down on the belly. After several weeks, a "second down" replaces this; it is shorter, less dense and more brownish-gray in appearance. By about two months of age, the down is entirely gone, replaced by its first juvenile plumage. This pattern consists of a white belly and grayish-brown feathers above, with the upper body feathers having a scalloped pattern, with the tips of the feathers being grayish-white. As for the head, the feathers on the cheek and on the throat are grayish-white in appearance, with these same colors appearing around the neck in the area where the "necklace" pattern will develop as an adult. In essence, though the bird at this stage is less striking, you can see the coming future in its feather patterns. Juvenile loons retain this less colorful plumage for two years, molting at various intervals, before adult plumage appears. Interestingly, biologists even today are not in full agreement on the matter of timing, and among some loons there may be an "alternate" plumage phase for another two years before the basic adult plumage appears. One other interesting possibility when it comes to aging first-year juveniles versus older juveniles, though not definitively studied or proven, is their feather patterning. Dr. Mark Pokras, commenting during a loon necropsy at the LPC in early 2023, noted that first-year juveniles had feather patterns on their bodies where the tips show a more rounded

Loon chick, Lower Baker Pond, Orford/Wentworth, June 2022. *Courtesy Cathy Eastburn.*

appearance, while those of older juveniles tended to show a more squared-off look indicative of their future adult plumage.

Once a juvenile has grown into an adult, the loon has two main plumages; its presentation from March through September is the one that everyone knows best. The head and neck are a jet-black color, with a greenish or purplish gloss, depending on the light. The forward part of the upper neck has a line of white spots, anywhere from 6 to 12 in number, that is often referred to as the "chinstrap," while at the base of the neck is a band of alternating white and black stripes, narrowest at the forward part of the neck and broadest at the back of the neck. This band comes close to meeting in the front where it tapers down in size, but does not completely meet, and is often referred to, especially in Native American lore, as the "necklace" of the loon. On the breast of the bird close to the waterline, there is also an alternating band of white and black stripes that borders the black neck, the white breast and the white spotted sides. The underbody of the loon is completely white, thought to be a camouflage against underwater predators. The upper body has a lot going on—most feathers have two white patches on them. These are round and small at the rear of the loon and on the sides but increase in size going forward and are rectangular in shape, appearing in rows on the top of the wings (the scapulars). All these elements come together to make for a stunning bird that, once seen, cannot be forgotten. Now, as to the reason for this distinct patterning, biologists really don't know the full answer. It may, perhaps, serve as a form of camouflage from predators above, the spotting pattern perhaps mimicking the various slants of light that occur on the tips of wind-whipped waves. According to the LPC, it may also serve as camouflage for nesting loons, as it breaks up the outline of a bird that is incubating, making it more difficult to see. Or perhaps there is something in loons to be seen that cannot be detected by the human eye? It's a fact that it it's nearly impossible, even for biologists, to distinguish adult female loons from male loons in the wild, except under several specific and fleeting circumstances (to be discussed later), as all have the same plumage. So, the exact reason for their plumage pattern remains a mystery.

The second main plumage of the loon, the one less seen by New Hampshire tourists and seasonal visitors, is present from October through February. By the end of summer, the spectacular plumage begins to fade and is replaced by a more subdued pattern with wing feathers that are a mix of white, gray, black and brownish-black in color. While the change is noticeable all over, its beginnings are distinctive, beginning on the head, just

Juvenile loon spreading its wings, September 2022, Post Pond, Lyme. *Courtesy Catherine Holland.*

behind the base of the beak. Here, the feathers drop and are replaced by new feathers that are light gray in appearance. During this change, the loon's facial appearance has a grizzled old man look, as if it's aging before our very eyes, as the feathers on the cheek and throat are also replaced by new light gray feathers. Likewise, the feathers around the eyes also change; while the top of the head will remain a blackish-gray, there develops a bright ring of white around the loon's eyes. As for the body of the loon in this plumage phase, the primary and secondary feathers remain black with white spots, though this is seldom seen by casual observers because the wings are folded. One may wonder why these feathers do not molt at this time of the year like the others. Interestingly, as was explained to me by the LPC's senior biologist Harry Vogel, these feathers are the only ones on a loon that are molted once a year because they are the bird's largest feathers and are all protein, therefore requiring a large amount of energy to replace. In fact, in this phase it is difficult to distinguish an adult loon from a juvenile except for these trailing edge feathers, as they otherwise look similar to one another. The feathers are a pale brownish-black with white tips, though the faded rectangular pattern is easily visible. It is interesting to note that in the late fall, many casual observers are unaware of this change in the loon's appearance and often mistake those loons that hang around after summer is over as a different kind of bird entirely. At this time of the year, when our weather has begun to turn and the summer is but a pleasant memory, though our loons have lost their flourish, they nonetheless remain, at close inspection, a beautiful bird to behold.

Finally, like all other birds, loons grow new feathers every year in a process referred to as "molting." This process of growing new feathers is important, as it replaces worn-out feathers with stronger, newer ones so that they can both keep optimum flight performance and stay warm during the winter. Adult loons undergo two phases of molting during the course of the year. As summer comes to an end in New Hampshire, by October they begin the process on their bodies, subsequently beginning their wing molt about mid-January, per LPC data. This typically takes place after their migration to New England coastal waters, their nonbreeding wintering grounds, and is a critical time in their annual life cycle. Because they molt their wing feathers all at the same time, loons are rendered flightless during the several-week period when new flight feathers are emerging and are more vulnerable because of the large amount of energy required for the process. For loons that have made their migration, this process is nonfatal, as they can swim and dive for food (ocean waters off the coast of New England don't freeze)

A loon beginning its fall molt. Note the graying around the eye, October 2018, Back Bay, Wolfeboro. *Courtesy Brooks Campbell.*

and they are less vulnerable to predators. However, worldwide climate change has affected our loons here in New Hampshire. In those years where the early winter weather is mild, some of our New Hampshire lakes, especially Lake Winnipesaukee, do not freeze over early on, resulting in large areas of open water. This can cause loons on the lake to linger longer than they should before migrating, or the open water can attract migrating loons passing through the area on the way to their wintering grounds. Some of these loons, if on the lake in January, may begin the wing molt process, rendering them unable to fly. However, all it takes is several days of extreme cold to cause lake waters to flash freeze, greatly reducing the amount of open water and icing in the loon, affecting its feeding options and leaving it vulnerable to predators. Once this occurs, the results are almost always fatal, unless the loon is rescued by the LPC. This situation has occurred many times on a number of lakes over the years, with notable instances on Lake Winnipesaukee in 2007 and 2022. These incidents often have tragic consequences, and the months of December through February have become increasingly concerning to those safeguarding our loon population. For those adult loons safely on their ocean wintering grounds, once the molting process is completed, they have their colorful breeding plumage again before heading back to New Hampshire's lakes and ponds after ice-out has occurred, usually from late March to early May at the latest.

How the loon gets around, whether on land, in water or in the air, is yet another fascinating example of this bird's unique adaptations and varying abilities. The loon, or great northern diver as it is sometimes called, is a champion swimmer, one of the most skilled birds of its type, and its feet and legs are what make it happen. The loon, though it can survive on land for a short period of time, spends most of its time on the water, both fresh and saltwater, and is uniquely suited to its environment. Though many inexperienced birdwatchers consider loons to be akin to a duck, they are actually, according to biologist James Paruk and others, more closely related to penguins based on a study of their DNA. Like the penguin, loons are excellent divers and swimmers, and their feet, located at the far rear portion of their body, aid them greatly in this endeavor. This positioning, however, makes them extremely ungainly on land. This is because much of their limb structure is located within the body cavity itself, including the hip and knee joints, and is not covered by skin, thus limiting the bird's upright movement. Chicks can walk upright until about three weeks of age; this ability disappears as their bodies grow and develop for life in the water. Adult loons typically go on land only to copulate and to prepare and occupy their nests. In other circumstances, often when ill or after being injured in a conflict with another loon, they beach themselves on dry land. While loons can move on land, sometimes aided by their wings if stressed, the distances documented have been well under a mile, and more often these distances are measured in feet. Either way, their survival on land in these circumstances is limited at best, since they are extremely vulnerable to land predators. Loons also do not have the ability to fly from land and only take to the skies from the water. However, wayward loons sometimes land on the ground by accident, in some cases likely mistaking the wet, black pavement on our roads as a body of water. This has occurred a number of times over the years in New Hampshire—sometimes with bad outcomes, but not always. In August 2008, in the town of Lee, a police officer reported an injured loon he found on the side of a road to the LPC. Field biologist Chris Conrod subsequently picked up the bird, discovering that the officer thought that the loon was injured because it could not move very well. Fortunately, an examination revealed that the bird was fine and it was soon after released on nearby Wheelwright Pond. Yet another loon crash-landed on dry land along Route 4 in Rollinsford in May 2015 and

Loon feathers, 2013. *Photo by Kittie Wilson, courtesy John Wilson.*

lived to tell the tale with help from locals and the LPC. Perhaps the most interesting incident of this kind occurred in the summer of 2017 along busy I-93 in the town of Lincoln, where a loon was spotted on the side of the highway. Motorists Jim Kegley and George and Sandy Frost stopped to help, and with the aid of the Lincoln Police Department, the loon was recovered by the LPC. It was subsequently released in a local body of water. In each of these cases, had these loons not been helped by good Samaritans and the LPC, they likely would not have survived.

Loon Locomotion

The webbed foot of the loon is large, and the leg, unlike many birds, is flat in its bone structure rather than round, the skin covering being tough and leathery, albeit smooth. The leg is grayish-black in color, the web being either a pale white or light pink in color when in their basic plumage and black when in their breeding plumage. Having seen several examples, both on live and deceased loons, their legs remind me of a paddle. Indeed, the loon can maneuver expertly underwater, zigzagging to catch its prey at high speed if needed. The loon can stay underwater for as long as 10 minutes in extreme situations, but most dives last less than a minute or two at the very most; they are able to dive to depths of 200 feet. The duration of their dives is directly related to the depth of the water in which they are operating, which makes long-duration loon dives in any New Hampshire lake extremely unlikely. Lake Winnipesaukee, for example, is just under 200 feet at maximum depth but averages less than 50 feet in depth in most areas. So, if a loon you've been observing dives and you lose sight of him for more than a few minutes, it's more than likely that he's already surfaced (and perhaps even dived again) in another direction out of your line of sight, rather than having stayed underwater the whole time. Being fast swimmers, loons can go quite the distance underwater in even a minute if they perceive your presence as a threat! In the water, loons control their buoyancy by regulating the air sacs in their bodies and often sit low in the water between diving bouts for food. Loons start their dives by thrusting their legs and likewise end their dives by using their feet to move them to the surface.

Interestingly, unlike most birds, whose bones are hollow and filled with air, the bones of the loon are denser, thus allowing them to dive quickly. This feat is also aided by their ability to flatten their feathers quickly in order to expel

The foot waggle, Back Bay, Wolfeboro, November 2022. Note the bands on this loon's leg. *Author photo.*

the air in their plumage. It's no wonder, then, that a diving and surfacing loon is often compared to a submarine. Though it was once thought by early naturalists like John J. Audubon that loons propelled themselves underwater with the aid of their wings, this idea has been disproven. Their wings are instead positioned flat against their body while underwater, making the loon a streamlined projectile. One other interesting aspect of a loon's foot is a type of behavior known as the "foot waggle." This occurs when the loon is on the surface of the water, the bird raising one leg high out of the water at a slight angle and resting in this position for a short time. It's a cool sight to see, especially the first time, but for many that aren't in the know, it's somewhat concerning, some thinking that the loon is somehow injured. So, why does the foot waggle occur? Biologists don't really know—it may have something to do with regulating the loon's body temperature, or it could be a simple comfort measure.

The wings of the loon are also a powerful part of their anatomy. The loon is certainly not the most graceful bird when it comes to getting and staying airborne, but it is impressive for its power. Adult loons have a wingspan of four feet or more, and they are fast flyers, able to reach speeds of up to 75 miles per hour during migration. However, their wings are smaller and narrower than a bird of similar weight like a goose. Thus, to stay aloft, loons must flap their wings constantly—about four times a second according to

Loon in flight over Odiorne Point, Rye, May 2022. *Courtesy Brett Hillman.*

the LPC—while in flight to keep their heavy payload aloft, their feet trailing straight behind them. Interestingly, because the loon has only vestigial tail feathers, their feet actually act as a rudder. In short, loons use a great amount of energy to stay aloft. They can fly as high as about 9,000 feet during migration, though when over water they often fly quite low. Loons typically do their flying during the day, whether during the fall migration or when they are returning to New Hampshire's lakes and ponds in the spring. They seldom travel in large groups, often flying alone or perhaps with another loon. As for the process of getting airborne, loons need a long water runway, at least 100 feet of open water, and it's an interesting process to watch. The loon lingers briefly at his starting point, probably gauging the wind, and just before beginning his takeoff rides high in the water. Once he begins the takeoff, his wings flap furiously, while his feet are doing the same, literally paddling across the surface of the water while slowly gaining altitude. Given his large size, the loon at this point somewhat resembles a big World War II bomber lumbering down a runway, yet he gets it done and, finally, is in the air and on his way. Loon landings are also dramatic, the feet trailing behind as he hits the water with a good-sized belly splash and then slides to a stop, his feet acting as brakes. While loons spend little time on land, when forced to move quickly, they use their wings to row them across dry land at a fast pace for short distances. This "wing-rowing" is also used on the open water, most often seen when in conflict with another loon, resulting in a lot of white-water action.

2

SIGHT, HEARING AND
THE MIND OF THE LOON

Eyesight and Sleeping Habits

Yet another distinguishing characteristic of the loon is the color of its eyes. Coincidental with the appearance of breeding season plumage, the iris of the loon turns a startling blood-red color. This feature gives the loon a somewhat eerie, almost prehistoric appearance. Though this color eventually fades as summer turns to fall, it does not go away entirely. Until relatively recently, there were many ideas put forth for the reason of this coloring, with many speculating that it might somehow enhance their night or underwater vision. However, biologists have now determined that this distinctive eye coloring, like their plumage in the summer, makes loons more attractive to one another, a secondary sexual characteristic. However, as Harry Vogel of the LPC has explained, the red eyes fade to a black color, in effect camouflaged, once the bird dives to a depth of 10 feet or more due to a lack of light. This change makes the loon better able to catch its prey. That said, loons are thought to have excellent vision, including at night, and feed by sight in the clear ocean, lake or pond waters that they inhabit. Should a loon somehow lose an eye, whether by accident or in conflict with another loon, the result would likely be fatal over time, as it would be more difficult to catch the food it needs to live.

It is also of interest to note that, when loons sleep, their necks turned to the rear, with their heads resting on their backs, they often sleep with one

Juvenile loon taking a nap, Pleasant Lake, New London, August 2012. *Photo by Kittie Wilson, courtesy John Wilson.*

eye open. Their sleeping periods, by the way, don't last long, typically several 15-minute periods, on average, during the day, while at night their sleeping period is longer, anywhere from about a half an hour to as long as an hour. Most of the time they sleep on the water, though during the breeding season they may sleep on their nests.

HEARING

The aural abilities of the loon are also excellent; they can hear the calls of other loons from a far-off distance, well beyond the range of human capabilities. Like many other birds, they don't have external ear structures like humans but rather small ear openings on either side of the head and just behind their eyes. Special feathers called "auriculars" cover these openings, offering some protection and resistance to the wind. These feathers have a slightly different color on at least one loon species but are almost impossible to distinguish on New Hampshire's loons by most casual observers. Combine their senses of sight and sound together, and it's no wonder that loons are almost impossible to sneak up on, and in most cases, they see and hear us humans out on the lake long before we can spot them.

Loon Intelligence and Learned Behaviors

In the realms of the brain, the loon has a lot to offer for observers. Even for a biologist, it's hard not to ascribe human characteristics (known as "anthropomorphism") to loons—it's what we humans do with many of our beloved animals. Regarding intelligence, as a bird lover, I've never been fond of the derogatory term *bird-brained*. It just isn't fair to our fine feathered friends and, I think, especially to loons. They, like the crow and blue jay, have amply demonstrated their intelligence by observation alone, even if it's not been tested in controlled scientific studies. One of the most important aspects of intelligence is the ability to learn and acquire knowledge and to apply that knowledge to everyday existence. Loons are pretty good at that. As young chicks, they are taught by both their mother and father how to feed, dive and, soon enough, care for themselves independently. LPC observations of breeding loons over the years show that not all are equal to the task. Experienced older loons have a higher success rate than loons breeding for the first time and still learning the ropes. They are better at selecting suitable nesting sites and, after a failed attempt in one location, are likely to change to a different site. Even among paired loons, the older loon, male or female, will often take charge during this important time, showing their younger partner what needs to be done, even if it is the male, whether young or old, that always chooses the nesting site. The LPC's Squam Lakes biologist, Tiffany Grade, has seen this in person on the Little Squam territory. As she recounted:

> There was a new female, and the male had been on territory for a decade. She was simply hardly ever around (I didn't even see her out on the lake, no idea where she went), and the male ended up doing the lion's share of incubation and caring for chicks. Finally, by their third year together, the female learned that she ought to contribute to the effort and began to take up her share of the duties, but he carried the burden for those first two years—kudos to him!

What is also interesting, though perhaps not surprising, is the fact that loons are not equal in New Hampshire when it comes to learned behavior. As the LPC has put it, "There are city loons and country loons....A loon in the channel of The Weirs on Winnipesaukee reacts to human presence much differently than a loon on Cummins Pond in the wilds of Dorchester." Indeed, loons living on our most crowded lakes, through their acquired knowledge and experience, have learned to live in proximity to humans. This can be seen almost every day in the summer months on our busiest lakes and ponds, where a loon may be idly floating, unfazed, when a paddle-boarder or kayaker glides by or a motorboat approaches. While the LPC advises the public to keep a distance from loons, at least 150 feet, many loon observers, myself included, have viewed them at closer distances simply because they have surfaced in our area and don't immediately flee when our actions are nonthreatening. However, on the quieter bodies of water, which seem to diminish year by year in New Hampshire, the loons that reside there are a bit more elusive and prone to avoid close encounters with humans, simply because it's not part of their learned experience. If crowded conditions persist, loons on once quiet lakes will either leave or adapt to the human presence.

Loon watching an angler in the channel between Upper and Lower Suncook Lake, Barnstead, August 2022. *Author photo.*

Finally, loons, like other animals living in proximity to humans, can also learn things that are detrimental to their well-being. Just like our black bears in New Hampshire have learned, sometimes with dire consequences, that it is easier to forage for food in garbage cans and dumpsters than out in the wild, loons, too, can gain, as LPC senior biologist John Cooley Jr. has discussed, "bad habits." One example of this has been reported by anglers on Lake Massasecum, a 409-acre body of water in Bradford. They have noticed that loons on this small lake have begun to hang around fishing boats, perhaps having learned that this is where the fish, their major food source, can be found. Luckily, the anglers on this lake have taken action in order that a loon might not be accidentally hooked by reeling in their lines and moving elsewhere. I have also witnessed loons hanging around fishermen in the shallow waters of the narrow channel that connects Upper and Lower Suncook Lakes in Barnstead.

LOON MEMORY AND RECOGNITION

Loons are also interesting in terms of their memory abilities. Some memory behaviors, like those associated with migration habits, are more instinctual in nature. As fall approaches in New Hampshire, juvenile loons will eventually leave the lake or pond on which they are born, almost always after their parents have already departed rather than with them. Interestingly, one exception to this norm has been the loons on Pleasant Lake in New London, where the late Kittie Wilson and her husband, John Wilson, well documented their behaviors. As John Wilson recalled, "If we had two chicks, father and one chick would depart the lake in October and mother and the remaining chick would depart the lake as the ice was starting to form in December. If we had one chick, father still seemed to disappear in October and mother and the one chick would still leave in December. I guess nothing is always." For those juveniles making a solitary journey to their ocean home, where they will spend the next several years of their lives, how do they know which way to go and what route to travel this first time around? And when they make their return several years later, how do they know the way back to the area close to their birthplace? In the first instance, it's almost certainly instinctual, something imprinted in their DNA, an inner compass that helps to guide them. On their return, this same inner compass may be at work, combined, perhaps, with some imprinted geographical memory of the landmarks encountered along the way. However, we are left to wonder about loons that find themselves in unusual circumstances.

Take for example the juvenile loon, thought to be a female, rescued from the ice on Kezar Pond in Sutton, New Hampshire, in early December 2022. As the bird was found to be healthy, and not willing to risk it being iced in again so late in the year, LPC biologist Caroline Hughes and wildlife rehabilitator Maria Colby, along with myself as an unskilled helper, banded the juvenile loon, took a blood sample and some physical measurements and released her into the ocean at Odiorne Point in Rye on December 7 at sunset. Though a commonplace task for LPC biologists, it was an amazing event to witness. Some discussion ensued—would this loon return to her birthplace near Sutton? How would she know the way, since she did not make it to the ocean on her own but was transported in a car? The fact is, biologists are unsure what may happen, though perhaps we will have an answer in several years if she is spotted and identified by her leg band color combinations. I hope she returns to the area and is again sighted in a few years. If this happens, I'll be paying her a visit, for she is the first loon I was able to handle and experience up close and personal during the course of researching and writing this book.

Beyond this type of memory, however, LPC biologists have determined by experience, as have many nonexpert loon observers, that loons can also recognize and remember individual humans that they encounter by facial features. As one LPC biologist stated, "I and a colleague of mine have had too many firsthand experiences to doubt this." I wholeheartedly agree, having had this same experience right here in Wolfeboro. Nowhere is this memory of individual human encounters more amply, and humorously, demonstrated than with LPC biologist Tiffany Grade and her experiences on Squam Lake in the summer of 2008. As she wrote of her banding experiences in the fall 2009 LPC newsletter article titled "Friend or Foe," after a night of loon banding exercises on the lake, "I feel exhilarated and relieved that the loon's ordeal is over and it can go back to the business of taking care of its chick and living its daily life on Squam. But as it swims away and calls out in distress to the night sky, I also feel a pang of dread. If this loon is typical, there is a good chance it will fear me for the rest of the summer." As Grade further recounted, during her daily activities on the lakes early on, everything is fine and the loons accept her presence, but after the banding activities, it all changes. The most extreme reaction came from an encounter in Squam's Yard Island territory in 2008. While Grade was checking in on the male loon banded the previous night, being careful to keep her distance, his mate, on sighting her boat, immediately dove and came up right alongside the boat "tremoloing in agitation." This same female was banded later on that evening, and for the rest of the summer she reacted negatively whenever Grade made an appearance, coming up to the boat and scolding her. While the behavior of this female was the most extreme to occur, it's been repeated enough over time to make it clear that Grade, despite her good work (even if the loons don't know it), was *recognized* and *remembered* as a threat. So, if you've spent a lot of time out on the water, bonding peacefully with "your" loon, and you think he recognizes you, you're not as crazy as your family and friends might think you are! Chances are, that loon has come to recognize you as a nonthreat and is willing to tolerate, and is curious about, your presence. Which comes to my next point: loons are curious birds as well and are often described as being "nosy." Not only do they want to know everything that is going on in their territory, but they are also interested in what's going on in lakes and ponds—other territories—in the immediate area. This curiosity often serves a purpose, keeping a loon in the know as to what other loons are occupying this territory and whether or not that territory might be a better opportunity for them to take advantage of in the future. Not surprisingly, loons are curious about humans too and what we're up to. Once their curiosity is satisfied, and you're determined to be no threat, they'll move on to something else.

LOON EMOTIONS

Finally, we can't help but talk about emotion. This is an uncomfortable topic among biologists, the issue of anthropomorphism always a concern, but many longtime loon observers insist that loons will at times exhibit emotions and have personalities all their own, even if, as longtime LPC LoonCam operator Bill Gassman states, "loons are more subtle" than your family dog. Outside of primates, there are other animals, like the elephant, that have been proven by scientific study and long-term observation to show such emotions as compassion, grief, joy and anger. As just discussed, loons do experience that most basic of all animal emotions, fear. But do they exhibit signs of sadness or joy? It's unlikely that few people in New Hampshire have more loon observation hours to their credit than Gassman, who stated, "You can't convince me that loons don't have

A loon parent and its chick, Pleasant Lake, New London, September 2011. *Photo by Kittie Wilson, courtesy John Wilson.*

personalities. I can tell when they're happy and mad and what they're thinking…not all the time, but I've seen enough over the years." Likewise, we can hear these emotions through their cries, when a loon is wailing for its partner in an attempt to find or call out to it. The face of the loon looks rather inscrutable, but perhaps their eyes tell the tale or how they carry themselves. Cathy Eastburn, a longtime observer (whose story is told later on) and LPC volunteer on the Upper Baker Pond in Orford and Lower Baker Pond in Orford and Wentworth, has seen it all, from the "frantic" searches and calls made by parents looking for their lost chicks to the "sad and miserable" look on the female bird that lost one of her chicks to an eagle in late 2022. In the end, while we all must be cognizant about ascribing to loons too many human behaviors and emotions, such as "rationality and sentience," the LPC also points out, "It's a mistake to de-animalize humans," and it's possible, even if unknowable (since we can't talk to them), that we have more in common with loons than we think.

3

THE CALLS OF THE LOON

In addition to the distinctive plumage that they wear in the spring and summer months, it is the sounds of the loon that make it a wildlife superstar. In fact, loon vocalizations are a standard feature of any film that has a wilderness background, whether set in New England, Alaska or anywhere in the country for that matter, even places where loon vocalizations are unlikely to be heard. They are a quintessential call of the wild, ranking right up there with the howl of the wolf. The most famous movie to feature the call of the loon, with loons playing a major part in the story, was the 1981 hit film *On Golden Pond*, which was filmed on Squam Lake. Its screenwriter, Ernest Thompson, lives in New Hampton and won an Academy Award for the film, as did its two stars, Henry Fonda and Katharine Hepburn. Her character not only enthusiastically celebrates the call of the loon ("The loons, the loons! They're welcoming us back") but, in quite humorous fashion, makes the call of the loon herself as well. So, yeah, the call of the loon is a big deal in New Hampshire and has been ever since that film came out. Of course, long before this time, the calls of the loon were a cherished part of the lake life experience. So, let's discuss these sounds. There are actually five vocalizations that the loon makes, examples of which can be heard on the LPC's website (https://loon.org/the-call-of-the-loon/).

The "coo" or "mew" is the softest sound the loon makes, and though it covers a wide range, they are used when a territorial pair is in close contact, often during courtship or when on the nest with their chicks. In human terms, it is the most intimate of the sounds made by loons. Though a distinct sound made by these birds, it is not classified by biologists as a "call" like the other vocalizations that follow.

The "hoot" is a soft call made over short distances that is also short in duration. It is most often heard between a territorial pair, or between a parent and its chicks, but is also used when communicating with other loons in low-level territorial interactions, as stated by the LPC.

Next up is the "wail," a frequent call used for long-distance communication between a territorial pair. It is effectively a call asking, "Where are you?" or, in its more frantic version, as when an intruding loon comes into their territory, "Come here, quickly!" The "wail" is also used in conjunction with two other calls, the "tremolo" and the "yodel," during times of stress or conflict. The wail is an iconic sound of night chorusing performed by loons on New Hampshire ponds and lakes on any given summer evening.

The tremolo is another iconic call of the loon, often described as a "crazy laugh," and it's the sound that has given rise to the saying "crazy as a loon." It is a call used when there is a threat to the loons, such as an intruding loon in their territory, predators like the eagle and unwanted human interactions. Loons will also use the tremolo during night chorusing and sometimes even as a duet between a territorial pair. It's also the only call that the loon makes while flying, usually over the territories of other loons.

Finally, there is the yodel. This call is interesting, as it is made only by male loons and is thus one of just a few ways to distinguish a male from a female loon in the wild. This call is made when a male loon feels threatened, either by intruding loons, a predator or close human contact, especially with his nest or chicks. It is also the only call that is distinguished by accompanying physical displays. When yodeling, a male loon will usually extend his neck forward and lie close to the water in order to project the call. The male loon will also sometimes yodel while rising out of the water, with neck extended forward and wings outstretched and arched toward the intruder. Either of these aggressive postures is quite the sight to see, a clear signal to intruders that they are not welcome and that trouble will ensue if they don't leave the area. Interestingly, studies from the 1970s suggest that the length of the yodel, specifically the number of repeat phrases within, transmits information about the male loon making that call, including not only his identity but also size, health and possible intentions, including a willingness to defend his territory at all costs. Makes sense, doesn't it? After all, these are all factors anyone considering a potential fight, loon and human alike, must take into consideration. A 1995 study by the LPC's Harry Vogel also found that territorial loons respond differently to the yodels from territorial neighbors and non-neighbors. The yodel is indeed a more complex communication tool than most of us may think.

Interestingly, the calls of the loon have been commented on by New Hampshire historians and others for well over 100 years now. Dr. Ebenezer Morse of Dublin wrote in prose form in 1852 of "the shrill note of the loon, which so found, is calling her mate from a neighboring pond." Silvanus Howard, in his 1881 history of the town of Gilsum, stated that in "every season is heard the ominous cry of the loon," while the 1886 history of the town of Washington, compiled by G.N. Gage, stated that the loon's "shrill cry is sometimes heard as it flies swiftly along from one pond to another." Finally, James Jackson in his 1905 history of Littleton (vol. 2) wrote similarly of "the loud, sad cry of the loon as it went sailing through the air high above us." The descriptive terms these early writers used about the calls of the loon—"shrill," "ominous" and "sad"—make us wonder about the status of the bird in the hearts and minds of our New Hampshire ancestors. Certainly, the loon was a mysterious creature to them, but as we will see, it was hardly the beloved bird back then that it is today. In addition to such older published accounts, lake residents all over the state have reminisced on the sounds of their loons over the years. My favorite is that of Dwight Crow, whose family has been on Pawtuckaway Lake in Nottingham since 1928. In an interview with Jeff Gurrier, he recalled that his mother would "complain," saying, "Those darned loons, they know when I'd go to the bathroom. They laugh at me all the way to the outhouse." The chorusing of the loons on summer nights in New Hampshire, no matter where they may be heard from, *is* the sound of summer and in more ways than one. While all these vocalizations occur on their breeding grounds, when wintering on the ocean, the loon, during a time when it has no mate and no young, and leads a somewhat solitary life at sea, with no territory to guard, is largely a silent bird.

FREQUENCY AND TIMING OF LOON CALLS

In addition to the types of calls, we may wonder about the frequency of these calls in relation to the time of day and the weather. Numerous studies over the years have confirmed what anyone who lives on a New Hampshire lake already knows—that most loon vocalization, except the hoots, take place at night rather than during the day, peaking anytime from several hours after sunset to the early morning hours. It has also been known for a long time now that vocalizations occur most frequently during the peak breeding season and decrease as the summer winds down. This coincides with the fact that by late summer, the hormone levels in loons have also decreased and territorial battles become less frequent as the breeding season comes to an end. Weather folklore has often related the call of the loon to stormy weather predictions. John Eastman and others, in their 1910 history of Andover, New Hampshire, related that "for many years, the old residents, when they heard the startling cry of the loon in its rapid flight between these ponds [Highland Lake and Bradley Pond], felt that a rainstorm was certainly coming." Likewise, in the August 1913 edition of the popular *Field & Stream* magazine, Arthur F. Rice wrote, in his discussion of woodcraft, that "the laughing cackle of the loon is an almost infallible precursor of a wind or rain storm." These assertions, like so much other weather lore, are romantic sounding but largely untrue based on scientific studies.

Loon Vocal Identification

Finally, we may wonder about vocal identification. Clearly, a loon and its mate can distinguish their own calls from that of intruding loons. This shows the acute hearing abilities of the loon, as discussed. But what about us humans? Is there a way for biologists to identify specific loons by their vocalizations alone? One study on this topic by Charles Walcott and David Evers, published in 1997 (*Loons: Old History, New Findings*, McIntyre and Evers), focused on the yodels of male loons. Through a study of loons in Michigan from 1990 to 1995, they did indeed discover that male loons occupying the same territory in successive years did have the same vocal pattern, based on tape recordings of their calls that were subsequently digitalized and analyzed. However, they also discovered that the yodels of some of these males changed when they moved to a new territory. Everything is not always as cut and dried as it seems in nature, and as stated in the beginning, loons do not always give up their secrets easily or quickly and there is much yet to learn from studying recordings of their calls.

4

THE LOON HABITAT AND FEEDING AND MAINTENANCE ACTIVITIES

Loon Ocean Habitat

Loons are a bird of two different worlds, one that is saltwater and the other freshwater. Anytime from the late fall into early spring, depending on when they migrate, New Hampshire loons live on the Atlantic Ocean, migrating as far south as Long Island and Block Island Sounds and northward to Massachusetts and Maine coastal waters. Birds from northern New Hampshire, including Lake Umbagog, winter as far south as Cape Ann on the Massachusetts coast, all the way north to Mid-coast Maine waters, according to LPC data. Those from central or southern New Hampshire lakes winter anywhere from the Maine coast down to Cape Cod, as well as in Long Island Sound, though they sometimes will go even farther south. In the winter of 2022, the male banded loon from Pioneer Pond in Stoddard was recovered after beaching itself on North Carolina's Outer Banks. Though this loon did not survive, the fact that it was found several hundred miles farther south than any other banded New Hampshire loon was previously known to migrate was an eye-opener. Most often, loons winter in waters just under seven miles offshore, while half of them spend their time less than a mile offshore. So, when you are checking out the ocean on a sunny winter day, whether from a beach in Rye or Hampton, our loons are possibly out there, even if out of sight. The waters in these areas average from 10 to 65 feet deep. Since loons feed by sight, the clarity of the water is important, which means they will avoid the more turbulent waters at the mouth of a river. As to their range in these coastal waters during the wintertime, according to the LPC, most will stay within a one- or two-square-mile area for the duration of their stay. Loons are interesting, too, in that they have special adaptations to live in this saltwater environment. This consists of two large glands above their eyes inside their head that expel the saltwater they ingest, which drips out like tears, while feeding or diving on the ocean.

LOON POND AND LAKE HABITATS

When the loons return to New Hampshire's lakes and ponds, they generally return to the area of their birth lake (within 10 to 15 miles) but not on that lake so as to avoid having to battle a parent for territory or potentially pairing up with a parent. Ofttimes loons return to the same body of water for many years in a row. The pond or lake in question must have plenty of fish and be large enough to feed a loon and his mate, and their chicks if mating is successful, from their return in the early spring into the fall months. The lake or pond must also have clear waters in which to feed. Since loons hunt for their prey visually, a body of water that is too choked with downed branches, weeds or vegetation or is too brackish will not be to their liking. Likewise, a body of water filled with lily pads may look charming to us humans, but for loons they are a major impediment to feeding. Loons also prefer a body of water with a gently sloping shoreline that offers some cover for their nesting sites. Loons do not live on most rivers, as these are too fast flowing, often have murky waters and their steep banks do not offer suitable nesting sites. Though loons are spotted on the Nashua, Connecticut or Merrimack Rivers from time to time, their sojourns are brief before they head on to their final, more friendly, habitat destination. The Androscoggin River up north near Errol is, however, an exception and actually has its own loon territories close to its source at Lake Umbagog. It is interesting to note that some lakes and ponds in New Hampshire and elsewhere may be enticing to loons, at least at first, but later are found to be "ecological traps." According to the biologists at The Loon Project in Wisconsin, such lakes may appear to have enough food to feed a loon family, but water quality can change with the seasons and what once looked to be a promising body of water turns out to be detrimental to loon reproduction rates. These bodies of water are ones that have little or no loon nesting success for multiple years in a row.

Loon Feeding Habits

Loon feeding on a perch. *Top*: bringing the fish to the surface; *center*: positioning the fish in its bill; *bottom*: swallowing the fish down its gullet. Back Bay, Wolfeboro, April 2023. *Author photo*.

Because loons live most of their lives on the water, it's not surprising that they are largely fish-eaters. They do all of their feeding during the day since they pursue their prey by sight. When they are young, loon chicks are taught how to catch fish on their own by both parents. At first, they are fed by their parents, but this quickly evolves, with parents bringing small fish to their young and dropping the prey in the water in front of them so that they can practice catching it. Early on, young loons will eat not only fish, but plant matter as well, while they're figuring things out. When feeding underwater, loons usually swim in a zigzag pattern to catch their prey. Once caught, their prey is often swallowed underwater, but sometimes loons will swallow the larger fish they catch while on the surface, working to get the fish positioned just right so that they may swallow it whole. Interestingly, when feeding on the surface, while the loon has little competition for their prey, sometimes opportunistic scavengers have been known to swoop down and try to steal the fish they have brought to the surface, including gulls, eagles and ospreys. I was lucky enough to witness just such an encounter between a loon and a gull on the Blackwater River in Seabrook in the winter of 2023, the loon easily shooing a herring gull away from his prey in this instance while rising high out of the water and flapping its wings.

The Loon's Beak, Tongue and Gizzard

The beak of the loon is a powerful tool for grabbing and holding onto their prey, while their long, slim tongue helps them to swallow. Interestingly, loons have denticles, rows of rear-facing spikes lining the roof of the mouth, which interlock with fish scales to prevent the fish from being able to slip out of the loon's mouth to freedom during this process. That's a pretty handy evolutionary trait. The prey, once swallowed, makes its way down to the gizzard of the loon. There are a number of small rocks or pebbles within, which, aided by the acids the gizzard produces, help to reduce the fish so that it can be digested properly. According to a 2009 study by Dr. Mark Pokras and others, New England loons have, on average, 14 such stones, most of which are about a quarter inch in size, in their gizzards to do this work. It is not surprising, given the size of our loons, that this amount is much greater in number than those found in loons from other regions. Loons will swallow these small rocks, usually obtained from the bottom of the lake or pond on which they live, to replenish them periodically as they become ground down and reduced to grit. The loon's favorite prey in New Hampshire is the yellow perch, bluegill and pumpkinseed, as they are easy to catch due to their erratic swimming patterns. Other favorite fish foods include suckers, minnows, catfish and smelt. They will also eat, when the opportunity presents, trout and salmon, but the pure speed of these fish makes them harder to catch. Though loons prefer fish, they will eat other forms of marine life, including crayfish, frogs, snails and leeches on New Hampshire bodies of water, as well as snails, crabs, shrimp, lobster and other crustaceans while out on the ocean. Loons have been observed feeding on crabs in their ocean environment, ripping their legs off so that they can be more easily swallowed, and even stingrays. Loons generally feed on their own once grown, though on the ocean they will feed cooperatively with other loons at times when large schools of fish are their target prey. The average loon, feeding periodically throughout the day, eats about two pounds of fish a day. Throughout New Hampshire history, loons have been viewed by fishermen as anything from a nuisance bird to a downright scourge, it being thought that they will eat all the fish in a given body of water. As the LPC's John Cooley Jr. has stated, "There's plenty of fish in the sea for everyone.…Fishermen tend to believe this myth when they see a loon on the surface swallowing a large fish, but this is the exception, as most of their food are perch that are about four to six inches in length." In short, anglers, there's nothing to worry about—the loon is not your enemy, and he's certainly not going to swallow a prize-winning fish the likes of which are seen in the annual Winni Derby.

LOON WATER CONSUMPTION

As to the liquid part of their diet, loons also drink water to stay hydrated, something we may not always think about when viewing them. Some of this water is ingested underwater while they are feeding on fish, but they also ingest water while floating on the surface, dipping their bills into the water to take a drink from time to time. Loons that are unable to feed or drink due to discarded monofilament fishing line that has become wound around their beaks may die of starvation, but they can also die of dehydration while floating on a New Hampshire lake in the hot summer weather. Dying such a harsh death, unable to take a drink while water is all around them, is sometimes a tragic irony for loons and, as will be discussed later, is one of many human-induced threats that they face.

LOON DEFECATION HABITS

Finally, as the variation on an old saying goes, what comes in, must go out. For you readers with a seven-year-old in the family, you know what I'm talking about—loon pooping habits. Loons, unlike many birds (especially raptors), do not regurgitate or "cast" pellets that consist of undigestible parts of their prey. They do, however, poop, mostly in the water. Their defecation comes in a largely semiliquid form, and they lift their tails when doing so. They also, on occasion, will defecate on land, up to about 15 feet from the shore and away from their pond or lake waters. Unlike the dreaded Canada goose, this activity does not usually take place on public beaches or other heavily used recreational waterfront sites. This "ritualized" act is thought to be a method of marking their territory. Loon chicks, even from a young age, respect their parents and while riding on their backs will defecate away from them and into the water. When in extreme panic situations, as when being flushed off their nest, or when they are captured, say for the rescue operations regularly performed by LPC biologists, loons will also defecate—a lot! In fact, in these situations, working with loons is not so glamorous; wildlife rehabilitator Kappy Sprenger reported that a loon can spray waste across an entire room when in a "terrified" state. However, once they get used to their new situation, after a day or two, loons will hold off defecating until they are placed in the water in their temporary home while being rehabilitated.

Preening and Feather Maintenance Activities

The process by which loons maintain their feathers is also an eye-opening one. So, you're out one summer day, walking around your favorite pond or lake site, when you see a loon, maybe two—your day just got better. But then you see one of these loons acting in an apparently weird way. He's contorting his body, rubbing his beak and bill on his back or rolling on his back or side and pulling at his feathers. Maybe he's got a leg sticking in the air and is paddling in circles, like a ship with a jammed rudder. Perhaps he's flapping his wings hard and rising out of the water, seemingly trying hard to fly, but failing. Or maybe he's shaking his head, wings and tail. To the uninitiated loon observer, these habits can be worrisome, perhaps indicative of a bird that is injured or sick. But, not to worry—what you're actually observing is a loon going through one of its daily periodic bouts of preening. Loons perform these maintenance rituals not to look good, but because their very survival depends on proper preening. Loons actually have a small organ at the base of their tail called the uropygial gland, which secretes oil. While the gland itself is not visible, you can easily spot its location at times by the tuft of feathers that is often visible at the rear of the bird, sometimes making it look like it's having a bad hair day. Loons use their bill and head to spread this

Loon preening sequence. *Left*: spreading the oil while floating on its back; *right*: rising out of the water to realign its feathers after it is done preening. Back Bay, Wolfeboro, November 2022. *Author photo.*

oil on their body feathers so as to maintain their waterproofing. This coating, along with the loon's interlocking feathers, comparable, says the LPC, to shingles on a roof, is what allows it to live on the water nearly year-round in all New Hampshire weather conditions, from a hot summer day in July to a frigid and blustery day in December. Without this weatherproofing, the loon could not long survive, so daily bouts of preening are required to make this happen. All of the contortions we can see are their efforts to take care of all these feathers by distributing the secreted oil, often dipping their bill in the water during the process. Once a loon has completed this maintenance chore, he rises out of the water and flaps his wings, perhaps to help in realigning their feathers. Loon pairs and families will typically preen together, and this activity overall accounts for about 5 percent of the loon's daytime activities, the time spent doing so ranging anywhere from 23 to 98 minutes. The average bout of preening, which takes place only during the day, lasts up to 6 minutes long. Not surprisingly, loons also take rigorous baths at times to rid themselves of feather lice or other parasites. These bathing activities also can be mistaken for a loon in distress, as they involve a vigorous flapping of their wings, rolling over on their backs, beating the water with their wings or thrashing about while their heads are submerged. In short, it not easy for this beautiful water bird to keep both its good looks and its incredible all-weather performance capabilities.

5

THE LOON'S PLACE
IN NATURE'S FOOD CHAIN

LOONS VERSUS EAGLES

The loon, with his large size and fierce countenance, is indeed a formidable bird. However, the loon actually occupies two different places on the food chain, and it all depends upon their age. Prior to being hatched, and in their first summer and fall on New Hampshire lakes or ponds as juveniles, they are extremely vulnerable and low on the food chain. Loon eggs are predated by any number of animal species, both from the land and from the air. Common culprits include eagles, gulls, crows, raccoons, skunks, foxes and minks, and due to these animals' abilities, nesting loons experience a high rate of failure. Once the chicks are hatched, even though they are well cared for and closely guarded by their parents, they are often preyed on by eagles, snapping turtles and even large fish like the northern pike and muskie. Indeed, as many a loon watcher has observed, with heartbreaking results, chick survival is always touch and go. However, this changes as they grow into adults and become the big birds we know and love. From here on out, they are near the top of the food chain, a so-called apex predator, with but few enemies. The loon's biggest natural enemy from this point forward during the months they spend on New Hampshire lakes and ponds are bald eagles. In fact, as LPC head Harry Vogel has commented, loons and eagles have been enemies "for millions of years." Of course, this relationship is a bit one-sided; loons do not eat eagles and would prefer to have nothing to do with them, but eagles are opportunistic predators. They will often swoop down to attack loon chicks or hope to distract their parents and separate them from their young to make them easy game. Sometimes eagles are successful in their efforts, but many times they are not, with adult loons fighting them off. Pictures of these encounters are generally hard to come by, since they happen in just an instant, but professional photographer Jon Winslow did just that on June 15, 2013, from his dock on Bow Lake in Strafford. As he recalled,

I was actually packing my gear up when the whole thing unfolded from my dock. About 100 to 150 yards away the two eagles began attacking the two loons and were swooping in driving them away from the baby. As hard as it was to watch I knew I had to try to document it. Unfortunately, my wife, daughter, sister-in-law and niece were there and very vocal when the eagles got close to the baby. Once the eagles drove the loons far enough from the baby loon, one of them came swooping in, and at the last second the three-day old baby dove (perhaps for the first time) and stayed underwater so long I thought he must have died. After what seemed like minutes he popped up and the two loons quickly swam to him, and the attack was over.

Loon parent fighting off an eagle, Bow Lake, Strafford, June 2013. *Courtesy Jon Winslow.*

That picture would soon become an iconic shot, for it dramatically demonstrates the ferocity of loon parents when it comes to protecting their chicks. That year, 2013, was actually a great one for Bow Lake, despite the presence of nesting eagles, as each of the three territorial loon pairs had a surviving chick, including the Bennett Island pair, whose spirited defense Winslow caught on camera. This pair actually had two chicks in 2013, the one defended here being the sole survivor. Overall, the results on Bow Lake were better than those on most other lakes in New Hampshire that year.

The loon's sharp beak is an excellent weapon, and when the eagle attacks, ofttimes they will fight to a draw, but not always. In the summer of 2022, the adult male loon on Canobie Lake died from an eagle attack. The loon pair were in the middle of a nesting attempt (on a raft with an eagle predation cover), so the female, who was incubating at the time, was not attacked. But LPC volunteers witnessed the eagle take a swipe at the male loon, which was swimming in the water. While the eagle didn't manage to kill the loon that day, the attack left the loon with a bad wound on its leg. They abandoned the nest shortly after, likely because the male was unable to pull his weight due to his injury. Despite this injury, the loon was able to dive well enough to evade LPC biologists' rescue attempts. Sadly, a few weeks after the initial attack, he was found dead. A necropsy revealed that this injury had compromised the loon and caused him to develop aspergillosis, a deadly condition, which will be discussed at greater length.

However, it was on Highland Lake in Bridgeton, Maine, in 2019 that an unusual event occurred, the first of its kind to be documented. A dead bald eagle was discovered along the shoreline by a Maine game warden, along with a dead loon chick. It was at first thought that the eagle was shot, but a necropsy (arranged with LPC involvement) proved that the eagle died in an instant. Incredibly, it was stabbed through the heart while battling an adult loon and was possibly the same eagle that had killed the loon chick. Despite their occasional success in attacking young loons, eagles are seldom successful attacking a healthy adult loon. However, if an adult loon is sick or injured, and thus less able to defend itself, it may fall prey to the eagle. This is also true of healthy loons that might become trapped in the ice in the winter months, with their movements restricted, as eagles have been sighted keeping an eye on the remaining small patches of open water, hoping to catch a surfacing loon. It is interesting to note that loon-eagle confrontations are becoming more and more common on New Hampshire bodies of water, much to the chagrin of many observers. This is because the formerly endangered bald eagle population has been restored due to conservation efforts and is now commonly found all across New Hampshire, especially in the Lakes Region. Indeed, it's not hard these days to spot this majestic bird, which, though still protected by several laws, was removed from the federal endangered list in 2007 and New Hampshire's endangered list in 2017. This strong eagle rebound, along with the slow increase in the loon population, has meant that encounters between these two birds are increasingly being reported. In reality, their enmity toward one another goes far back in time and has, since the early 20th century, ebbed and flowed as the populations of the two birds have gone through cycles of decline and increase.

Other Loon Enemies

Other than eagles and humans, adult loons have few enemies that will endanger their lives. Snapping turtles and large fish, like the northern pike, that live in New Hampshire's lakes and ponds will certainly eat loon chicks but are no match for an adult loon. However, from time to time an encountered loon has a damaged, scarred or even missing leg thought to be the result of such an encounter. As the LPC's Betsy McCoy recalls, one such incident took place on Pea Porridge Pond in Madison, where a canoeist reported seeing a turtle drag a loon by his leg before the bird eventually escaped. An even more dramatic encounter of this type was captured by the LPC's LoonCam in June 2022 when a loon was heard to, as described by the LPC's Chris Conrod, "let out some hideous sounds and began splashing in the water…beating his wings against the water"; the "contortions went on for a few minutes." This loon appeared to have escaped his attacker and swam off, "only to begin his own bizarre behavior all over again. He worked his way to the middle of the lake, [and] his efforts seemed to slow down as if he were wearing out, he dropped lower in the water, went under once, twice, three times, then he sank out of sight." Luckily, this loon survived the attack, and while some observers didn't believe it was a turtle attack, Conrod disagreed, commenting, "The only aquatic critter in the lake that could hold down a loon from swimming away would be a large snapping turtle." As to enemies on their ocean wintering grounds, loons are vulnerable to large fish, including sharks, as well as seals on occasion, but as on land, their survival rates are pretty good once they reach adulthood, if they are lucky enough to avoid human threats.

6

LOON TERRITORIAL
AND SOCIAL INTERACTIONS

T his aspect of a loon's nature is one of the most interesting and surprising to many: looking at these birds in the summer, one may view them as peaceful birds floating about without a seeming care in the world beyond catching enough fish to eat or caring for their young. But this easygoing demeanor belies a bird that, in the months from April to August, can be a fierce and ruthless creature that, at times, might even be a violent killer.

In the late fall and through the winter months, loons are peaceful birds that live a largely carefree existence. They often swim alone and have no mates, no young to care for and no territory to defend. But this changes when they return to New Hampshire every spring after ice-out. Unlike New Hampshire's millions of human tourists who come here annually to relax and have a good time in the great outdoors, our loons are returning here with serious work to do, that of propagating their species on their breeding grounds. This means that on their return, they have to find a suitable place to live, either on a lake or pond that will support just one loon pair, or a suitable territory if it's a large body of water that can support more than one pair of loons. Then, of course, they must find a partner with which to breed, and once they have nested, they have to incubate their eggs so that they might hatch. Finally, once their chicks have emerged, they must then care for, teach, feed and defend their young so that they may fledge and survive to the end of the breeding season. And that, in a nutshell, is the work of an adult loon, both male and female, in New Hampshire. This period runs from approximately April, depending on when ice-out occurs, to November or even into December if a chick has fledged.

It's not as easy as it sounds, for there is much competition among loons, and as their hormones increase during breeding season, they become very territorial. What they have claimed as their own they will defend at great lengths, even if they have to kill another loon. A newly mature loon, returning to the area of its birth lake in New Hampshire for the first time, immediately begins the search for a territory of its own. It may take several years, but eventually, it may gain its own territory after battling it out with another, older, loon already established in a territory. When we think of territorial battles in nature, we often envision the males of the species battling it out for supremacy, but quite surprising for many, this territorial nature of loons applies to both females and males. In other words, a female loon will just as often fight another female loon occupying a territory in an attempt to oust her, just as males will do the same.

Territorial Disputes

The territorial fights among loons can, at first glance, look quite comical and funny and are sometimes thought by the uninitiated to be rituals of courtship. Conflicts start when an intruder arrives in another loon's territory. The loon occupying the territory will then approach the intruder, the two swimming in circling fashion. This often takes place as close as nine feet distant from one another, though LPC biologists have seen them happening at a much closer proximity, perhaps as little as one to two feet apart. During this time, loons may splash, dive or peer into the water at frequent intervals. Such activities can quickly escalate, with one loon rising high out of the water and lunging at its enemy. The territorial loon will often rush at the invading loon vigorously, wing-rowing its way on top of the water at a fast pace to drive. This is always an interesting occurrence, most of this being a ritualistic display of strength and endurance. In fact, according to the LPC's Harry Vogel, wing-rowing is a loon's way of saying to an invader, "do not mess with me," and once one loon stops, the other will also do so. If the two loons stand their ground, a close-fought battle may ensue, the combatants jabbing or striking at each other with their strong bills or even grabbing at each other's bill or neck. However, it's what we can't see during these fights that often results in the most trauma and death. During these encounters, one loon may dive underwater and attack from below, using their long and sharply pointed bill to pierce the sternum of their enemy. Some of these kinds of wounds are not life-threatening, but others can be deadly. A pioneering study published in 2022 by Mark Pokras, Amanda Higgins and Meghan Hartwick documented the sternal punctures in loons and how they relate to gender and territorial aggression, and what they discovered is eye-opening. The sternal trauma inflicted as a result of these encounters is found in more than half of the loon population in New England, based on necropsy results from 2008 to 2015. Interestingly, female loons exhibited a slightly higher rate of these punctures than males. Observations by LPC biologists and others, coupled with the physical evidence compiled over the years, makes it clear that female loons are just as much in the thick of these territorial fights as are their male counterparts. One striking example of female loon conflicts and drama occurred on Squam Lake, which is often

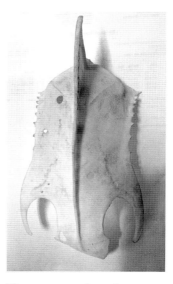

The sternum, or breastbone of a loon. The small holes are puncture wounds, some of which are healed, that show this loon endured several territorial fights during its lifetime. *Courtesy LPC.*

filled with strife, beginning in 2010. As biologist Tiffany Grade recounted, early in 2010 the female in the Sturtevant Cove territory was "evicted," and she was a floater wandering around the lake until midsummer 2014, when she "teamed up" with the ex–Yard Islands female (also driven from her territory) to drive out the resident Moultonborough Bay female, which was nesting at the time. After succeeding in that, the two females then turned on each other to "duke it out for victory." At that point, the ex–Yard Islands female won the fight; but the ex-Sturtevant female came out on top in the long run by being the territorial female in Moultonborough Bay in 2015. She nested that year, but the nest was predated. Then she was a single again from 2016 to 2018 before regaining the Moultonborough Bay territory in 2019–20. Having a hard time keeping track of all that? Well, now you know how difficult it is to be a loon biologist on Squam Lake these days.

Another incredible example of female loon aggression was documented in 2021 on Pleasant Lake in New London. As LPC biologist Caroline Hughes related,

The female loon there, one that was originally banded as a chick on Squam Lake, found herself ousted from her position as a member of the pair at the start of the season. Though she tried repeatedly to win her spot back, she could not stop her old mate from nesting with the new female, and they produced a chick. When the chick was still young, the old female decided to make a stand. She started a brutal fight with the new female. Typically, these fights end on the water—if one loon beaches itself, the other may swim back and forth in front of it, but won't continue the attack. That was not the case on this day. The old female drove the new female up on shore, then followed her up about 20 feet from the water line and continued the attack, the old female totally on top of the new female and continuing to poke her. The old female finally decided she had won, and she returned to the water. The new female returned to the water a bit later, battered and bruised but alive. But she never rejoined her mate, and the chick soon disappeared. By the end of the season, the old female was being regularly spotted with the male, and in 2022, she was once again the pair member, and they nested successfully. We don't know where the new female went, but hopefully she moved on to a new territory!

Following the harrowing physical encounters described earlier, a victor will often emerge. The defeated loon, whether invader or territory holder, will skulk away to a distant part of the lake or pond to find shelter. Battered and bruised, perhaps wounded, it might even beach itself on land. At other times, neither loon may achieve a resounding victory, the invading loon strong enough to come back and fight another day. Most often, these territorial battles take place on larger bodies of water, like Squam Lake or Lake Winnipesaukee, where every square foot of territory is contested, and where one territory ends, another begins, with no unoccupied ground in between the different loon territories. A loon invader may try to fly in without being detected, perhaps landing in an adjacent territory, but this seldom lasts long, as a territorial loon pair knows what is going on in their backyard. In contrast, on small lakes and ponds that constitute a single territory, any potential invader is more easily detected by the occupying pair and may be warned off by sharp cries, especially the male yodel call, even before they land. Overall, it is estimated that the annual turnover rate for loon territories is 20 to 23 percent, with about 41 percent occurring through forcible eviction. That's quite a bit of yearly conflict.

ROGUE LOONS

With all this action, just as with human physical encounters that turn violent, there is often collateral damage, and when it comes to loons, such damage is suffered by loon chicks. On some of New Hampshire's lakes, both big and small, territorial conflicts among loons are becoming more and more common, even in places where none existed before for a variety of possible reasons that will be touched on later. In some cases, "rogue" loons looking for a territory will come into a territory and try to break up the pair there by attacking their chicks, for once there are no chicks to defend, there is no "imperative," as Harry Vogel states, for that territorial pair to stay together. Rogue loons are well aware that loon parents will defend their young at almost any cost and often use a divide-and-conquer approach. Through relentless attacks that may last hours, they will separate first one chick from its parents and then kill the chick instantly, and if there is a second chick, they will work to do the same. If they're lucky enough, they may even exhaust one of the territorial pair and succeed in driving it away. Very often, the rogue loon will subsequently pair up with the remaining loon in the territory. Any chick that may have survived to this point would be subsequently killed very

A loon territorial dispute on Lake Umbagog, Errol. Here, the ritual of wing-rowing across the water is demonstrated, one loon chasing another but stopping short of actual contact. *Courtesy Nordel Gagnon.*

quickly in a Darwinian display of the survival of the fittest. It's not a pleasant situation to envision, nor is it one that you would ever want to witness, but unfortunately, that was the misfortune that residents on Swain's Lake, a 341-acre body of water in Barrington, suffered in 1991. On this single-pair lake, an aggressive intruding loon swooped into the lake, and soon a fight ensued between it and one of the defending parents. This bird was subsequently badly wounded in the attack and was out of action. The invader then went to the other parent, which was defending two loon chicks. As graphically described by LPC biologist Betsy McCoy, "the rogue…in a quick flurry had cleanly killed one of the young with a stab to the belly," all of which action was witnessed by local residents. With "moral support" from the LPC, these folks mobilized and took to their canoes and small boats and subsequently formed a "human barrier" between the rogue loon and the remaining parent and its chick. Though they never directly interfered with the loons and neither pursued nor harassed the rogue loon, their actions did offer some hope and gave the parent "a well-deserved break." In the end, though, these human efforts went for naught, and the relentless loon eventually killed the other chick. It was, indeed, a rough time for the traumatized folks on Swain's Lake. Back in 1991, these events were rare, but they have become more commonplace today as the competition for territories in some areas has greatly increased.

Aggressive Behavior in Older Male Loons

However these territorial loon battles play out, one might wonder if these conflicts take place for the entirety of the birds' adult lives, or is there a time when they decline in frequency? The answer here is a multilayered one: loons are long-lived birds, and for females, these battles do decline in intensity with age. Though older females are often ousted from their territories by younger females, fights to the death seldom occur. As a result, those females on the losing end will join the floater population and move to a nearby lake, one that is either unoccupied or unproductive in terms of breeding success. Sometimes, as we have seen happen on Squam Lake, they may regain their old territory or settle a new one. On the other hand, older male loons increase their territorial aggression as they age and can become quite cantankerous. According to biologist Walter H. Piper and others, who detailed their findings in a 2018 article, those male loons aged

14 and over show increased "hyper-aggressive" behavior, including a large increase in making their yodel calls in defense of their territory. So, why do older male loons act this way? It is simply their way of holding on to their territory as long as they can, their aggression warning off potential usurpers. One interesting example of this behavior for loons took place in New Hampshire around 2013 and finally ended in 2016. As the LPC's senior biologist John Cooley Jr. noted in 2016, "'The Angry Old East End Loon' might sound like a bad movie, but it's become the nickname for a male loon on Northwood Lake. Northwood loon watchers swear they've watched this loon get crankier and crankier in recent years, fending off mergansers, other loons, innocent human bystanders and would-be swimmers with a brashness seldom rivaled in loon lore. And then this spring [2016] as loons returned and pairs formed on the lake, the angry loon was gone, replaced by an unbanded newcomer. The demise or displacement of the East End loon on Northwood after years of bad temper was a perfect case study." Whatever the end may be for some males, it is interesting to note that, among the oldest known loons in New Hampshire, a majority of them are males.

LOON AGGRESSION AGAINST OTHER WATER BIRDS

Though unsettling to waterfowl lovers, the territorial nature of the loon does not just apply to their own kind. It is true that, other than the fish and related prey that they eat, loons are not normally predatory toward waterfowl like ducks and geese on their home lake and do not eat them. However, during the breeding season, loons will aggressively defend their area, especially when loon chicks are present, from any perceived threat, even other waterfowl with which they may otherwise normally peacefully coexist. For reasons hard to discern, with no apparent threat looming, loons have been observed brutally killing mallard ducks and other waterfowl, including their ducklings, that stray into their territory. This kind of aggression is certainly disturbing to witness, but it is a stark reminder that loons are wild animals and that one of their strongest instincts is to protect their family and their home turf.

LOON SOCIAL GATHERINGS

Now, lest it be thought that all loon social interactions in the summertime are aggressive in nature, have no fear. There are actually social gatherings that happen during these months that are more friendly in nature. The earliest of these gatherings take place between floaters in the early summer season and generally occur on a neutral site where there is no territorial pair. In fact, in the early summer months, at the height of the breeding season, it is almost always the case that, if three or more loons are seen together in proximity, acting civil toward one another, they are floaters. Similar gatherings also occur late in the summer, often in mid- to late August, when the territorial nature of loons has dramatically decreased. This coincides with a decrease in their hormone levels. With fall migration close at hand, loons, whether floaters without a territory or a territorial pair, will often gather together on a neutral lake or pond with no territorial pair and sometimes on a body of water with a territorial pair. These late summer social gatherings are usually larger in size and can consist of 10 loons or more in some cases, which makes for an impressive sight to see. Whether it's floaters in the early summer or a mix of loons in the late summer, the same social behaviors are exhibited. These gatherings usually take place late in the day or in the early morning hours just after sunrise and may last anywhere from one to three hours, the shortest sessions occurring early in the season.

If there is a territorial pair on the gathering site with a chick or two, their young will usually be hidden away in a small cove or inlet during the social gathering. Nobody, not loons and not humans, really wants little children at a party, right?! The beginning of these social visits is often signaled by hooting calls, and the loons will begin by circling each other, their movements accompanied by bill dipping, peering into the water, head turning and even a "vulture" posture. Sometimes, either early on or at various intervals during the gathering, more aggressive actions, including running across the water, wing flapping and the vulture posture, may briefly occur before everyone settles down a bit. However, mutual splash dives take place frequently, with one loon initiating the sequence and the others following, emerging from the water some distance away and spaced out from one another. In this manner, they move across the lake together, sometimes covering quite a distance depending on how long the gathering lasts. Eventually, as the gathering comes to a close, the loons begin to depart, usually diving away from the group singularly for

Loon social gathering, Lower Suncook Lake, Barnstead, August 2022. Note the varied behaviors: the loon at far left is peering into the water while the two with wings spread are just ending a display of aggression. The other loons are taking it all in. *Author photo*.

the last time and then flying off the lake. Sometimes when they are flying off over the lake, they may circle and make their tremolo call. Once the party is over, if there's a territorial pair on the lake with a chick or two, the male will dive and survey his territory, making sure the coast is clear before returning to his mate, the two subsequently returning to where the chicks were hidden away. I have witnessed just these kinds of late summer loon gatherings while kayaking on Lower Suncook Lake in Barnstead in August 2022 and 2023, and both were wonderful experiences that lasted for over two hours.

One may wonder what the purpose of these gatherings may be, especially those taking place late in the season. Most loon biologists agree with expert Judith McIntyre that these "ritualized behaviors prepare loons for cooperative feeding en route to wintering grounds" and serve as a "unifying" type of event. An unusually large gathering of loons, 80 in number, was sighted in Otter Cove on First Connecticut Lake in Pittsburg on October 8, 2005, possibly an inland record count. This same flock, 74 in number, had been previously sighted in the same town on Back Lake four days earlier. These loons were almost certainly using these lakes as a stopping-off point for their ocean migration voyage and likely originated from Vermont, New York or southern Canada.

LOON SOCIAL HABITS
IN AN OCEAN ENVIRONMENT

Finally, as to social activities on their winter ocean home, loons lead a mostly solitary existence, though there is some cooperative feeding that takes place at times with other loons. Aggressive behavior is not common during this time but has been observed taking place during interactions with other waterfowl species. Loons will also sometimes feed or raft near red-throated loons and horned grebes, and at times, when chasing schools of fish, herring and ring-billed gulls will forage with them. There are even anecdotal accounts of dolphin and loon interactions, though these are likely quite rare in the waters of the Gulf of Maine. As with the fall migration time, loons will also congregate prior to their spring migration back to New Hampshire and beyond. One example of a large pre-migration gathering was that of 450 loons spotted off the Rye coast on May 26, 2005, based on *New Hampshire Bird Records* accounts.

7

STARTING A LOON FAMILY

Mating, Nesting and Egg Incubation

With the onset of their spring and summer plumage beginning about March, the time for New Hampshire's loons to return to the state's inland water bodies is imminent. They generally begin to appear within a day or two of "ice-out," that famed time that all New Hampshire residents, especially from the Lakes Region northward, look forward to as the end of winter. It is "officially" declared when the main ports on Lake Winnipesaukee, Alton Bay, The Weirs, Meredith, Center Harbor and Wolfeboro are free of ice and open to visits from the famed ship MV *Mount Washington*. This event, which is currently determined by aerial survey by Dave Emerson of Emerson Aviation, occurs sometime in March, April or May, with records dating back to 1887. The earliest ice-out date on record is March 18 (2016), while the latest occurred on May 12 (1888). No matter what the date may be, loons are sure to follow, nature's call to begin their breeding season an uncannily accurate one.

RETURNING TO INLAND PONDS AND LAKES

Adult male loons are the first to appear on our lakes and ponds, almost acting as scouts, with females arriving a day or two later. This is interesting, as territorial pairs from the previous year do not spend the winter together, but each, nonetheless, has the instinct to make their return. One common myth about loons that has remained strong today is that they mate for life. In New Hampshire, according to former LPC director Jeff Fair, this notion began to be dispelled in the 1990s after LPC loon banding efforts—and resulting gathered data from loon re-sightings—made it clear that the reality is more nuanced. Loons, indeed, often will mate with the same partner for years on end on the same body of water, these tending to be pairs that are successful at producing chicks year after year. However, there are events that can occur that often disrupt this tendency toward serial monogamy. Birds, male or female, can be ousted from their territory by invading loons, but why? I used to think that it was younger loons displacing aging loons, but the LPC's Harry Vogel explained to me that it was not age, necessarily, but the more fit birds that will likely be the victor. As he explained, an older, larger male "will beat the tar out of a younger male that weighs less." It really is all about that idea of survival of the fittest. In many cases, following such a battle, the remaining loon in the territory will pair up with the victor. It is also common for loons that are unsuccessful nesters, ones that fail to produce chicks, to break up and seek other partners. This is not really surprising, as the loon's strongest instinct at this time of year is to reproduce, and when failure occurs, they seek other, better opportunities. Of course, the death of one of a territorial pair for any number of reasons, whether by human or natural causes, means that the surviving loon now must work to find a partner. Perhaps it will be a younger, newly mature loon, male or female, coming into a newly opened territory on or near its birth lake. Or maybe it will be another bird that was ousted from its previous territory, either on that same lake (a larger one with multiple territories) or from a neighboring lake. Then again, maybe the surviving loon is now ousted from its old territory and is forced to seek another. Whatever the case may be, it's not always easy being a single loon of breeding age, even if there are many possibilities.

Loon Pair Bonds

In the end, pair bonds last, on average, about 5 years, though bonds that have lasted more than 2 decades have occurred. The world record for known loon bonding is the paired couple found in the Seney National Wildlife Refuge in Michigan's Upper Peninsula. As of 2021, they had been together for 25 consecutive summers, though in 2022, the streak was broken when they were ousted from their territory. In New Hampshire, we have also had some long-lasting loon pairs, this data gathered through banding efforts and subsequent yearly observations. The championship of loon pairing overall goes to the pair on Pleasant Lake in New London, which were first recorded in 2010. This pair, well documented in the photos of Kittie Wilson shown in this book, was together for 11 straight years from 2010 to 2020, then were separated for a year before reuniting in 2022. During their long time together, this pair hatched 21 chicks and successfully fledged 18 of them, a truly remarkable accomplishment.

Interestingly, during the year they were separated in 2021, the male remained on the territory and hatched but a single chick, which did not survive, with a new mate, while his old mate remained on the lake as a floater and did not reproduce. The current longest continually bonded pair of loons in the state as of 2022 is that on Wakondah Pond, just 94 acres in size, in Moultonborough. The pair there was first documented in 2013, and they have remained together ever since. Through the 2022 season they have hatched 12 chicks and fledged 9 of them, a great success on such a small body of water. Not far behind these pairs is the pair on Hawkins Pond in Center Harbor. This pair was first documented in 2011 and was together through 2019. However, the male of the pair was missing in 2020 (where he went no one knows), only to return in 2021 to reunite for one last time. During their time together, they hatched 12 chicks and fledged 7 of them. The female of the pair remained on the territory in 2020 and had no reproductive success that year and none in 2021 as well. The male of this pair returned for 2022, but his mate was a different female. Other notable longtime loon bonded pairs in New Hampshire include those on Middle Pea Porridge Pond in Madison (2014–21), Squam Lake, Long Point territory (2011–13, 2015–17, 2020–21), Lake Winnipesaukee, Poplar Island territory (2014–20), again on Buzzell's Cove territory (2022) and Bow Lake, Kooaukee territory (2014–16, 2018–22). And last but not least, there is that grand dame of the Sweat Meadows and Harper's Meadow territories on the Androscoggin River in northern New Hampshire, which was banded in 1994. She had the same mate on two different territories (Sweat Meadows 2006 and 2010, Harper's Meadow 2011–18) for 9 straight years and 10 years overall. We shall read more about this notable bird later on. As can be seen in the cases of the pairs on the last of the four lakes listed, there were varying degrees of mate changes at several intervals and on different territories, indicative of both the heavy competition for territories and low reproductive success in the years preceding a change. Despite such challenges, these New Hampshire loons are doing quite well for themselves, especially when we consider the fact that most loons don't live beyond 20 years of age (more on that follows), and every year that a pair remains bonded means we learn a little bit more about loon tendencies in this area overall.

Loon Courtship Behaviors

Once the male and female loon are on the same territory, the season of love—their courtship if you will—begins. While there are a number of displays that often appear to casual observers as some kind of courtship ritual between loons of the opposite sex, this is not the case at all, and most of these interactions are territorial in nature. Many denizens of the bird world have elaborate courtship dances or rituals, including eagles, which lock talons together during a magnificent aerial display, or western grebes, which literally walk on water, but that is not the way of the loon. Though brilliant in their plumage, loon courtships are quite subdued, quietly graceful in manner. Early in the breeding season, pairs that return to a lake will get to know each other, or reacquaint themselves, by swimming and foraging together, often diving together in synchronous fashion and surfacing at the same time. While swimming together, several bonding rituals are noticeable, including quick bill movements in and out of the water, known as "bill dipping" and "bill flipping," as well as bowing their heads down, with their bill resting on their chest, known as the "pelican" posture. The pair will also swim together in circular fashion, positioned head to tail, in a ritual known as "circling." And that's about it—no elaborate wing flaps or crazy displays.

When their mating is about to be consummated, either of the loons will lead the other to shore, likely the one, male or female, that is a more experienced breeder, this accompanied by soft mewing or hooting vocalizations and perhaps head and bill movements motioning toward the shore. They will choose a clearing on land, often close to their eventual nesting site and close to the water. As the Cornell biologists noted, the male then approaches the female "from behind, and mounts the female by climbing over the female's back, standing half upright. The female raises her tail and cloacal contact occurs." The whole process takes less than a minute. Interestingly, other than spotting a male loon making a yodel call, the position of the male during the act of copulation is the

Loon pair in the act of copulation, Meetinghouse Pond, Marlborough, 2016. *Courtesy Brian J. Reilly.*

only reliable way that a male and female loon can be distinguished in the wild. Afterward, the male "dismounts," and while the pair may remain on shore together for a time, the male is usually the first to return to the water. His mate "may remain on the land and engage in ritualized nest-building (grabbing nest material and placing it around her body) before returning to the water." A mated pair of loons will copulate on successive days, but there have been no definitive studies regarding frequency of copulation. Anecdotal information on this topic from the late Kittie Wilson, a reliable observer and renowned photographer of the loons on Pleasant Lake in New London for many years (as relayed to the LPC), suggests that copulation took place much more frequently than is usually thought to be the norm. The interval of time between copulation and when egg-laying occurs is also uncertain but requires at least two days and likely longer so that egg formation may develop. Once again, there's much about loons that is still to be learned.

Choosing a Nesting Site

Once copulation has occurred, the nesting process begins. This includes choosing a suitable nesting site, as well as building the nest itself. Widespread studies show that it is the male that chooses the nesting site, even if his mate has been on the territory longer and would, presumably, have a greater knowledge of the terrain. The site of the nest is critical for success, so loons, in general, know what to look for and what will work best. The loon's nest is usually on dry land, preferably an island, but whether located there or on the shoreline, it will be built very close to the water's edge, on the sheltered side of an island facing the mainland or on the lee side of a body of water with no islands. Ideally, the water will be at least a foot deep, allowing a submerged approach to the nest, and there is often some cover, whether it be a small shrub or bush, cattails or marsh grass. In some areas, nests may be constructed on the tops of bogs, sedge mats or even on top of floating logs or muskrat houses. Regarding a nest's location in relationship to the loon's territory, biologist Tiffany Grade put it best:

> *Good nesting sites are limited in any given territory—that really good spot may be deep in the territory or it may be near the edge, and the loons choose it because it is The Good Spot, regardless of its proximity in relation to the territory boundary. Even if they are nesting near the territory boundary, they may position themselves so that the view is into the territory rather than to the outside just because the configuration of the site is more favorable for nesting that way (leeward side of island, more protected in general, etc.).*

Loons will also nest on artificial rafts, which are today used extensively by the LPC in areas where other options are limited due to human development. However, while all of the above sites are ideal locations, there have been many cases over the years where loons have built their nests in unusual locations that don't conform to the norm. Nests have been found much farther away from a pond or lakeside than is typical, as was found under the porch of the camp home of Mrs. David Gregg in 1979 on Squam Lake's Perch Island. That family kindly "abandoned' their home, going above and beyond so that the loons could nest without human interference, and two chicks hatched as a result. Indeed, the Gregg family has routinely given their home and dock over to the loons on Squam's Perch Island territory for over 40 years now during the nesting season. Perhaps the most unusual nesting site chosen by a loon in New Hampshire in recent memory, one that broke all the rules of what a "good spot" entails, occurred in the summer of 2022 on Lake Winnipesaukee. There, in the Weirs Channel to Paugus Bay, a loon pair built their nest in May on the end of the North Water Marine dock, a place where hundreds of boats would eventually pass close by every day during the boating season. This was a pair of loons that were new to the area, and as LPC biologist Caroline Hughes commented, "It could be that these are inexperienced loon parents." While the loons on the nest certainly appeared to be unfazed, they were unsuccessful in their first nesting attempt, and their second attempt on the same site also failed, with one egg turning out to be inviable, while the other one was smashed under unknown circumstances, before they vacated their nest in late July. While inexperience may have been a factor, it is also entirely possible that the loons chose this location because there were few or no other options for shoreline nesting in this heavily developed area.

As to nest construction, it is thought that the male is the one most likely to begin the construction process, since they choose the nesting site, but the female participates as well. The nest is constructed from whatever

Loon pair gathering nesting material, Upper Baker Pond, Orford, May 2022. *Courtesy Cathy Eastburn.*

vegetation is available close by, often within reach to the loons while sitting on the nest itself according to Jeff Fair. Suitable materials include dried cattails and reeds on shore, or plant matter growing in the shallow water, and the nest is contoured in a circular or oval shape to fit the loon's body, measuring about two feet in diameter and four inches deep. Construction takes about a week to complete, although if renesting occurs later in the season, it can take as little as a day. Sadly, there are many reasons why a nest might fail at a given location, and it's not always the loon's fault. Sometimes shoreline development, climate change and other human causes are the culprit, as will be discussed further on.

EGG LAYING AND INCUBATION

Once the nest is ready, and sometimes before it is even finished, the female loon takes her place and begins to lay her eggs. This usually takes place in the month of May or June, though eggs are sometimes laid even in July, albeit with lower hatching success. The eggs themselves average just under four inches long and are a brownish olive color with speckling that is dark brown or black. The texture, as with the coloring, can vary from a granular matte finish to a glossy look. The weight of a loon egg in America overall averages about .316 pounds, with a high of .44 pounds, somewhat smaller than the eggs laid by a Canada goose. After the first loon egg is laid, subsequent eggs are slightly smaller. It is interesting to note that the thickness of the shells of loon eggs has changed over time, demonstrably so. The LPC has what is probably the largest archive of loon eggs, both complete examples and fragments of broken or predated eggs, anywhere in the world. During a tour of their facility in Moultonborough with LPC senior biologist John Cooley Jr., I was shown a fragment that dated from the 1930s, the shell clearly thicker than samples from modern-day loon eggs, almost certainly due to environmental factors that will be discussed later.

The number of eggs a loon may lay, known as a "clutch," averages about 2, with the second being laid about a day apart, though this interval can increase to up to three days depending on their nutrition. The average clutch size of New Hampshire and New England loons has possibly changed over time. In his seminal work *The Birds of America*, John J. Audubon strongly asserted that a loon's egg clutch was usually 3 in number, and perhaps that indeed was the number in 1840. However, the LPC now knows, through

Loon egg, recovered from a washed-out nest, Back Bay, Wolfeboro, June 2019. It would not hatch. *Courtesy Brooks Campbell.*

extensive study and fieldwork, that the average clutch size here averages 1.7 eggs. Indeed, the loon has a low reproduction rate, and each egg is a precious resource when it comes to growing their numbers, a negative that is offset by their relatively long life span, as will be discussed at greater length. The egg laying process is normally trouble-free, but in rare instances female loons may have difficulties. A loon on Waukeena Lake in Danbury died in 1996 because she was unable to pass an egg, death resulting from either infection or internal tissue damage. This condition, called "egg-binding," can occur in other birds, especially chickens, but this was the first documented instance amongst loons and is considered a rare occurrence. While 1- and 2-egg clutches are commonly found among New Hampshire loons, 3-egg clutches are extremely rare and occur in New Hampshire only .0052 percent of the time, and even then, they are rarely successfully hatched. Several examples of a 3-egg clutch have been documented over the last 47 years, including two on Squam Lake. One 3-egg clutch was laid on a nesting raft in 1990, which was immediately abandoned by its parents, while another was laid in the Heron Cove territory in 2015 that was affected by a territorial dispute (see the full story that follows).

Once laid, the business of incubating the egg(s) so that it will, hopefully, hatch is immediately begun by both loon parents. Interestingly, loons do not have an incubation patch on their underside like many birds. However, the posterior part of their underbelly, between their feet, where the eggs are incubated has a dense network of veins, "extensive subcutaneous vascularization," as it is described by the experts at Cornell, whose blood flow provides the needed warmth. The warmth from the feet themselves is also thought to aid in the incubation process. The time of incubation from laying until the first chick is hatched averages about 26 to 27 days in New Hampshire, with the second egg coming about a day later. About 6.8 percent of the time in New Hampshire, an egg is nonviable and will not hatch. This could be due to any number of reasons, including an egg that was not successfully fertilized or something that went awry in the incubation process, including stressors relating to territorial invaders, predators and human disturbances. Loons will abandon eggs for any number of reasons, but in other cases some pairs will continue to incubate their unviable eggs long after the time for hatching has passed, sometimes over 70 days.

When it comes to incubation duties, loon behavior in this area is surprising to many. First and foremost, it's not just the female sitting on the nest, as loon parents share incubating duties on an equal basis. In fact, in the first week, studies have shown that males perform about 60 percent of incubation duties, possibly due to the fact that the female, after egg-laying has been completed, needs more time to forage for food to replenish her bodily nutrients. On the other hand, by week four, as the hatch time approaches, females usually are doing 60 percent or more of the incubating while their mate is occupied elsewhere. LPC data also indicates that females tend to be on the nest at nighttime during the whole period of incubation more than males.

Incubation and nest attentiveness does vary depending on location and the size of the body of water where a loon pair is located. Those loon pairs whose territory encompasses an entire pond or small lake spend anywhere from 96 to 99 percent of their time tending to their incubation duties and will generally have greater success in hatching chicks. For those loon pairs that occupy a large lake where there are multiple territories, their nest attentiveness runs anywhere from 78 to 96 percent and can result in less success. This is understandable because loon pairs on larger lakes often have to spend a great deal of time and energy defending their territory from invading loons looking to usurp them. This is especially prevalent on Squam Lake and Lake Winnipesaukee, where chick production is usually well below that of other lakes and ponds across the Granite State, both for this reason and many other factors. One interesting example of this kind of territorial disruption, one with tragic consequences, took place in 2015 in the Heron Cove territory on Squam Lake. As the LPC's Squam Lakes biologist Tiffany Grade relates,

The curious backstory is that the longtime male was *extremely* *late coming back that year, not returning until Memorial Day weekend. In his absence, an unbanded male had taken the territory. He got kicked out by the male from the Moon Island territory, who then got kicked out by the Heron Cove male once he finally showed up. So, by the end of Memorial Day weekend, that poor female had already had to deal with three different males! With the regular pair finally re-united (they had been together in Heron Cove since 2009), they quickly settled on their* [nesting] *raft and produced three eggs. Two of the eggs hatched. The day the second chick hatched I had gone in to check on the family. The female was coming out of the raft cove and the male stayed in the cove brooding the two chicks. I went to put out chick signs* [warning local boaters of their presence] *and about 15 minutes later I heard the male yodeling and saw him reared up in the water, then chasing another loon out of the raft cove. At the same time, the female of the pair (who had been elsewhere in the territory foraging) came wing-rowing back toward her mate. As the intruder headed out, the pair swam to the raft cove hooting, the male yodeled again, and I saw only one chick in the cove. I then got distracted getting the bands on the intruder. When I looked again, I still saw only one chick with the male. The female headed out of the raft cove again after a few minutes, and the male climbed on the raft to incubate the third egg, and I still could only see one chick. As the parents were dealing with the intruder, one of the chicks must have gotten taken by a predator—fish, snapping turtle, something. I have this very distinct memory of seeing the two chicks in the raft cove, glancing away for a few moments toward the adults, and, when I looked back, the one chick was gone—just that fast. The intruder was back again in the afternoon—ironically, she had been previously paired for six years with the Heron Cove male in a neighboring territory (from 2001 to 2006). But, after getting chased away again, she seemed to have gotten the message. I collected the egg two days after these events, by which time they had abandoned it. The egg had a fully formed chick in it that appeared to be in the final stages of absorbing the yolk sac. Whether it would have been able to complete the absorption and hatch had they given it another day or so of incubation, or if it ran into a problem right at the end with absorbing the yolk sac, I can't say for sure. But we were so close to having three chicks hatch! The pair did end up successfully raising their remaining chick.*

A loon incubating its eggs, Lake Massabesic, Auburn, June 2010. *Courtesy John M. Rockwood.*

While this example is an extreme one, it does show all the challenges that loon parents face with successfully hatching any eggs and protecting their chicks, let alone the extra complications a three-egg clutch entails.

Studies show that the average bout of incubation for an individual loon can last anywhere from 2 to 6 hours, though bouts as short as a half an hour and as long as 12 hours have been documented in New Hampshire. While one loon is on the nest, the other is out foraging, patrolling their territory, preening or sleeping. The loon that remains on the nest, whether during the day or at night, remains constantly vigilant, alert for any possible predators and loon intruders. Other waterfowl, turtles, raccoons and even beavers may approach the nest, and loons are not shy about chasing them off if they are deemed a threat. However, one of the biggest threats to loons and their eggs, and it's been a growing one for over the last decade now, is bald eagle predation. The first documented incident of an eagle killing a loon on its nest occurred on Baxter Lake in Rochester in 2012, when LPC volunteer Joe Roy reported a destroyed nest and a dead loon just in front of it. Several days earlier, Roy had reported the presence of eagles at one end of the lake, and a necropsy of the dead loon determined that the otherwise healthy loon was killed during the attack. More recently, an eagle predation attempt on a loon nest was documented by the LPC's LoonCam in 2019 when an eagle twice landed on an untended nest but failed to take the eggs early on; it eventually predated one chick a few days later, hours after it hatched.

Depending on how long the incubation bout may last, the parent in charge will periodically stand up and, using their beak, turn the egg(s) before settling back down to continue their incubation duties. During this process, the loon looks remarkably like a penguin. Incubation activities take place at all times, in all kinds of weather, and whether it be hot and humid or driving rain conditions, loon pairs are intrepid in performing their duties. However, some extreme environmental conditions (not including human factors) can cause a loon pair to leave their nest or even abandon it altogether. This includes prolonged periods of heavy rain that can wash away a nest or even instances of severe black fly disturbances, swarms of which caused the abandonment of two nests on Squam Lake in 2014. The summer weather is also a potential problem, as the days become increasingly warmer by late June. That's ideal for vacationers but not so much for loons, which are, it must be remembered, northern birds that are at the limit of their southern range in New Hampshire. You know how you feel on those hot summer days and nights outside, dripping with perspiration? Well, as the LPC's LoonCam shows every year, loons too feel the effects of the heat. Just like your family dog, loons can be seen with beak open, panting in an effort to regulate their body temperature. LPC data indicates that temperatures above 78.08 degrees Fahrenheit will cause this panting, but studies also show that adults are more likely to stay on their nests when temperatures are high to protect their eggs, even if it is to their own detriment. In some extreme cases, incubation periods are ended because the loon must take a dive into the water to cool off, leaving the nest vulnerable to predators.

The nest exchange between a loon pair most often takes place within an hour of sunrise and again between 11:00 a.m. and 1:00 p.m. Sometimes the nest is left unattended as the one loon departs and goes to meet its mate in the middle of their territory for the exchange. In other cases, the loon parent coming in for nest duty will swim right up to the nest area, often circling, making sure the coast is clear, before climbing up on land and waiting for its mate to get off the nest. At times, the exchanges don't always take place to the satisfaction of the incubating loon. In these cases, the loon will wail for its mate, calling it to the nest. In some cases, when its mate does not appear in good time, the incubating loon will leave the nest unattended and go off in search of it, wailing all the while. While such an action leaves the eggs in the nest vulnerable to predators, loon eggs can still remain viable even if they go un-incubated for up to 24 hours. It's a dicey situation and, as anyone who has tuned into the LPC's annual LoonCam proceedings over the years knows, can lead to a nesting failure. The LoonCam has also shown that loon pairs will often leave their nests and the eggs within unattended in the early morning hours between dawn and 8:00 a.m.

Finally, after about 27 days or so, the loon egg(s), if all has gone well, is ready to hatch. For those successful loon pairs that reach this point, their true work—the drive to propagate their species—has only just begun.

8

RAISING LOON CHICKS

Observations into this phase of a loon's life, that of raising a newly hatched chick or two, are a rare treat for wildlife enthusiasts in New Hampshire. They are also full of events that we humans can easily understand and identify with, as the way of loon parents in many ways mirrors our own actions when it comes to how we tenderly and patiently care for our young. This process, raising a young loon from hatching to the time, about 12 weeks later, when it can fly, is called "fledging" and is important to the survival not only of individual loon chicks but, collectively, for the whole species in New Hampshire as well. It is for this reason that the LPC invests large amounts of time and resources in the summer, the busiest time of year, monitoring the state's lakes and ponds, putting protective measures in place where possible and gathering data about nesting successes and failures. Here's one figure that every loon biologist in New Hampshire knows, and one that all loon lovers should know—0.48. That is the minimum number of surviving chicks, ones that have successfully fledged, per territorial pair that needs to survive in our state in order to keep the loon population viable for the long term. Put in stark terms, that means that if a pair hatches two eggs, and only one chick survives to fledge, that is a success. Sounds easy, right? But it's not. When both chicks survive to fledge, it's a cause for celebration. Some years, as will be discussed, are better than others. For example, 2021 was a down year, but 2022 was a success. Additionally, 1981 saw record success at the 0.70 rate, almost certainly due to the actions of the LPC as it ramped up operations, a rate that has never since been matched, while 1998 dropped to an all-time low of 0.30. There are so many reasons why the fledging rate fluctuates, and that is what the LPC is continually at work on, being both proactive (research and legislation, for example) and reactive (weather condition–related rescues) to help our loon parents in New Hampshire have optimal breeding success.

Egg Hatching

Prior to the actual hatching of the loon egg, the fully formed chick can be heard peeping inside the egg. The loon chick, as with other birds, has a specially formed egg tooth that it uses to "pip" or crack the shell of the egg so that it may emerge. This pipping action usually takes place at the large end of the egg, the hole cut in a circular fashion. The time it takes for a loon chick to emerge can vary widely, ranging from about 8 hours to nearly 20 hours, experience showing that the longer it takes, the lower chance of survival for the chick due to its weakened and exhausted state when it finally emerges. LPC field biologist Jack Noon inadvertently witnessed this process in June 1987 when checking out the nesting pair on Lake Umbagog's Leonard Marsh territory. He arrived on the scene in the morning while both loon parents were off the nest and noticed "pencil-sized holes in the tops of both eggs. Suspecting avian predation, I went right to the nest. Both eggs were warm and both eggs started cheeping at me! Left quickly." Three days later, Noon was able to observe both chicks with their parents.

Loon Chicks

Once fully hatched, loon chicks are described as "semi-precocial" by Cornell biologists. This simply means that, from day one, loon chicks are born with their eyes open, are covered with down and can leave the nest but still need to be fed by their parents. (Fully precocial birds can feed themselves.) In short, they are able to do many things an adult can do, even if they will need much practice and help to hone their skills so that they can survive on their own. Within a few short hours, if the weather allows, loon chicks, their down now dried, can enter the water and swim with their parents and even make short, shallow dives. Interestingly, loon chicks will first use their tiny wings to help

Loon chick testing its wings, Lake Massabesic, Auburn, July 2011. *Courtesy John M. Rockwood.*

propel them underwater, but this ends after the first week. Within two days, loon chicks, while still totally dependent on their parents for feeding, have the ability to peer into the water and dive and chase after small minnows, although their success rate is low. One of the most fascinating things about loon chicks and their care is the fact that by the end of their first week of life, they can be spotted riding on the backs of their parents. Both parents provide this safe space for their chicks, where they can keep warm, rest, sleep and even feed, but observations show that male loons tend to provide these "piggy-back" rides more often than females.

Not surprisingly, the loon parents' early days are all about feeding their chicks and teaching them how to feed on their own. One of the loon pair will stay on the surface closely guarding the chicks, while the other dives to bring small minnows and other prey to the surface and present it to the chick, whether in the water or on the other parent's back. The prey is offered sideways so that the chick will learn the skill of manipulating it with its beak and tongue so that the food can slide vertically down its gullet. This soon enough progresses to a parent dropping a small fish into the water in front of the chick so that they can practice catching it on their own. Loon chicks remain dependent on their parents for food for at least the first two months of life; by week eight or so, they are able to capture 50 percent of their daily needs and progress to 90 percent or more another month later. Even at this age, loon parents will sometimes still feed their young, usually at night or in the early morning hours. In the first weeks, loon chicks are voracious eaters, and there are frequent bouts of feeding. To indicate their hunger, loon chicks will beg by cheeping or yelping loudly and even peck at their parents' cheek, side of the bill or neck to make their wants known.

SIBLING RIVALRY

One aspect of the development of loon chicks, when a loon pair hatches more than one chick, is the common phenomenon known as "sibling rivalry." In a two-egg clutch, the second egg will typically hatch about a day later. During this interval of time between hatchings, the LPC has noted one interesting behavior by loon parents. After the first egg has hatched, they have often been observed removing the egg membrane and large fragments from the nest, a behavior that is not common for many bird species. So, what may be the reason for this bit of housekeeping? As the LPC explains,

> *The first chick ends up spending a lot of time on the nest while the family waits for the hatch of the second chick. Loon eggs and newly-hatched loon chicks are brown in color, and as such, they blend in with their surroundings on the nest. The egg membrane and the inside of eggshells, in contrast, are a creamy white color. That makes them much more conspicuous and, if left on the nest, could increase the chance of nest predation. Therefore, it is believed that in removing egg membranes and large eggshell pieces from the nest, adult loons may be protecting their chick and the second egg from being easily noticed by predators.*

To continue, once that second egg hatches, there are now two chicks vying for the attention of their parents. This is especially true when it comes to feeding, and it is often the case that, when food is scarce, parents will feed only the first chick that gets to the offered food. However, even when food resources are plentiful, the older loon chick will assert its dominance over its sibling so that it will be fed first and most frequently. In essence, it is the dynamic that exists between two chicks that is the deciding factor, not loon parents. This dominance, which is allowed by loon parents without interference, occurs in the form of the dominant chick pecking at the head of the submissive chick.

According to LPC biologist Tiffany Grade, "Pecking on the head can occur almost immediately once both chicks are in the water. It has certainly happened on our LoonCam, much to the horror of the viewers!" While the two chicks don't compete directly for food, the elder chick intimidates its sibling to become first in the pecking/feeding order. Sometimes the submissive chick will fight back and hold its own, and sometimes it can gain food by eating prey that is rejected by its older sibling simply because the dominant chick is full and can no longer cram any more food down its gullet. But if these circumstances don't prevail, the submissive chick will be fed up to 50 percent less than its sibling, and eventually, all parental feeding ceases. The submissive chick then grows malnourished and is unable to keep up with the rest of the family. In this situation, submissive chicks that fall outside the family orbit easily fall prey to predators of all kinds and often die within several days. In other situations, the rivalry can take an even darker turn, with the oldest chick violently attacking its sibling and either pecking it to death or holding its head underwater and drowning it. Both scenarios are a stark illustration of Darwin's ideal of the survival of the fittest, which is common in the animal world. However, they're also some of the most difficult events to observe, no matter if you're a casual observer or a trained professional. In New Hampshire, LPC biologists are trained not to intervene in these deadly situations, and the public in general is advised by the LPC and New Hampshire's Fish and Game Department not to interfere with the activities of wild animals.

For the chick that does become displaced from its family, all may not be lost. In extremely rare instances, such a chick might be adopted by another loon family, as happened on Bow Lake in Strafford in the 1990s and on both Bow Lake and Silver Lake in Madison in 2014. In the case of Silver Lake, the displaced chick was a week older than its new siblings, while on Bow in 2014 the displaced chick was a few days younger. Another incident took place in 1995, beginning on Mendums Pond in Barrington. Here, the second chick of a brood was seen to have been attacked by its sibling and subsequently trailed behind its family before being entirely abandoned. Local residents intervened and took the chick into their care and called the LPC. Their biologists took the chick and first tried to introduce to it a nesting pair on another lake, without success. They then made a last-ditch attempt, releasing the chick onto Silver Lake in Madison. The territorial pair there already had a chick that was larger than its potential foster sibling. Quite surprisingly, and touching to many, one of the adult pair, on spotting the transplanted chick, immediately broke away from the family to dive and came up with a small fish to feed it. It was a nice outcome.

Threats to Loon Chicks

Of course, loon chicks are extremely vulnerable to predators of all kinds, and next to their feeding duties, loon parents are kept most busy defending their young from all manner of threats. These threats don't just come from predators like bald eagles or snapping turtles but other loons as well. As previously discussed, loons are extremely territorial during the summer months, and there are many floaters out there seeking a territory of their own. In many cases, they will begin their assault on a new territory by attacking loon chicks, with the knowledge that by killing the chicks, they can break up the pair bond. These attacks show a different side of the loon, for they can be relentless and brutal in nature. In many cases, one loon chick may be killed but a second survives. Should an intruding male loon be successful in taking over a territory, even if he pairs up with the surviving female, any surviving chicks are doomed, as they are usually killed by the new male on the scene. Why isn't the surviving chick simply adopted? Once again, it's a case of survival of the fittest; the male, like all loons, is instinctually hardwired and interested only in propagating his own bloodline and not that of a weaker rival loon that he has conquered. One example, among many, of this type of threat occurred on Pool Pond in Rindge on the evening of August 15, 2022. In this case, the female of a pair with two chicks died of unknown causes, leaving the father to be his chicks' sole provider, both feeding them and defending them. When an invading loon came into the territory, this father loon defended his chicks fiercely, one of which subsequently flew off to another nearby body of water. However, his other chick was badly injured in the attack, suffering a compound fracture to its wing, which was broken in four places. This chick subsequently beached itself and was recovered by the LPC. Sadly, the chick had to be euthanized due to the severity of its injuries. A subsequent necropsy of the loon in January 2023 showed that the father loon had kept his chick well fed and cared for. As for the hard-fighting father, he survived the attack and may have returned for the 2023 season, though his unbanded status means that he cannot be positively identified. Whatever the case, the pair on Pool Pond this year did meet with success, hatching one chick in June after an initial nest failure in May, and it has so far survived to the end of the season.

EARLY FLIGHT

In other areas, loon chicks develop rapidly. Not only do they grow quickly in size, but by the end of the first week they also can access their uropygial gland and perform all the preening and maintenance activities, including the foot waggle, observed in adults. They will early on, during their exercise periods, rise up out of the water in so-called mock battles in imitation of their parents' actions. Flying comes along at a later time. Chicks flap their wings early on, at as little as 8 days old, and even instinctually orient themselves into the wind. At the age of 3 weeks, juvenile feathers "erupt," then grow rapidly for the next 8 weeks, their down replaced by gray juvenile feathers, with the development of the bill, head and legs coming before flight feathers fully develop. Some may attempt to fly by the age of about 45 days; the capacity for flight is more developed by 75 days. Their first flights are short in both duration and distance, the young loon having difficulty staying aloft, sometimes even falling out of the sky. Interestingly, our New England loons are late flyers in comparison to their midwestern brethren, which learn to fly several weeks earlier, perhaps because their upcoming first migration journey is a much longer one than the short flight to the ocean required by New Hampshire's loons.

9

THE MYSTERIOUS LIVES OF IMMATURE LOONS

With the end of summer and fall fast approaching in September, juvenile loons, now about 13 weeks old, will soon be separated from their parents for the first time. While it has often been said about humans that "a mother's work is never done," this is not the case for loon parents, and it will soon be the case that they are separated forever.

FIRST MIGRATION

In terms of fall migration, one parent, often the male, will depart his summer home for ocean waters, sometimes as early as when his offspring is 9 or 10 weeks old. However, one of the parent loons remains on the body of water with its chick(s), usually for another 3 or 4 weeks, eventually departing for the ocean and leaving its babies behind. The juvenile loon will then linger on its birth home for another 1 to 3 weeks before eventually departing for the ocean during its first migration. In some cases, according to the LPC, juveniles will leave their birth lake to travel to another nearby larger lake to swim and feed with other loon chicks before migrating.

EARLY OCEAN LIFE

From here on out, the activities of immature loons, as they are called once they have left their birth lake, have not been well documented or studied and are somewhat of a mystery. It is known that they migrate to the ocean, but whether alone or with other juveniles is not certain. Once they reach the ocean, this becomes the immature loon's home for the next three years. In this environment, they swim and float, feed and forage, often in solitary fashion, though sometimes ocean loons will forage in a cooperative manner and perhaps even raft together at times. They periodically molt during this time, and by the approximate age of 24 to 26 months, they attain their adult breeding plumage. But this occurs too late for them to join the adult loons in their journey back to New Hampshire's inland waters. So, their return to inland waters is delayed for another season.

RETURNING TO INLAND WATERS

Once the newly mature loon has returned to its New Hampshire home, it lives an unsettled and semi-solitary life for at least the next year and quite possibly the next 3 years or even possibly a bit longer. Indeed, Cornell biologists state that the average age at first breeding for males is 5.9 years, while that for females is 7.4 years. In fact, no male younger than 4 years of age has been documented as part of a breeding pair, while the youngest female documented in a breeding pair was 5 years old. So, what are these adult, unpaired loons (floaters) doing in the meantime? At any given time in New Hampshire in the summer, as of this writing, the LPC estimates that there are about 100 floaters, these loons spending their time on lakes and ponds that are either marginal or not suitable for nesting, or are otherwise unoccupied. Floaters also scope out other nearby lakes that do have territorial pairs, seeking out opportunities to gain a territory, and a mate, of their own. These solitary floaters can often be seen on New Hampshire's smaller bodies of water, oftentimes ones that are heavily developed and have a large amount of recreational activity, and they frequently travel from one body of water to another alone, without a true place to call home.

Eventually, both male and female floaters may gain a territory in one of several different scenarios. These include occupying and holding a territory that somehow became vacant (perhaps by an untimely death) or even carving out a new territory in a body of water where none had existed before. Of course, these loons, both male and female, will also try to oust other loons from their established territories to gain it for their own, an event that occurs multiple times during the course of an adult loon's life. As in the rest of the animal world, the stronger always supplants the weaker in a cycle of generational changes, although in the case of loons, this change usually comes with conflict and confrontation. Nothing comes easy to a young loon, and they usually have to fight to find a mate and a territory all their own. Once a territory is attained, it may be kept for years on end, but usually not without a spirited defense at varied intervals.

10

LOON LONGEVITY

This is one aspect of the loons in New Hampshire that I never gave much thought to before, but it's yet another part of their fascinating history. Loons, in fact, are long-lived birds, though knowledge about the ultimate age they may attain is continually evolving and changing. The world's oldest known loon is the previously mentioned male of the banded pair at Seney National Wildlife Refuge in Michigan's Upper Peninsula, he being known exactly to be 35 years old in 2022 because he was banded as a chick. His mate is thought to be about a year older due to the loon's minimum age at first breeding. Every year these birds return, they set yet another record. So, the fact remains that we don't yet know how long a loon can ultimately live in the wild.

Loons in Captivity

Incidentally, and in sharp contrast, there's a reason you don't see loons in a zoo or wildlife preserve, even though captive loons were advertised by one bird dealer in New England early in the 20th century. Loons do not do well at all in captivity. If captured as a chick or adult on their home lake for whatever reasons, they will most likely die due to stress alone within a short period when taken out of their natural environment. Even those loons that have been hatched in captivity do poorly, rarely surviving for more than a year and usually for far less time. However, there is a novel approach that the Biodiversity Research Institute (BRI) of Portland, Maine, one of the LPC's partner organizations, has pioneered, that of raising loon chicks translocated from New York to help repopulate Massachusetts waters in specially constructed "rearing pens" on a natural body of water. This method minimizes the amount of human contact and keeps the chicks in a somewhat natural environment. However, this captivity is only designed to last a short time before their release into their new home waters, anywhere from several weeks to a month later. The short lesson to be learned here is simple: if you see a loon chick left alone on your own New Hampshire lake, do not take it into "protective custody" and put it in your bathtub. Instead, call the experts at the LPC for guidance. By leaving it alone, you may actually save its life. Indeed, "Caution before action" is the LPC's motto, formulated in the wake of two instances on New Hampshire waters in 1992, when loon chicks, thought to have been abandoned, were taken into people's homes and subsequently died overnight. Both losses were categorized as "preventable."

Loons in the wild seldom live more than 20 years, though, as we have seen, the possibilities are there for a much longer life. As is the case in the wild for all birds and animals, there are many dangers that can end a loon's life, both human and natural causes. Some of these causes we'll touch on later; others have already been discussed, including loon territorial conflicts. According to the experts at Cornell, about 77 percent of juvenile loons survive for the first three years of life. Thereafter, the annual survival rate for adult loons ranges from 90 to 94 percent. As they age, this rate does go down, especially among the male loon population, whose survival rate dips to 75 percent annually between the ages of 14 and 18. By the way, it is hard to accurately determine the age of adult loons that have not been banded, though there have been studies that examine such things as the telomeres of their DNA, but these methods have yet to be perfected.

NEW HAMPSHIRE'S OLDEST LOONS

To conclude this chapter, it is only fitting that we look at New Hampshire's oldest known loons, as determined by banding efforts, which first took place in the 1990s. Who knows, maybe one of these grand dames or gentlemen is on your lake? The oldest known loon in New Hampshire, and indeed all of New England, is the female loon that was banded on the Sweat Meadows territory on the Androscoggin River in Errol as an adult in 1993. This bird was estimated to be about 6 or 7 years old at the time of banding, meaning that she has attained the ripe old age of about 35 or 36 years as of this writing. This makes this loon one of the oldest documented loons in the world. As of the end of the 2018 season, this female loon had hatched 19 chicks and fledged 10 of them, a good success rate. However, from 2019 to 2022, she was not part of a territorial pair and was instead a floater, hanging out either on the Androscoggin River or near her old-time nesting places at Sweat Meadows and Harper's Meadow. Part of a territorial pair with eight different males from at least 1993 to 2018, she had during this time 7 years where, though paired, she produced no chicks, though she also had 7 years where she produced two chicks. In no year did she and her mate have two chicks successfully fledge. This area around Lake Umbagog has been a difficult one in terms of reproductive success, especially in the early 2000s. The Sweat Meadows female had a most difficult year in 1998; she and her mate were so involved in fending off invading loons that she did not even nest. If you were up in Errol over the years past, perhaps you got to see this true survivor—her original orange band has by now faded to brown. Happily, during the 2023 season, this history-making old gal made her annual return yet again. Certainly, time is now against her, but every year she returns she adds to our loon knowledge. No one knows what 2024 and beyond may bring, but we do know that LPC biologists will be on the lookout with bated breath for this beloved loon.

Next in line in terms of age for New Hampshire loons, with ages estimated as of this writing in early 2023, are the following birds:

Female banded as an adult on Squam Lakes Five Finger Point territory in Center Sandwich in 1998, estimated age 30 years

Female banded as an adult in 1998 on Middle Pea Porridge Pond in Madison and on territory (and nested unsuccessfully) in 2022, estimated age 30 years

Male on Swain's Lake in Barrington, banded in 1999, estimated age 30 years

Male banded on Martin Meadow Pond in Lancaster in 2000, estimated age 29 years

Male banded on Squam Lake's Swaney Brook/Great Island territory in Holderness in 2001, estimated age 28 years

Male from the Harper's/Sweat Meadows territory on Lake Umbagog in Errol banded as a chick in 1994 and on territory in 2022, hatching a chick at the known age of 28

Male banded on Lake Massabesic's Birch Island territory in Manchester in 2005, estimated age 23 years

Male banded in 2005 on Little Sebago Lake's Policeman's Cove territory in Gray, Maine, on Lake Winnipesaukee's Back Bay territory in Wolfeboro since 2019, estimated age 23 years (read more about this bird further on)

Male banded on Lake Winnipesaukee's Lincoln Island territory in Moultonborough in 2006, in later years sighted on the adjacent Whaleback Island territory, estimated age 22 years

Female banded as a chick on Squam Lake's Moon Island territory in Holderness in 2001, in recent years seen on Pleasant Lake in New London, known age 21 years

Finally, there are a number of banded loons that were long-lived whose fate is unknown, having either died or moved to another area and not resighted in subsequent years. These include the female on Lake Massabesic's Yacht Club territory in Manchester, banded as an adult in 1999, last sighted in 2021, likely 29 or older; and the male banded on Sand Pond in Marlow and Lempster in 1998 as an adult, which moved to Millen Pond in Washington and was last seen in 2021. At that time, he was likely 26 or older. He may have died over the winter, as in 2021 he showed up on Lake Massasecum in Bradford acting lethargic, then ended up in a small pool of water below a dam on Sunapee, then apparently was able to fly off but did not return to Millen Pond in 2022 (interestingly, he was one of the loons rescued off the ice on Lake Sunapee in 2016). Other unknown loons include the female banded as a chick in 1998 on Meetinghouse Pond in Marlborough, sighted until at least 2020, known age 22 years old; and the adult male banded in 1999 on Squam Lake's Moultonborough Bay territory, not sighted since 2015, estimated age of 22 years old.

Of course, these are just the banded loons that we know about in the wilds of New Hampshire, and it's entirely possible that there are other similarly aged loons out there that have gone un-banded and unnoticed. It makes you think, doesn't it? But no matter what, we hope that the older loons detailed here continue to survive and thrive and that through them we may learn even more about their species.

PART II

SAVING OUR
NEW HAMPSHIRE LOONS

1

THE LOON AND ITS SLOW DECLINE

New Hampshire was a very different place some 13,000 years ago. It was the end of the Pleistocene epoch, what we today call the Ice Age, when the glaciers that covered North America and beyond began to recede. The entire Northeast, as well as most of Canada, was covered by the Laurentide Ice Sheet, which was as much as two miles thick in some places. But as it began to recede, it carved and gouged out huge chunks of the landscape, creating many glacial lakes, including the five Great Lakes, from the Midwest and throughout New England. In New Hampshire, most of our lakes were created by glacial action. Lake Winnipesaukee had been created in a previous ice age, but the retreating ice sheet caused the flow of the "Big Lake" to change drastically. The lake once drained into the Atlantic Ocean via its outlet at Alton Bay and down through the Merrymeeting River, but the debris left by the receding ice blocked this outlet, shifting the lake's water flow to the west, it now reaching the Atlantic through Paugus Bay and the Winnipesaukee River, flowing subsequently into the Merrimack River. Following this glacial action, New Hampshire was a barren tundra, but soon enough, at least in terms of earth time, once the dust settled, plant life returned, spreading from the south, and animals returned soon after that. Among them were loons, which surely thrived in our clear and cool glacier lakes. Indeed, loons existed even in the Pleistocene era, fossilized remains having been found from that epoch in California and Florida. Way back then, loons had a much larger range in North America than they do today, their summer breeding grounds extending as far south as Maryland and the

Ohio River valley. By about 8,000 years ago, the forests of New Hampshire were populated by the same kinds of trees that are still here today, including pine, oak and spruce. Once the animals returned, humans followed not long after, they being of the Clovis culture and referred to today by archaeologists as Paleo-Indians. They are thought to have crossed into North America via the land bridge that once connected Siberia and Alaska about 11,000 years ago. And that's when humans' relationship with the loon, and other wild animals in our state, got its start.

The Loon and Native American Culture

While we know little about the Paleo-Indians and their customs, we do know about their successors, the Indigenous people who were living here when the first Europeans arrived in the 1500s. These Native American groups were divided into several different tribes or bands—the Penacooks, the Winnipesaukee, the Ossipee, the Cowasuck, the Pigwackets and the Sokoki—collectively known as the Abenaki for their common language dialects. The Abenaki were not only hunters but also farmers and fishermen. Long before Europeans arrived here, about 9,500 years ago, the Abenaki people had established a summertime settlement at Acquadoctan, what is today known as The Weirs, in Laconia. Here, they set up fish traps, weirs, in the narrow channel to provide abundant food for a large summertime population. Not only did these Indigenous people share the lake with loons, which were likely much more abundant than today, but they also developed a spiritual kinship with them, as many Native American groups have done with the wild animals in their environment, and celebrated them in tribal lore, legends and stories highlighting their cultural and world beliefs. One of the central figures in Abenaki creation legends is Glooscap; he was created from the dust of the body of Tabaldak, the creator of all humans, along with his brother Malumis. While his brother was an evil spirit, Glooscap was given the power to create a good world. One of Glooscap's concerns was for hunters who would take too many animals and destroy the good world he had created. He kept an eye on men with the aid of a loon named Medawisla, which means "spirit bird" or "magic bird." Medawisla's calls, the haunting wails or tremolos of the loon, were said to be his reports or findings to Glooscap after spying on the Abenaki people. Because Glooscap was viewed by the Abenaki as a "benevolent" figure, Medawisla the loon was seen as a friendly figure, albeit a bit of a trickster. All of these mythical qualities of Medawisla truly fit in with the nature of the loon itself, its cries and its abilities to appear and disappear quickly. Interestingly, there are quite similar loon legends among the Mi'kmaq's of Maine and the Canadian Maritime provinces, where, according to folklorist Charles Leland, Kwemoo (the loon) is taught "a strange long cry like the howl of a dog" and becomes Glooscap's messenger and faithful friend.

One other Native folklore tale that has made the rounds in recent decades is that of the blind man and the loon, as described by historian Craig Mishler, an "ancient" tale about ritual healing that also tells how the loon got its necklace markings. This was an oral tradition that has origins in Greenland and the northern Arctic, where loons are plentiful and a species of "least concern" even today. This tale was first recorded in print in 1827 and since that time has spread in popularity all over Canada, the western United States and in modern days even into New England in the form of children's books. This almost universal tale, of which there are a number of variants, tells of a blind man who is out in the woods hunting with his wife, who leaves him out in the wilderness to starve after they shoot a bear with their bow and arrow. Left alone, the man crawls for a long way on his hands and knees until he hears a loon calling in the distance. He follows the sound to the shore of a lake, where a loon comes up and talks to him, telling him to wrap his arms around his neck. The loon subsequently takes the blind man out to the center of the lake, and after the third dive, the man tells the loon he can see clearly. The loon takes the man back to shore and is thanked by him. Early versions of the story tell of the subsequent revenge the man gains on his wife, while later versions focus on the reward, the "necklace" decoration, the loon receives for helping restore the blind man's sight.

While such folklore is indicative of the loon's importance to Native American culture, what do we really know about their actual relationship with Native peoples? No matter how highly regarded, the loon was not so sacred that it couldn't be killed. Though the evidence is scant all around, there is no doubt that loons were taken from time to time by the Abenaki people in New Hampshire, though they were likely a prey of opportunity and not a major food source. And unlike later-day white hunters, Native Americans did not kill loons simply for sport. Such actions were not a part of their culture, and all indications are that Native Americans had little or no impact on the loon population here or anywhere in New England. When loons were taken, as was customary of any animal they hunted, they used as much of the bird as possible. In addition to eating its meat, the sharp beak and leg bones were used as awls, the tough skin used as seat coverings or articles of clothing and the feathers used for ceremonial or decorative purposes, as well as for bedding. In short, very little would have gone to waste. To this day, Indigenous peoples in northern Canada are permitted to hunt loons for these very same purposes. Interestingly, the only actual account I've been able to find regarding loons and Native American peoples in New Hampshire comes from the experiences of John Stark, the originator of New Hampshire's "Live Free or Die" motto much later in life. Stark was captured by Abenaki warriors in April 1752 while on a hunting and trapping expedition along the Baker River near Rumney with his brother and some other men. He was taken as a captive to Canada, where, according to Concord historian James Lyford, he was made to run a gauntlet of warriors, being "smitten with the conventional pole tipped with a loon skin." Legend has it that Stark grabbed this stick from the first warrior and attacked him, surprising the other warriors. The chief, impressed by this act of courage, adopted John Stark as an honorary member of his tribe and protected him from further harm until he was eventually ransomed in the spring.

Finally, regarding Native American associations, we may wonder if they used any loon-related place names in the state. George Waldo Browne, in his *History of Hillsborough*, asserts, "The largest and most picturesque body of still water in town is the Indian's Che-sehunk-auke, meaning 'great place for loons,' which was immediately Englished by the white settlers as 'Loon Pond,' as they found a large number of that fowl in the vicinity." It was "a frequent meeting-place of the Indians in their journeys hither and yon." Browne also records one Indian legend associated with this body of water, but whether any of his Native American references have any factual basis or were a modern-day romantic construct is unknown. Interestingly, this pond was devoid of its namesake birds by the 1970s, and they would not return until 2003. For every year since 2007, there has been a territorial pair on this lake, and from that time to 2019, nine chicks have been hatched, with seven fledging, though no chicks have been hatched for the last three years.

THE LOON IN COLONIAL NEW ENGLAND

It was the coming of white European settlers to New Hampshire that would eventually result in major changes for New Hampshire's loon population, but this change would evolve slowly over the course of 200 years or more. The loon was not unknown to early English settlers, as the great northern diver inhabits the British Isles, but it was something of a bird of mystery and its habits were not well known or understood. The great northern diver, sometimes called the greatest speckled diver, probably gained its alternate name, loon, from either the Swedish word *lum*, meaning something that is "lame or clumsy," or the Old English word *lumme*, from which the modern word *lummox*, the term for an awkward person, is derived. Both words pertain to the loon's clumsy abilities when walking on land. The common loon's scientific name, *Gavia immer*, also has some interesting roots from Europe. *Gavia* was the Latin term for the sea smew, a small sea duck that is also black and white in color but otherwise has no relationship to the loon. Interestingly, in Scotland, according to historian W.H. Mullens, noted physician and sometime naturalist Robert Sibbald noted that the loon was called "the Goose of our country folk called the Ember Goose, which is said to make its nest under the water and hatch out its eggs there." The term *ember* (or *immer*) refers to the black coloring of the loon, and we are left to wonder whether or not the Scotch-Irish settlers who first came to New Hampshire in the early 1700s and settled in the area of modern-day Manchester and Londonderry referred to the loons they saw on Lake Massabesic as ember geese.

With the settling of New England and the establishment of colonies in Massachusetts and New Hampshire, there was a great interest in the flora and fauna of the region, and many of the animals and birds encountered, loons included, were commented on in widely popular accounts of the New World. The first account of the loon in New England comes from William Wood's book *New England's Prospect*, which was first published in 1634. He describes them as such; "The Loone is an ill-shap'd thing like a Cormorant; but that he can nyther goe nor flye; he maketh a noise sometimes like a Sowgelders horne." This last reference refers to a horn that a man who practiced the trade of gelding sows blew whenever he entered a town during his travels in old England to advertise his services. It is perhaps the most unusual description of the call of the loon, but how apt is anybody's guess. We may easily surmise that Wood encountered his loons off the coast of Cape Ann or even in the waters of Boston Harbor during his four-year stay in Massachusetts.

Our next account of the loon in early America comes from the Englishman John Josselyn, who spent two periods of his life in Massachusetts, the first for 15 months beginning in 1638 and again from 1663 to 1671. His published work *New England Rarities* (1671) provides a fascinating, and somewhat odd, account of the birds and animals of early New England, touching on their medicinal value in many cases. Josselyn traveled widely, including going as far north as New Hampshire's White Mountains, as well as spending time at the Maine coast at Black Point (Scarborough), so we know that he saw his share of loons. Of them, however, he has little to say, stating, "The Loone is a Water Fowl, alike in shape to the Wobble," that is, "ill shaped," a rather common description of the bird in early times. He recommended that both birds were good for "Aches," stating it was best "to salt them well, and dry them in an earthen pot well glazed in an Oven; or else (which is the better way) to burn them underground for a day or two, then quarter them and stew them in a Tin Stewpan with very little water." Doesn't sound very enticing, does it?

Interestingly, while there are seven loon-named bodies of water in the state, Loon Pond in Fremont is the earliest to be identified on a New Hampshire map, so far as I have been able to discover. It is identified on a survey map by Samuel Lane, a Stratham surveyor hired to run lines for Benjamin Cram and Josiah Robinson in the town of Poplin, now Fremont, in October 1774. Lane's map denotes Loon Pond as being 16 acres in size, located in a remote location in the western part of the town. Today, Loon Pond in Fremont is classified by the LPC as a "zero tier" body of water, which means it has not had a territorial pair of loons since the LPC began keeping records in 1975. The size of the pond itself, which is just over 14 acres, is on the small size for a territorial pair, and the water clarity is poor, so loon activity

Map detail, Loon Pond, Fremont, from "Lines Run & Land Measured for Benja Cram & Josiah Robinson at Poplin by order of Court, Oct. 24, 1774" by Samuel Lane. *Courtesy NH Division of Records Management and Archives.*

has been sparse or, as LPC biologist John Cooley Jr. put it, "ephemeral," here. An 1887 account of a summer boating excursion on the lake makes no mention of loons, and town historian Matthew Thomas commented in his 1998 *History of Fremont, N.H.* that he "has visited Loon Pond many times over the past 26 years, finally had the great privilege of hearing for the first time on September 24, 1992, the sound of a single loon near the shore of the pond....After more than 200 years the pond's namesake still occasionally inhabit its beautiful and glistening shores."

As far as can be found, the loon was largely ignored in New Hampshire nature writings until the late 1800s, though Jeremiah Belknap, in his *History of New Hampshire*, vol. 3 (1792), does include it in his list of birds found in the state. Another possible mention of New Hampshire loons is found in Audubon's *The Birds of America* from 1840. He related that he had received three eggs "taken from the nest of a Loon, made in a hummock, or elevated grassy hillock, at Sebago Pond, in New Hampshire." However, whether this is a mistaken reference to Sebago Lake (which can by no means be deemed a pond) in Maine or a misnamed New Hampshire lake is, unfortunately, unknown.

HUNTING THE LOON

By the time loons began to be mentioned again in print, they had largely already disappeared from southern New Hampshire. Why was so little attention paid to the loon, despite its striking plumage and unforgettable calls, and what happened to cause its disappearance? Early New Hampshire biologist Ned Dearborn perhaps stated it best when he wrote in 1901 in the popular *Granite Monthly* magazine that "the common loon is a picturesque element in the scenery of our northern lakes in summer." However, he also commented that "in the economical balance, they have little weight either way. The fish they consume are generally worthless, while their own flesh is hardly better." Simply put, the loon was perceived to have no economic value for our state. In terms of hunting the loon for food, it was a difficult bird to hunt due to its elusive nature and the fact that it does not generally congregate in large numbers in comparison to waterfowl such as the mallard duck, meaning the time required for such a small harvest was wasted effort in comparison. Too, loon flesh was generally undesirable due to its fishy taste, once again considered poor fare when compared to the tasty flesh of other game more easily taken. Of course, this was not just true of the loon—fish-eating waterfowl such as the cormorant and the merganser were also deemed lesser fare. No doubt, just as today there are many who state that such flesh is always a delicacy if prepared properly, there were those who consumed loon flesh in the past, albeit the number of people who did so was likely quite low. Audubon, in his account of the loon, stated, "Although the flesh of the Loon is not very palatable, being tough, rank, and dark colored, I have seen it much relished by many lovers of good-living, especially at Boston, where it was not unfrequently served almost raw at the table of the house where I boarded." In discussing the attributes of the loon as a food source, New Hampshire writers are silent on the subject, but decoy historians have had their say. Quintina Colio stated, "It is well-known to bag a few 'tinkers,' or young loons for a delectable dinner," but does not say in what part of the country this was a tradition. Closer to home, decoy historian Joel Barber documented the work of decoy carver and lighthouse keeper Albert Orme of the Hendrick's Head Light in Sheepscot Bay, Maine. He decoyed loons as food for his table mainly to break the monotony of his other fare. To prepare the loon for eating, it was parboiled first and then roasted. Whether the loon was widely consumed in New Hampshire is unknown, but we do know that it was shot for sport. And that, perhaps, was the main allure of the loon for the outdoorsman, for to bag a loon required quite a bit of stealth, in addition to being a good shot. However, by the late 1800s, even this sport in the southern tier of New Hampshire was a waning one. Writing in 1892, Benjamin Read, the town historian of Swanzey, recorded that "wild ducks… [and] loons have had their haunts here, but their numbers have been too limited to afford sportsmen more than an occasional opportunity."

In the end, it is quite likely that inland hunters in most cases were not the main culprits when it came to killing loons in terms of numbers; more probably, those responsible were the market gunners hunting from small barges, called punts, mostly on the ocean in the Seacoast area marshes in such town as Hampton and Seabrook, as well as farther south in Massachusetts from Newburyport to Cape Cod. These hunters, looking to sell their harvest as table fare for guests in hotels and restaurants in large cities like Boston and New York, used small swivel cannons to kill hundreds of waterfowl indiscriminately in one blast, both in the fall and spring migration periods. While ducks were their primary targets, other water birds, loons included, were also brought down (and left in the ocean) as collateral damage, with Massachusetts ornithologist Edward Howe Forbush noting in 1912 that as many as 60 loons might be killed in this manner on a given morning near

Cape Cod from the middle of April to June back in the 1890s. Lest we think that such activity in Massachusetts has nothing to do with New Hampshire, it should be remembered that then, as now, many loons from southern New Hampshire wintered in Massachusetts waters. Forbush also stated that "probably the spring shooting of loons has had something to do with their decrease in numbers" and recommended that such activity in the spring should be prohibited. Forbush also wrote of the loon in his book *Birds of Massachusetts and Other New England States* (1925) that "the bird once bred in most of the ponds in the northern tier of states. Now its breeding places in the United States are comparatively few.…Fifty years ago it nested about many ponds in Massachusetts. Now I know of none where a breeding pair may surely be found…They were 'shot out'…or driven out by continual persecution." Finally, though such large-scale hunting is largely documented on the New England coastline, ornithologist William Brewster noted that such activities also took place on remote Lake Umbagog in northern New Hampshire. This hunting, legal at the time, took place from about 1838 to 1849, "the huge gun mounted on a swivel" used by the Stone brothers on their farm "near the Narrows." These brothers hunted "systematically and very successfully" and "were especially devoted to the pursuit of water-fowl" for their meat and feathers. While loons were certainly not their main target, an unknown number likely fell as incidental victims of this large-scale slaughter.

EARLY HUMAN IMPACTS ON LOONS

The loons' disappearance was slow and gradual and varied widely from one region to another in the state, so much so that there never was a general outcry about its status. These diminishing numbers occurred in New Hampshire towns from the Lakes Region southward even before the mid-19th century. In his 1845 history of Gilmanton, Daniel Lancaster wrote that Loon Pond in that town was named for the "water fowl of that name, which formerly abounded upon its shores." Loon Pond would remain largely loon-less, according to LPC records, with no loons recorded here until 1997 and no nesting pairs again until 2021. In 2022, two chicks were hatched there for the first time in modern history. Interestingly, both juveniles stayed later than they should have due to warm weather conditions. One of them flew off the pond early in the day on December 22, but the other had to be rescued by LPC biologists John Cooley Jr. and Caroline Hughes, with the

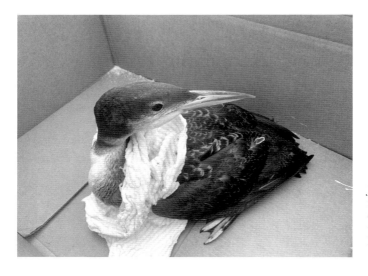

Juvenile loon rescued by LPC on Loon Pond, Gilmanton, December 22, 2022. *Author photo.*

author present as an extra hand, on that same day after the ice had firmed up and taken over most of the pond, leaving the bird without enough room for a takeoff. This loon was subsequently examined by wildlife rehabilitator Maria Colby, found to be healthy and released into the ocean successfully on December 24, a nice Christmas present.

Massachusetts naturalist Edward Samuels also wrote about the loon in his book *Birds of New England* in 1867. He raised no alarm as to their decreasing numbers but did mention that "they are abundant during summer in the high northern latitudes, both on the seacoast and on inland lakes. In winter they migrate to the south." He further stated that "the Great Loon is a rather common species on our coast in the autumn and winter" and spoke of their "favorite breeding location" on Lake Umbagog. He made no direct comment on the presence of the bird anywhere in Massachusetts or southern New Hampshire.

In 1903, American Ornithologists' Union member Ralph Hoffmann wrote in his *A Guide to the Birds of New England and Eastern New York* (revised in 1923) that loons are "occurring sparingly on the more remote bodies of water from the neighborhood of Mt. Monadnock northward" and that the loons' "weird notes are a familiar sound on the northern lakes." Though brief, Hoffmann's comments paint a clear picture of the scarcity of loons by this time in southern New Hampshire and even farther north.

In 1909, Gerald Thayer wrote (reprinted in the 1920 history of Dublin) that "loons are still faithful to Dublin Lake as visitors, but not as nesters....We summer folks are too much for them. They have now forsaken Breed Pond in

Nelson. The loons that still honor us with frequent summer visits probably come from Long Pond…north of Harrisville. There, a pair or two still nest." Likewise, in Bradford, it was noted in 1885 that "Loon Island in Massasecum Lake is evidence that the great northern diver once frequented the waters of that lake. It is now occasionally seen there." The 1906 history of the town of Andover offers up a unique perspective on Highland Lake in that town. This lake was once called Loon Pond "because it was a favorite haunt and nesting place of that peculiar water fowl.…For nearly half a century this pond has been referred to as Highland Lake." While it is not exactly certain why the name changed, it is likely because the loons had disappeared from there by 1840 due to intensive human activity of an unusual nature. Andover was the site of "frequent and extensive" religious revivals from 1803 to 1840, and this "led to the selection of certain spots on the shore of Loon Pond, or on the grassy banks of the outlet of that body of water, for the celebration of the ordinance of baptism.…The white sands on the south shore was a favored locality." These revivals and rites—which included a significant amount of praying, singing and splashing in the water in numbers that were variously described as "great" and "large"—were celebrated in the spring and summer months, at the height of the loon's breeding season, and it is quite likely that these continual human disturbances caused loons to abandon the lake. Notably, loons did not consistently return to Highland Lake as nesters until the year 2000, an absence of 160 years, and since then, 15 chicks have fledged on the lake.

So, what were the causes for the shrinking of the loon population in New Hampshire beyond that of hunting activities? While we have no contemporary reporting on the subject beyond anecdotal accounts, there were certain trends happening here that point to the likely causes, this bolstered in part by the current trends regarding the loon population. The earliest of these influences were changes to land use patterns throughout the state, beginning by the 1850s. This included clearing the land for farming and sheep pasture usage, as well as lumbering operations. These activities affected the watersheds that were present in any given area as the original ground vegetation was cleared and different patterns of erosion and water runoff occurred. This in turn led to changes in the water quality of nearby bodies of water. We don't often think of these common activities as having an effect on our lakes and ponds and the creatures, including loons, that inhabit them, but they did (and still do), and sediment core sample studies from these lakes prove it. One such study by Sushil Dixit and others looked at Willard Pond in Antrim, now part of the dePierrefeu-

Willard Pond Wildlife Sanctuary, a 1,793-acre site that is New Hampshire Audubon's largest property. It is now a loon sanctuary as well as a popular birding spot. The pond was reclaimed by the New Hampshire Fish and Game Department in 1962, and core sediment samples taken in 1999 demonstrate that the water quality has changed here over the years in such aspects as inorganic matter (increased beginning about 1860, stabilized by 1940, now at normal background levels), trace metals (most levels peaked by 1960, except lead, which peaked in the early 1970s) and chloride (increased between 1850 and 1910, high but stable between 1910 and 1950, decreased since 1950). As water quality goes, based on human activities, so goes our loon population. These changes don't happen instantly, but they are inevitable if we don't change our land and water use practices. Willard Pond, as a protected body of water since 1962, demonstrates that we can reverse loon declines. Ever since the LPC began keeping records, this recovered body of water has consistently supported a pair of nesting loons from before 1975–85, with 16 chicks hatched there and 6 that fledged. This is significant, as this success came at a time when loons were floundering elsewhere in the state. While output here would decline from 1986 to 1998, it has since rebounded, with 12 chicks fledged between 1999 and 2022.

Water quality, especially when it comes to the loons, has another component that must be considered, for contaminants affect not only their bodies but also their ability to catch their prey. Remember that loons feed by sight and prefer a clear-water environment, so increased soil runoff due to land being cleared of vegetation can result in turbid or murky waters that make it harder for loons to feed and may also promote plant growth that can choke smaller bodies of water. Early human industrial activities, as harmless as they may seem to us today, caused the same problems, including water-powered sawmills that might choke a body of water with large amounts of sawdust, not only affecting the clarity of the water but also reducing the oxygen levels in water, killing fish and other organisms consumed by loons. Other early industrial activities that harmed water quality include shoe factories and textile mills, both of which were active on such bodies of water as Lake Winnipesaukee. Of course, in the 20th century, even more toxic chemicals, such as fertilizers and insecticides, came into use around our lakes, and just when we seem to get a handle on one substance, other man-made toxins come to the fore, some of which are discussed further on. It is, indeed, a never-ending battle when it comes to the delicate balance of protecting our wildlife versus so-called human progress and the chemicals we use to make our lives easier.

Yet another human influence on our loon population in New Hampshire was the growth of the tourism industry, which took place overall in conjunction with the state's economic development. It was a two-phased development that spanned a century. First, as our state's transportation network, including roads, bridges and railroads, grew, so was our tourism industry born. It actually began as early as the 1820s, as the natural wonders of the White Mountains became more widely known. Even the site of the 1826 Willey landslide tragedy in the White Mountains brought thousands of tourists to the area, and it increased even more after the Civil War. Really, from these early days up to the present, New Hampshire has been a tourist mecca—not just the mountains up north but throughout the state. The loon population in the southern tier of the state was the first to be affected, as that area not only became more populous but also had its own tourist spots. With all these visitors, development along many of our lakeshores, as well as boat traffic on our larger lakes, increased at a steady pace. Bodies of water that were once the haunts of loons all on their own now had to be shared with humans, and this too has remained a constant in our state.

The second phase of the tourist, or recreational, industry, that affected loons ramped up after World War II. While there were hotels and many primitive camps (when a camp truly was a camp) on our pond and lake shorelines, they were not as numerous as they are today. After the war, the national economy was humming along, and jobs were plentiful. With the GI Bill, many young men acquired a college education and gained jobs that provided not just a good income but also vacation time. The concept of the vacation, a time to get away from it all and restore one's physical and mental health from the worries of everyday life, was not a new one but was largely only for the upper class in America, those folks who could afford such an unpaid luxury. Now, however, the middle class had that option too, and they fully embraced the concept. With the aid of our newly formed and continually expanding interstate highway system, including I-95 along the New Hampshire Seacoast and I-93 straight through the heart of central New Hampshire, Americans and Granite Staters alike took to the roads in droves to enjoy their paid time off. To get away from it all, thousands came to enjoy the lakes and ponds in our state, and many would buy properties here that served as refuges from their busier lives elsewhere. And so it was that shoreline development expanded exponentially, with unintended consequences for loons. With all those people now spending time on our lakes, more garbage was generated. Stored outside camp homes, this garbage attracted raccoons, a smart and determined scavenger, to lake shorelines in record numbers, resulting in a population explosion. Being the opportunistic scavengers that they are, raccoons found other tasty morsels in the form of loon eggs during the early summer season. This decades-long problem was a difficult one to solve; it is estimated that in 1977 some 75 to 95 percent of loon nesting failures in the state were due to raccoon predation.

All the aforementioned developmental factors served as clanging chimes of doom for the New Hampshire loon population. While no systematic loon censuses were taken statewide before the LPC began operations, both anecdotal accounts and early census data confirm the decline. Many older folks in New Hampshire today, based on my informal discussions, can recall their parents talking about loons in abundance at their lake homes, but when they were growing up in the late 1950s and the 1960s, they seldom saw the loons in numbers their parents had talked about. Early LPC census data would later confirm this on Lake Winnipesaukee.

The Loon and Our Changing Climate

Climate change in New Hampshire since colonial days has also had a large effect on our loon population, even though such changes have only been tracked for about the last 100 years. Prior to modern times, since the LPC began its monitoring program, it was hard to quantify these effects on loons. You will recall that loons are generally a cold weather bird—they thrive in the Arctic in huge numbers, but their numbers in the southernmost part of their range have diminished greatly. As mentioned previously, New Hampshire is now ground zero when it comes to loons and climate change as we are at the effective southern limit of their range. Meteorologists know from early records that since 1900 the average temperature has increased in our state 3.06 degrees Fahrenheit overall, with winter temperatures increasing by 4.5 degrees. These numbers may not seem huge, but scientists agree that even a 2.7-degree change in temperature worldwide could have catastrophic results, and when it comes to loons, we are seeing those on a relative scale even today. Given that loons were largely gone from southern New Hampshire by 1900, our warming temperatures may have been a contributing factor, though not a sole determiner, in their numbers decrease.

One thing we do know is that severe weather events in the form of excessive rain and flooding in the spring and early summer months can disrupt loon breeding activities and will often cause nest failures, with resultant lowered reproductive success. Long before anyone was monitoring the weather, these catastrophic events were taking place. For example, Newfound Lake suffered severe flooding in June 1843, one of the earliest of the severe summertime weather events to be recorded for a New Hampshire lake. A small sampling of other notable flooding events that likely caused loon nesting losses include the following: Squam and Newfound Lakes, as tributaries of the Pemigewasset River, saw severe rains in July 1830 and April 1852 and 1895; the Contoocook River, which flows from Poole Pond in Rindge, saw severe flooding in the spring of 1818, April 1852, April 1862 and April 1870; and Lake Winnipesaukee and the Winnipesaukee River flooded in April 1852. Of course, this does not take into account the many catastrophic floods that took place in our two major river systems in New Hampshire, the Merrimack and Connecticut Rivers, and their tributaries. Indeed, New Hampshire had its share of catastrophic weather events in the first decades of the 20th century, leading experts to rethink what a 100-year flood event really was. Severe floods, some in the springtime, some in the fall, took place in 1895 (March), 1927 (November), 1936 (two weeks in March) and the hurricane of 1938 (September). While some of these events would not have directly disturbed loons during their breeding season, the damage they left in their wake almost certainly did in subsequent years. This includes resulting shoreline erosion and runoff.

William Brewster and the Loons of Lake Umbagog

While little is known with certainty about what was happening with the loons on most of New Hampshire's lakes and ponds in the 19th century, there is one body of water that was an exception: Lake Umbagog in northern New Hampshire and Maine. Here, William Brewster, a famed ornithologist of Cambridge, Massachusetts, would spend a part of many summers from 1871 to 1909, noting the birds he encountered in his diaries, the bird data only published (in four parts between 1924 and 1938) as *Birds of the Lake Umbagog Region of Maine* after his death in 1919. Though Brewster typically resided on a houseboat or at an inn or camp on the Maine side of the lake, his observations covered the entire lake, most of which is in New Hampshire. Brewster's comments are also enlightening in that they highlight the evolution of the science of ornithology. It is important to remember that how we view nature and wildlife today in the 21st century is vastly different than how such things were viewed in the 19th century. We cannot look at what was taking place in New Hampshire regarding its loon population without realizing what was happening elsewhere in America at the same time, when birds and animals deemed more economically viable than the loon were being slaughtered to extinction, or nearly so. This includes the bison on the Great Plains, the great auk (extinct by 1844), the passenger pigeon (extinct in 1914), as well as the snowy egret and over a dozen other bird species whose feathers were prized as women's fashion accessories. Ornithologists struggled to find their way amid the bird slaughter of the late 19th century, with Lake Umbagog in New Hampshire and Maine serving as a battlefield of sorts, in which loons were caught in the crosshairs. Early ornithology wasn't just about bird observation; it was about collecting bird "skins" and eggs, the gun being the primary tool of the ornithologist. Even though he was conflicted about killing some of the beautiful birds he depicted, John James Audubon was still driven to kill birds so that they could be examined and studied, stuffed and mounted and put on display. This was at a time when optical technology was still in its infancy and there were no powerful binoculars, so the rule was simple: if you didn't shoot and collect the skin of any bird specimen, rare or otherwise, you didn't see it. Eggs, too, were collected from bird nests of all kinds, loons included, and not just by ornithologists, but egg collectors too, some of them wealthy individuals who traveled the world over looking to add unusual specimens to their collections. On Lake Umbagog, Brewster noted that loon eggs were collected there by two local men, who sold them to egg collectors and sportsmen for a dollar each in the early 1900s. By the 1880s, ornithologists faced a growing moral quandary when it came to specimen collecting, and the diaries of Brewster tell the evolution of that story.

August 27, 1873: In his first mention of the loon, he writes about "the melancholy quavering cry of the loon."

September 15, 1873: Brewster describes his first loon kill on the lake, stating, "In the p.m. we saw a fine loon and followed him for a short time until at the fourth shot I was lucky enough to put a rifle bullet through his neck at about 250 yards, and after a most exciting chase for a short distance I finished him with a charge of no. 6 shot; it was a very large adult and weighed 11lbs, 2oz. and although his jugular vein had been cut by the bullet and the neck more or less shattered, she was still able to dive and swim for a long distance underwater." On the following day, Brewster "skinned and made up the loon, the job occupying about 2½ hours."

The following summer, Brewster was again hunting loons. For what? Surely not study, as he'd already collected one skin, but for mere sport. Sometimes he was lucky, sometimes not.

AUGUST 18, 1874: Brewster "took to my boat at the outlet and after firing about 25 rifle shots at a loon (who by the way seemed to rather like the fun paying no more attention to my shots then to occasionally rise and flap his wings when I came very near him). I paddled across the flooded meadow into the pond. In one of the most secluded nooks, I was most surprised at suddenly coming upon a very large loon: he dived instantly and marking his course by a line of bubbles on the water, passed nearly under my boat and escaped into the river."

However, a few days later, one loon's luck would run out.

AUGUST 22, 1874: Brewster "shot a very fine loon in the pond, hitting him first with my rifle at about 100 yards distance and killing him instantly. The first bullet I found passed through his throat severing the tongue at its base, the last through the back of the head. As he lay dead on the surface of the water among the green lily pads, he presented a most beautiful appearance, frosted over as he was with minute air bubbles, and we paddled around him several times before picking him up." Three days later, Brewster skinned and made up "my loon."

Less than two weeks later, the ornithologist was somehow surprised at Lake Umbagog's loons' wary behavior in his presence.

SEPTEMBER 3, 1874: Brewster, while "coming down the lake the wind blew almost a gale and to my surprise nearly every loon that we saw would rise easily at our approach."

For the next 19 years, Lake Umbagog's loons are not mentioned in Brewster's diaries. Perhaps he had enough "skins," but changes were happening in the ornithology world. In 1886, when the idea of observing birds rather than killing them was coming to the fore, Brewster "scoffed" at the idea, according to historian Elizabeth Meyer, of studying birds through an opera glass. But she also noted that by 1890 "his thinking was encouraged by Frank Michler Chapman, a younger friend and colleague working at the American Museum of Natural History." In that year he wrote to Brewster about "this miserable collecting....We proclaim how little we know of the habits of birds and then kill them at sight. Sometimes I am completely disgusted with our ways....I long for an outing where the gun will be secondary....Will you embark with me on a novel ornithological expedition…where the gun shall be a servant, not a master, where days may pass without skins being made?" Weeks later, Brewster responded to his friend, stating that he had been off on a monthlong expedition, and "I left the gun at home for the first time in my life and did not once regret it, either." Change was indeed coming, but would it stick on Lake Umbagog?

Brewster's next diary entries mentioning loons in 1893 and 1894 highlight their calls but nothing about killing them. However, he would revert to his old self in 1897 in an unsuccessful attempt to bag a loon, this being his most lengthy loon entry in all his journals. His comments suggest he had forgotten the loons he killed on Lake Umbagog over 20 years before and his old skin-collecting habits got the best of him.

SEPTEMBER 5, 1897: "As we were nearing the mouth of Sturtevant Cove we saw an adult loon of exceptionally large size floating about 100 yards off on the glassy surface. Ordinarily I do not molest these noble birds but I coveted the skin of this gigantic fellow and at once gave him a charge of buckshot. Either one of the pellets hit him or he was a loon of peculiar habits for he began making a series of short dives after coming up within less than 40 yards from the spot where he had previously disappeared. He moved for the most part in a circle of about 200 yards in diameter but often doubled back. He came up repeatedly within half gunshot but on every fresh occasion merely broke water and immediately disappeared again like a big fish. Had I enough shells to risk snap shots freely I would certainly have killed him but as it was, I kept my two charges of heavy shot for fair chances at his head and neck and missed with both at rather long range. When we left the bird, he stood erect and flapped his wings heading his long quavering cry back at us as if in derision."

Score a rare victory for the loon!

In the late summer of 1898, Brewster was again back at Lake Umbagog, the loons, as always, drawing his attention. On August 24, he notes, "Loons often fly over Pine Point in the early morning, but seldom or never by day." Brewster hunted no loons this year, nor did he do so in 1900, when they are next noted briefly. His last encounters were noted for the summer of 1909, by which time Brewster's perspective had changed and so had the laws about hunting loons. It is to be wondered if he saw any incongruity in his criticism of a local hunter and his hunting activity in light of his previous loon-killing actions years before.

JUNE 10, 1909. "A Loon flew over us high up early this morning. I hear that one was seen in the lake near B. Point yesterday. A native vandal shot at it with his rifle and cut some feathers from its wing or back. The law protecting loons in Maine was repealed last summer."

June 22, 1909. "About 7am, before the wind had risen, a fine loon in fully adult plumage surprised us by appearing in our little cove which is now almost everywhere grass-ground due to the recent fall of water."

By the early 20th century, the loon was in trouble on Lake Umbagog, with Brewster classifying it as "formerly a very common summer resident, now comparatively seldom seen." He detailed the fact that loons were once seen across the lake once it was ice-free. Brewster, as I have previously noted, documented some of the early large-scale hunting of waterfowl in general on the lake. Of loons, he noted that loons "offered conspicuous and attractive targets for rifle practice and were wholly unprotected, either by law or popular sentiment, and it was customary to shoot at them whenever opportunity offered." Brewster interpreted the loon's reactions to these threats in a curious manner, he believing that they seemed to "rather enjoy the excitement of occasional hair-breadth escapes from injury of death." Brewster also reports that only a few loons were taken in the early years, these mostly being juveniles, but that as improved rifles came to be used, "loons began to suffer more and more seriously" and "continued to hold their own fairly well up to almost the close of the last century. Since then, they have been growing fewer and fewer year by year until they have almost, if not wholly, ceased to breed in any part of the lake." In concluding his account of the decline of the loon, it is interesting that Brewster actually places more emphasis on the "recent introduction of motor-boats, with which the Lake now swarms and which, in my opinion, would alone have brought it to pass." This statement was a harbinger of what was to happen on such lakes as Squam and Winnipesaukee in the 1950s. However, though accounts are lacking for New Hampshire's other lakes during this period, it is not hard to believe that the scenes detailed by William Brewster weren't also being played out in similar fashion elsewhere.

Early 20th-Century Oil Spills

Yet another factor that affected loons was the rising use of fuel oil. We tend to think of oil spills as a relatively recent environmental effect, but the dumping of oil into the ocean has caused loon deaths since the early 1900s after our nation's merchant marine and naval vessels transitioned from coal to oil for their powerplants. This fuel oil might be spilled through maritime disasters, but oil was also dumped into the ocean (at a time when environmental regulations were lax or nonexistent) during routine maintenance procedures. The New Hampshire Audubon Society first took notice of this in 1936, mentioning the after-effects of the steamer *Edward Luckenbach* going on the rocks off Block Island in 1930, resulting in oil being dumped into the sea and leaving thousands of waterbirds, loons included, dead or dying. Closer to home, in the fall of 1952, C.F. Jackson, the president of New Hampshire Audubon, noted the "troubled oil on water" at Great Bay in Newington, when he saw "a black greasy line which stretched from shore to shore." As the United States, and the world, used more and more fuel oil, it was inevitable that oil spills would become not only more common but also larger and more far-reaching in scope.

Early Loon Protective Measures

As to efforts to help preserve the loon population in general, there were some measures put into place at the state and federal level that helped protect the economically useless loon. Or was it still seen as an economically insignificant bird? Perhaps folks were getting the idea that loons on our picturesque bodies of water in the summertime were a good thing after all. In 1905, the State of New Hampshire passed a law making it illegal to kill loons on our inland lakes, ponds and rivers. That same year, the use of swivel cannons or punt guns, any gun not fired from the shoulder, was also outlawed, thus putting to an end the practice of market gunning. This was a start, though how often these laws were enforced is questionable, even if NH Fish and Game wardens surely made arrests from time to time. One such incident was reported in the *Manchester Union Leader* for July 21, 1912, when two young men from Meredith were arrested by Inspectors Clark and Wentworth from Concord and charged "with molesting two young loons, which were taken away from the parent birds. They were found guilty and fined $14.62 each." Whether these loon chicks died is not stated but highly likely. Adjacent to this article was commentary that Meredith was expecting its "largest influx of visitors for the month of August ever."

Loons received federal protection in 1918 with the passage of the Migratory Bird Treaty Act. This was passed after the kind of overhunting mentioned previously, which laws at the state level failed to mitigate.

Despite this important federal protection, the slow decline of the loon in New Hampshire continued, mostly for a combination of all the reasons listed above. However, there was perhaps another reason for the continued slide. Did the State of New Hampshire really protect loons like it should have? It is now known that none other than officers of the New Hampshire Fish and Game Department were encouraged to shoot loons on sight during the 1950s–60s. If we realize that the first designation of this state agency's mission name is "Fish," such activities are not surprising. Not only was the agency tasked with regulating and stocking the state's lakes and ponds, but also many in the department held to the old mistaken notion that loons will eat all the fish in any given location if allowed full range, leaving none for our state's anglers. While I've found no official "shoot on sight" order for loons in any state records, the very first director of the LPC, David Hammond, confirmed the practice when assuming his new role in the 1970s. He was in the know for sure, for he had been a Fish and Game officer since the 1950s up to his retirement and even joked that he grew to be a poor shot so that he would not kill loons. Luckily, this practice was discontinued, and the department now works in full partnership with the LPC.

Recognizing the Plight of the Loon

Finally, the decreased loon numbers became a concern for New Hampshire conservation organizations. The New Hampshire Audubon Society, which was established in 1914, gradually took note. At its formation, the society was most concerned about the prime issue of the day, the killing of birds for their plumage used in women's fashion, and loons received little attention. The loon first receives prominent mention in the society's second quarterly bulletin of 1931, when the pair of loons and their chick on Jenness Pond in Northwood is discussed in detail, their presence so far south and on such a small body of water being deemed "not common." That the occurrence of loons on Jenness Pond was unusual back then is interesting considering that pond's subsequent history. While loon records for the next 40 years are uncertain, in light of what's been happening since the advent of the LPC, it is likely that the loons never left Jenness Pond. Since 1975, there has always been a territorial pair of loons on this pond, they collectively hatching 40 chicks in 47 years and fledging 32 of them. The pair of loons currently on

DOWNY YOUNG OF LOON

Loon chick, Jenness Pond, Northwood. This may be the earliest photo of a New Hampshire loon chick. Photo from Mrs. Jean T. Stimmell, from *Bulletin of the Audubon Society of New Hampshire*, April-May-June 1931. *Courtesy New Hampshire Audubon.*

the pond in 2022 were banded in 2012, and they have been here ever since and fledged 7 chicks, the last in 2020.

When the New Hampshire Audubon Society's newsletter morphed into the publication *New Hampshire Bird News* in 1951, it is fitting that the image of a loon appeared on the title page and has ever since. In October 1953, the society's Vera Wallace asked the question, "Are these lovely birds also among those being deprived of the opportunity to raise young with the steady encroachment of civilization around our waterways?" The following year, the society's publication noted that the common loon was a "moderately common migrant and summer resident on most of the larger lakes" from Bow Lake in Strafford northward. In 1955, society president Tudor Richards noted that "loons seem to have increased somewhat," noting "recovered numbers" at Lake Umbagog as well as in Rockingham and Strafford Counties, they not noted as previously having breeding pairs since around 1900. However, in 1958 it was noted that loons were "only able to hold their own on the larger lakes, Umbagog, the Connecticuts, Squam, and Lake Winnipesaukee." In 1961, it was noted that loons were once found in the area of Webster, where the well-known ornithologist

Charles Goodhue documented the birds of his hometown, but not any longer, and that they last nested in the town of Andover in 1945. Sightings on our lakes were listed yearly by the society, but it was in 1970 when New Hampshire Audubon began one of its first-ever wildlife programs when it started an annual Loon Survey. The following year, the society even reported one of the first cases of a powerboat endangering a loon family, even though these incidents had no doubt occurred in the past. So, there were many ups and downs on reporting regarding the stability of the loon population in New Hampshire.

Even the choosing of a New Hampshire state bird perhaps reflected the prevailing attitudes toward the loon—out of sight, out of mind. When the state legislature finally chose a state bird in 1957 (efforts having begun in 1939), there were advocates for the hermit thrush, the bluebird, the goldfinch and even the New Hampshire Red, a selectively bred chicken. However, the New Hampshire Audubon Society lobbied for the eventual winner, the purple finch, as did garden clubs and women's clubs nationwide and across the state. The loon was never in the conversation, it subsequently chosen as the state bird of Minnesota in 1961. No offense to the purple finch—it is a lovely bird—but the selection seems like a lost opportunity. Based on my admittedly unscientific and informal polling, many folks in New Hampshire today actually believe the loon *is* our state bird. It is interesting to note that when the U.S. Postal

New Hampshire Flags of Our Nation stamp and postal cachet featuring a loon, 2010. *Author collection.*

Service issued its Flags of Our Nation series, the New Hampshire stamp, issued in 2010, featured the loon, indicative of the restored status of this now beloved waterbird.

Finally, another group to take early action in reaction to the loon's declining numbers was the Squam Lakes Association, formed in 1904 and the oldest such organization of its type in the country. They began conducting an annual loon census on Squam in 1967 after the loon decline on their waters became readily apparent and have served as a model for the many other New Hampshire lake associations that came into being. In fact, these lake conservation groups have been frontline partners in the fight to save New Hampshire's loons since the very beginning.

By the late 1960s, New Hampshire was at a definite tipping point. If changes were not made, if protections were not implemented, and soon, the state was on the verge of losing its loons. Even the efforts at recognizing the problems may have already been too late, had not one man stepped up and led focused conservation efforts to a new level with the establishment of a brand-new organization dedicated solely to loons. It was a clarion call for change and a novel approach to a dire problem.

2

RAWSON WOOD AND THE LOON PRESERVATION COMMITTEE TO THE RESCUE, 1975–81

He first came to Squam Lake in 1950, not on a mission to save loons, but rather to get away from the cares of his business world with his family. At first, he rented a house on the west side of the lake in the Gurney camps. Later, in 1959, he bought a simple house on Pine Needle Point in order to be close to the lake. It needed repair, but he was up to it, and over the years he added to the lake home. The journey from New York was well worth the effort, as it was for so many families in the postwar era. Later, when he retired from business in the 1970s and moved to Boston, his trips to Squam became even more frequent and prolonged. It truly was a home away from home, a refuge from city life. It's a common enough story on our New Hampshire lakes, one that has occurred countless times over the years for countless families. But as it turns out, Rawson Wood was no common man, not at all.

Rawson Lyman Wood was born in New York in 1908. Wood's family was a well-to-do one, with his father operating a highly successful jewelry company that had been founded by his grandfather in 1850. He grew up in New York and went to the finest schools before entering Harvard University, but even as a child the die was cast—he having had, as his daughter Ellen Barth recounted, "an exposure to the outdoors" and an "inclination for conservation." Wood graduated from Harvard in 1930 and enrolled in Harvard Law School but withdrew after the untimely death of his father to take over the family business. While at Harvard, he met and married his wife, Elizabeth Francis Ford of Cambridge, Massachusetts. The two would spend a wonderful 70 years together, and among their shared interests were birds. It may not have been his first career choice, but like everything Wood put his mind to, he made his family business a success and carried it to new heights, it being the oldest jewelry company in the United States and the largest manufacturer of rings. During World War II, Wood's business turned to wartime production for the military—not only did he patent a lost form of metal casting to make precision metal parts for such things as Norden bombsights, but his firm was also awarded the prestigious Army-Navy E Award for excellence in production. While Rawson Wood was involved in precision manufacturing for many years until his retirement and move to Boston in the 1970s, he also had many other interests. A social justice warrior and devout Catholic, Wood was vice-president of the New York Urban League, served on the Human Rights Commission of Nassau County and in 1967 was appointed by Pope John Paul VI as an American delegate to the Third Roman Catholic World Congress of the Lay Apostolate in Rome, just a few of his many activities. Indeed, as daughter Ellen stated, Wood "had a broad scope of liberal causes."

Important to our story, Wood was also a nature lover and avid birder. He established his family's homestead on an old orchard farm on Long Island, not far from New York City. Here, he and his wife would raise their five children, and birds always seemed to be a part of their life. Wood and his children would also make local birding expeditions around New York. Rawson Wood's first interactions with loons originated with his visits to the Adirondack Mountains and Elk Lake. His daughter Ellen has many fond memories of these visits and their stay in rustic cabins. While her siblings were not quite as interested in birds as she, Ellen later recalled that "you can't miss loons….They were very much a part of our experience." While her mother's favorite bird was the hermit thrush, clearly Rawson Wood was a loon guy and would remain so for the remainder of his life. As to his other birding activities, Wood was heavily involved in New York, helping to found today's North Shore Audubon Society on Long Island, as well as serving on the boards of the American Ornithological Union and the Linnaean Society. He was introduced to the wilds of New Hampshire by his wife, whose family had a summer place in Peterborough. Eventually, though, the Woods found a summer refuge of sorts in Center Harbor on Squam Lake. By 1959, as their daughter Ellen Barth recalled, the family had two canoes and Rawson was always out on the water, paddling around the islands.

By the early 1970s, after moving with his wife to Boston, Rawson Wood, ever the astute observer, began to notice that, as his daughter put it, "the loons were going down" on Squam Lake as compared to their numbers from the 1950s. Once this became abundantly clear, the resourceful businessman was not about to sit on his hands. He wanted to do something and, luckily for New Hampshire's loons, had the resources to make it happen. When a speedboat killed two loon chicks one summer, Wood used his own money to print out posters and leaflets reminding boaters to keep an eye out for loons. Since 1970, the New Hampshire Audubon Society had been counting loons, but it was in 1974 that Wood, under the auspices of New Hampshire Audubon, commissioned a young zoologist at Duke University named Robert Ridgely (later to become an acclaimed ornithologist and the recognized expert on the birds of Central and South America) to do a summer-long study of the loons on Squam Lake. Ridgely's parents, Dr. Beverly and Barbara Ridgely, not only had a place on Squam Lake but also were avid birders, something they instilled in their son. Bev Ridgely, a distinguished professor of French studies at Brown University, was not just a Classics scholar and birder who first and foremost focused on loons; he also wrote a book about the birds on Squam Lake that is a classic today and was a stamp collector who specialized in bird stamps from all over the world.

Using his parents' home as a base, Ridgely made his observations from mid-May to mid-August in the summer of 1974, most of the work carried out on the water and within a respectful distance of Squam's loons. This study is important, as it is the first focused scientific study in the modern era to be conducted strictly on a population of New Hampshire loons. Ridgely's conclusions were perhaps surprising to some, as he wrote, "Squam's loon population is close to being stable at the present," and "one cannot discern any significant trend in the number of offspring produced per season." However, Ridgely also made it clear that this was just a one-season study and that several years of loon data would need to be accumulated "to answer many important questions." He also recommended that the plight of the loon in New Hampshire overall should continue to be publicized, that the Squam Lakes Association should consider a program of land acquisitions and conservation easements, as well as stop the establishment of a proposed marina that would increase boat traffic, and that the predations of the local gull population on loon nests might be mitigated by area towns plowing under daily the exposed garbage in their landfills. Ridgely also visited Lake Winnipesaukee, and though he did not study it intensively, it was alarmingly clear to him that the lake might be "a classic case of 'too little, too late,'" and that "the lesson of Winnipesaukee should not be lost on those concerned about Squam loons—a few decades ago, Winnipesaukee looked much like

Squam does today." Wood took these recommendations to heart, and in 1975, as writer Kristen Laine related, "Rawson Wood stood to his full six-feet-plus height at an Audubon board meeting and announced that he was forming a committee for the preservation of loons. The Committee would be self-funded, and he would chair it. He sat down, and that was that." The Loon Preservation Committee (LPC) subsequently began operations that same year, Wood using his own money to the tune of $5,000 to get things started. It was an important moment not just in New Hampshire conservation history, but well beyond our state's borders, as the LPC was the first conservation organization in the world devoted solely to loons.

Putting a team together for this first-of-its-kind organization was Rawson Wood's first challenge, but for him it all came naturally. Indeed, as his daughter Ellen emphasized, and would become clear to everyone who knew him, Wood "took those skills he developed in business and social organizations, the skills of getting people working together. Building things up was a skill he had. Loons got to take advantage of all his experience." Rawson Wood was no biologist or loon expert, but he knew how to gather experts around him who could work together to further the cause of the LPC and to get results. He could be stubborn at times, not especially a bad trait when working with some Audubon Society board members, but was

LPC founder Rawson Wood (*left*), field biologist Jack Noon (*center*) and LPC director Jeff Fair (*right*) out on Lake Umbagog, circa 1988. *Courtesy LPC.*

a generous donor, the primary one in the beginning, to the LPC and kept it afloat during its formative period when donations were just beginning to come in. It was also, frankly, Rawson Wood's connections in terms of social and business networking that gained the LPC quite a bit of publicity that would normally be hard to come by for a small New Hampshire nonprofit group. When the story of New Hampshire's loons appeared on the front page of the *Wall Street Journal*, many wondered what loons were doing there—that was Wood's doing. Despite all his connections and all his money, Rawson Wood was really all about a few simple things when it came to the LPC: the loons and the small, dedicated band of people at the LPC helping them. As his daughter recounted, "He enjoyed the personal part, working with the Loon Rangers. It was such a different thing from the city and business offices." In fact, for Rawson Wood, despite his towering form, intellect and organizing abilities, he was never engaged in his causes to become famous or to have something named after him. It was all about doing what he believed to be right. It was an ideal, a mindset, that worked. For his entire career with the LPC, Rawson Wood was a powerful force, primarily interfacing with New Hampshire Audubon and high-level donors and overseeing financial operations. But while he followed his biologists' advice on the best scientific approaches, Wood enjoyed getting out on the lakes, whether it be on Squam or Winnipesaukee, floating nesting rafts in the early years or going out on "patrol" with those dedicated LPC volunteers who gained the moniker (a catchy one that still sticks today) Loon Rangers, protecting nesting loons in the summer. Rawson Wood would continue as the chairman of the LPC from its founding in 1975 until his retirement in 1989. For some years afterward, he remained an honorary trustee and continued his devotion to the loon cause. Even in his twilight years, after his move to Florida, when he was unable to travel to New Hampshire any longer, he retained an interest in the loons of Squam Lake and was eager to receive the yearly reports of loon activities there from the LPC's Squam Lakes biologist Tiffany Grade. When Rawson Wood died in 2012 at the age of 103, he concluded a career of loon preservation, among many other notable causes, that spanned over five decades.

In the beginning, only a few individuals were hired to staff the LPC. David Hammond served as director and Scott Sutcliffe, Ralph Kirshner, Connie Manville, Kimberly Young, Geoff LeBaron and Ted Levin as staff biologists. Hammond was a former conservation officer for the New Hampshire Department of Fish and Game with over 20 years of experience. The early operations of the LPC were headquartered out of the ell between his house

Longtime LPC volunteer and Loon Ranger extraordinaire Jane Irwin (1932–2012) of Laconia, out on Lake Winnipesaukee in her loon patrol boat training a new generation of Loon Rangers. *Courtesy LPC.*

and barn in Moultonborough. Hammond, of course, ran the early LPC like a Fish and Game program and, in contrast to the biologists, had a law enforcement background in addition to his outdoors experience. He was, however, respected by his staff biologists and served as a bridge of sorts between those in New Hampshire's Fish and Game department, some of whom had been tasked with shooting loons in the not-too-distant past as he had been, and the biologists who were formulating a scientific approach to saving New Hampshire's loon population. Much of his early activities included attempts to solve the problem of raccoon predation of loon nests, primarily by trapping and killing the pesky creatures. It was a constant battle during his three-year tenure and even beyond that.

Scott Sutcliffe was an important choice made by Rawson Wood, as he would eventually set the tone and way forward for the LPC by taking a multipronged cooperative approach to loon conservation. A native of Massachusetts, Sutcliffe describes himself as being "a product of the Massachusetts Audubon Society from a young age." His family had a summer home on Lake Waukewan in Meredith, so he got to know the local birds well. He attended Cornell University and graduated with a bachelor's degree in wildlife ecology in 1975. Prior to graduating, during his junior year, Sutcliffe did work for the Squam Lakes Association, and on New Year's Eve during his senior year, Rawson Wood called on him to work on the LPC's loon program on Squam Lake in the summer of 1975. After working at the Manomet Bird Observatory in Plymouth, Massachusetts, for a short time, Sutcliffe came to New Hampshire. Here, he gained a master's degree in wildlife ecology at the University of New Hampshire while at the same time working for the LPC. Sutcliffe recalled humorously that "it was the longest ever masters program at UNH," and he graduated in 1980. His time at UNH was indeed interesting, coming at a time when most students in his major were focusing on game animals like deer or moose. Sutcliffe was, as he recalled fondly, "a dickey-birder, the only non-game person in the UNH program at the time.…I've never shot anything, never wanted to." Indeed, the idea of conserving loons was a novel one, but for Sutcliffe and Wood, "it was a team of collaboration," with Sutcliffe helping to educate Rawson Wood on the science of loons. While the task of bringing back the loons looked to be monumental, Sutcliffe recalled, "I was young and I could work. Our number one goal was to learn more about why loons were declining, especially on Squam.…There were a lot of unknowns and we were just learning. We decided to go statewide and I set it upon myself to visit every lake to set up a state monitoring system, trying to set up a volunteer network." This collective team became known as the Loon Rangers, many of them lake or pond residents who were recruited to watch out for loons and the LPC biologists who guided them. Not only was Sutcliffe "shocked at how many lakes used to have loons but now didn't," but he also recognized "people's willingness to cooperate and activated them through education." Indeed, Sutcliffe acknowledged, "there were a lot of nice lake land owners who cherished loons and were enthusiastic and energetic, willing to work with the LPC, and really considered them 'their birds.'"

In building the early LPC, Sutcliffe brought on board another Cornell graduate with New Hampshire roots, Ralph Kirshner. He was a native of New York City who graduated in 1969 with a degree in conservation wildlife biology. As Kirshner recalled, "A city kid going to Cornell to learn wildlife was not a common thing." He came to New Hampshire in 1974 to stay but had been coming to Lake Winnipesaukee since 1959, where his family had a summer camp. He earned a master's degree in education at Plymouth State University and taught sixth-grade biology for some years until he "had enough of four walls." He later helped set up the newly founded Nature's Classroom outdoor environmental program and through that program met Scott Sutcliffe, who soon recruited Kirshner to be the LPC's first Lake Winnipesaukee biologist, in which position he served from 1976 to 1979. Kirshner was an excellent choice and had no delusions about the job. As he recalled, "We started from scratch, and it was a lot of work for little money." While Kirshner respected the LPC's first director, Dave Hammond, he also noted that "the atmosphere changed when Scott Sutcliffe was appointed director" in 1978 to succeed the retiring Hammond. The early working conditions, truth be told, were difficult, according to Kirshner, with "horrible boats and secondhand equipment. In the early days we didn't know a whole hell of a lot and Lake Winnipesaukee was too much for one man. But you did the best that you could. I hadn't been aware that reproduction levels [among loons] was so low….That was the main thing, getting the reproduction rate up." Like Sutcliffe, Kirshner's job on Lake Winnipesaukee involved educating local residents: "I had specialized in education, and that was most of the job, educating people. Anglers were not at first happy that 10 acres out of a 46,000-acre lake were being restricted because of loon breeding sites. I think maybe we were getting some place." Indeed, that first year for Ralph Kirshner on Lake Winnipesaukee was an eye-opening one, and not in a good way. On the "Big Lake," Kirshner documented only seven nesting pairs, with one chick fledged, while the summer census counted only 16 loons overall, substantially fewer than the nearly 70 loons that made the lake their home in the 1950s. That number would increase by exactly a single chick in 1977—not a sustainable reproduction rate by any means, but a minor victory nonetheless.

Another young loon ranger was Constance "Connie" Manville, one of the first women to do fieldwork for the LPC. She was a local, raised in Center Harbor, and was a bird lover from a young age, having banded birds since the age of 16. She would eventually graduate with a bachelor's degree in wildlife management from the University of New Hampshire in 1979 but worked for the LPC that first summer. She worked on several lakes, including Winnipesaukee, Squam and Willard Pond, with Sutcliffe, Kirshner and Squam volunteer Bev Ridgely. Her favorite part of the job was getting out on the water early, at 4:00 or 5:00 a.m., and as she later recalled, "I liked finding and watching loon nests….It was so exciting to discover them, but so, so sad when we found them predated by raccoons." She recalled LPC director Dave Hammond as an organized and efficient leader but serious, and humorously recounted one loon incident that took place around Becky's Garden, the smallest charted island on Lake Winnipesaukee, located near Center Harbor: "There was this speedboat just going in circles and circles just off the island, and it was really disturbing the loons, though I don't think the people even saw them. I hailed them down and took their license number and reported it to Dave. He tracked them down and gave them a very stern talk ashore, and they were so worried about being arrested. But that was part of our job, the public needed to be educated, and they were in this instance."

With the retirement of the LPC's first director in 1978, Scott Sutcliffe took over the position and helmed the day-to-day operations. His three years of leadership, with the guidance and financial efforts of Rawson Wood, were crucial in firmly establishing the mission of the LPC. As he would later describe the organization's activities, "I got to work with people on lakes all over New Hampshire, using a mixture of public skills, good science, and innovation....We developed relationships with people all over the state and introduced them to the wonders of these birds." Sutcliffe further reflected that the LPC had "a challenge on lots of lakes" and that he himself "gave programs [on loons] everywhere, every type of local organization, at innumerable places. I got into public speaking, which is something I hadn't done before." Sutcliffe and the small LPC team also disproved many misconceptions about loons. By the end of his LPC career in 1981, Sutcliffe and the LPC had made great strides, yet he maintained, "Helping getting it going was just plain fun." As to the other early biologists, LeBaron worked on Squam Lake after Sutcliffe took over as director, while Connie Manville worked on Willard Pond with Ted Levin, as well as on Lake Umbagog with Kimberly Young and Sutcliffe and on Squam and Lake Winnipesaukee. Both Manville and Young helped Sutcliffe gather inviable loon eggs and fragments, which were subsequently tested for harmful chemicals like DDT and mercury. The results were published in scientific papers. Sutcliffe later commented about his team, "I interacted with them at many levels, as friends and fellow Loon Rangers. We had lots of fun and all shared in the discoveries about loons."

During the LPC's formative years from 1975 to 1981, the loon population in New Hampshire remained small but stable. In 1975, there were 93 territorial pairs (186 loons overall) on 58 lakes, with 23 lakes having a successful nesting pair. The gains were very modest, but at least the decline of the loon population had been halted. By 1981, the number of territorial pairs had increased to 95, with 74 pairs nesting and 42 of these successfully. The number of chicks hatched on a yearly basis ebbed and flowed, with a high of 67 in 1979 and a low of 45 in 1977. In 1981, the number of chicks hatched was 62. Likewise, the number of lakes hosting territorial pairs rose to 62 after a low of just 44 in 1978, and the number of lakes with successful nesters increased nearly 50 percent to 34.

The LPC's success resulted from a multipronged approach, which remains a hallmark of the organization to this day. First, and perhaps foremost, was the building up of a solid and enthusiastic grassroots base. Hammond and Sutcliffe found that all across New Hampshire, lake and pond residents were eager to learn about loons and help them in any way they could. Patrols were established on some lakes early on during the breeding season to protect nesting sites and afterward the areas where loon parents brooded their chicks. Scott Sutcliffe happily recalled that "every cove had a family that was active, and we developed a cadre of volunteers." Of course, there were countless volunteers who also donated to the LPC to help fund these efforts; these donations came in varying amounts as well as in-kind donations of the supplies that the LPC needed to do its job on the water. Indeed, the Loon Rangers was a growing and emotionally invested group; its contributions in all forms then and down through the years have been what has kept the LPC a successful organization. Early volunteer efforts of this kind in the first several years included those on Squam Lake and Lake Winnipesaukee as well as Bow Lake in Strafford; Conway Lake, which produced seven chicks total in 1976–77; Pea Porridge Pond in Madison; and Willard Pond in Antrim, which in 1976 produced the only chick in all of Hillsborough County for the second year in a row.

A second approach developed by the LPC in the early years was that of collaboration with both the public at large as well as a variety of state, local and business organizations. For members of the public, and those recreating on the lakes, it was all about implementing a program of cooperation through education. As biologist Ralph Kirshner found out during that first summer as a biologist on Lake Winnipesaukee, it was all about educating the public, boaters or anglers, as to the ways of the loon and how human actions can negatively affect them, even if unintentionally. One of the biggest misconceptions early on about the harm done to loons was that involving powerboats, the majority of loon lovers believing that they were the major culprit on our lakes in terms of disruptions. While it is true that powerboats can and do cause harm, the LPC found out early on that small vessels like kayaks or canoes and the folks who operate them could potentially cause even greater harm. Many operators of these small boats like to "play Columbus" by exploring every nook and cranny along the shore of a given lake, which can have unintended consequences, including the disturbance of loon nesting sites (even if they're not visible).

By their inshore visits, small boaters flush loons off their nests during the breeding season, leaving the untended eggs within vulnerable to failure due to predators or decreased incubation time, resulting in lowered reproduction rates. Once again, early efforts took place on a number of bodies of water, including on Bow Lake, where residents worked with the LPC to buoy off the only successful nesting site in 1977. That same year, Dave Hammond and Rawson Wood reported that on Pea Porridge Pond in Madison, "Residents and landowners, vitally concerned with the problems, are moving toward a more effective conservation of the natural area remaining in this heavily developed community." Interestingly, this educational approach was not just aimed at adults. The annual Loon Festival was begun in 1978 and has been held every year except for the COVID years of 2020–22. This was an event where loon lovers of all ages could gather, especially children, with activities organized for both fun (the loon calling competition) as well as educational purposes.

However, it wasn't just the public at large that needed to be educated—so did a variety of organizations, including some that were formerly not so friendly to loons, whose activities affected these birds. Perhaps the greatest success in this area was gained with the New Hampshire Department of Fish and Game. Scott Sutcliffe recalled that the department, during his tenure, "became a conservation organization" and "totally jumped on board" with the LPC's mission. Many officers, indeed, "grasped" what was being done, Sutcliffe recalling the efforts of conservation officers, men like the late Carl Carlson (1931–2021) up in Pittsburg on the Connecticut Lakes and Lake Francis. He was "a great proponent of saving the loons" and built the first nesting raft on the Second Connecticut Lake. Carlson was just one example among many such conservation officers.

Yet another organization that was brought on board with the LPC mission was the power company that controlled the dams and waterflow on Lake Umbagog in northern New Hampshire. Sutcliffe called the company "incredibly cooperative" when it came to working with them to control the fluctuating water conditions there that threatened loon nesting sites. Surprisingly, this is one area where the leaders of the LPC had some disagreements with their then parent organization, New Hampshire Audubon. Some members were critical of the LPC's cooperative approach in the belief that to sit down at the table with power company officials was akin to making a deal with the devil. In fact, because the LPC was an entirely private entity with no regulatory control, without the financial muscle to engage in any legal battle, it was a smart move to engage with the power company directly and make the leadership see that it was in their best interests to help in the fight to save the loon population.

Lastly, the LPC also worked with local lake organizations, recreation groups and other conservancy groups to help protect the loons and their habitat. The Squam Lakes Association was an ally right from the start, while up on Lake Umbagog, the Seven Islands Land Company, which rented campsites to visitors, agreed to set aside known loon nesting sites as sanctuary areas. At the same time, in 1977 conservation easements were being established on Pea Porridge Pond in Madison, while relations were also established with the Chocorua Lake Foundation in Tamworth, which had not been known to have nesting loons since before 1957. Meanwhile, down on Bow Lake in Strafford, the Camp Owners Association met with LPC officials to come up with a loon plan for the future, which would meet with great success in the coming years.

Finally, the most important component in the LPC's mission to save New Hampshire loons was the scientific approach, which was at the heart of its efforts. All the education and cooperative approaches in the world would mean nothing if the LPC could not learn what was at the heart of the loon's decline and what realistic actions could be taken as a result of the knowledge gained. While it is true that the scientific staff of the LPC has always been small in terms of numbers, their tireless (and tiring) work has truly added to the science of loon conservation efforts, both in the beginning and down to this day. The earliest activities in this area were seemingly simple, but they brought results. Raccoon predation of nesting sites was known to be the largest single factor in nesting failures, so the first year an intensive program was established to trap and harvest raccoons. However, it was soon realized that this activity would never be the solution, so the use of nesting rafts was adopted. These consist of framed timber islands with natural materials placed on top that would make for, hopefully, an attractive nesting site for loons. These were placed in small coves and anchored offshore so as to protect them from shore-based predators like raccoons (though gulls were still a problem). The LPC did not invent the nesting raft concept, but it was an early proponent and practitioner of the method, one that today remains a primary tool in the attempts to increase loon reproductive rates. Help in this area was gained from Dr. Judith McIntyre, then the nation's foremost expert on loons, and both she and Rawson Wood, along with LPC biologists, worked together to put these rafts in place on New Hampshire lakes. Five rafts were placed in a pilot program in 1977, with two of them being used as nesting sites and one of them producing a pair of chicks. It was a small but important step.

Left: LPC loon nesting rafts. At top is a simple, first-generation version from the 1980s, location unknown. Note the lack of an avian guard/cover. At bottom is the latest version of the LPC's rafts, this one floated on Upper Baker Pond, Orford, in 2022. One egg was laid on the nest here but failed to hatch. *Courtesy LPC (top) and Cathy Eastburn (bottom)*.

Below: Signs like these are placed on lakes all over New Hampshire by the LPC to warn boaters of sensitive loon chick brooding areas. This chick on Lower Baker Pond, Orford/Wentworth, October 2021, seems to be reading the fine print. *Courtesy Cathy Eastburn*.

Today, the LPC has the world's largest collection of loon eggs and fragments, and this collection got its start in 1979 when Scott Sutcliffe and his team collected 15 failed eggs and in 1981 collected another 21 failed eggs. However, these eggs were not just put on a shelf and forgotten— they were tested to see what might be learned from their failure to hatch. The results were comforting, in a way, but also revealed another potential danger. First and foremost, the chemical DDT, a once commonly used insecticide that was banned in 1972, was not found present in any of the loon eggs. This was a relief, as the chemical, when ingested by other birds, most notably the bald eagle, caused a decrease in the thickness of their eggshells and led to large-scale reproductive failures. So, this was good news. On the other hand, while some trace metals were low, mercury was "found in biologically significant levels." This would point to other problems for loons, especially for those in the Monadnock Region, that would later be addressed.

One other important scientific initiative in loon science in which the LPC was involved was that of examining—performing a necropsy on— any recovered loon carcasses. This procedure, the wildlife equivalent of a human autopsy, is an attempt to find out the causes of death of an individual loon. It is an invaluable tool, and in the beginning, the LPC partnered with the U.S. Fish and Wildlife Service because, unlike now, it did not have the facilities to conduct necropsies. The very first New Hampshire loon necropsy took place in 1976 on a bird recovered on Squam Lake; the loon was found to have died from lead poisoning due to ingesting a fishing sinker. A second loon was necropsied in 1977 and found to have died from the same cause. This discovery was of historical importance, as it identified a primary cause for the loss of New Hampshire's loons, and ever since that time, initiatives have been put into place to combat the problem. The lead problem, as will be discussed, remains a primary cause for loon deaths to this day, but the early revelation of this human factor allowed for subsequent mitigation efforts to be put into place by the LPC that have allowed the loon population to recover and grow.

While these examples are just a small sampling of the loon work that was being done by the LPC, they nonetheless offer a glimpse into the organization's extensive operations. Its early success was highlighted at both the state and national level in 1979, a mere four years after its formation. In New Hampshire, the data gathered by the LPC resulted in the loon finally receiving the state status of a threatened species. Also in 1979, Rawson Wood and Scott Sutcliffe co-founded the North American Loon Fund (NALF).

This was an effort to expand the loon conservation model established by the LPC to other states in the northern tier of the United States, where loons were also under threat. Not only did NALF serve as a clearinghouse for current loon research, but it also offered grant money to fund scientific research and hosted a yearly conference where the latest loon research was presented. This exportation of the New Hampshire model was successful and eventually resulted in over 20 loon conservation organizations being established nationwide.

In 1981, Scott Sutcliffe departed the LPC and headed off to other birding organizations, first with the Nature Conservancy and subsequently to his former roost at Cornell, where he played a major role in developing the Cornell Lab of Ornithology's eBird platform. Of his time in New Hampshire, he stated simply, "It was a wonderful part of my life. Rawson [Wood] enabled our work, and it wasn't just me, it was we. It was a really nice team." Ralph Kirshner, too, had departed by this time, the physical work, "pounding around in a boat 12 hours a day" having taken its toll. However, his work with the LPC in reality did not end, as he still served as an LPC volunteer and spent over a decade on the LPC's board of directors. For Kirshner, "It was fun while it lasted, but for me it was not just about the loons. They are the canary in a coal mine. If we lose the loons, it's not going to go well for us humans.…Loons were and are the charismatic megaphone in that respect." Indeed, as the LPC continued its mission with a new director and a continually evolving team in the 1980s and beyond, new science would be developed, new threats would be identified and the loon population would make significant gains.

3

SETTING THE GROUNDWORK FOR THE LONG TERM, 1981–97

Following the departure of Scott Sutcliffe in 1981, the mission of the LPC continued without a break in the action. The organization grew in the scope of its scientific work as well as membership. In further developing partnerships with other scientists and biologists, wildlife rehabilitators, legislators, New Hampshire Fish and Game, a wide variety of lake associations and other loon conservation groups, the LPC has steadily grown to become more than just a reactionary organization but the foremost loon conservation group in the country. At the same time, the LPC has maintained its historical grassroots organizational approach to growing New Hampshire's loon population, a major key to its success. The LPC has had a number of directors, chairpersons and board members and trustees, as well as hundreds of biologists (both full-time staff and summer interns) and thousands of dedicated volunteers who have contributed to its success over the years. While a work such as this cannot name every individual involved in these efforts, there are some who stand out in the history of the organization for their work directly with loons, as well as those who staff the LPC's everyday current operations. Here follow a few highlights of these individuals and the LPC's work from 1981 to the present.

THE FAIR YEARS, 1981–91

Sutcliffe's replacement as LPC director was a man with a passion for the great outdoors—the more remote, the better, his inner compass pushing him ever northward. Jeff Fair was born in Philadelphia and raised in Hershey but knew from an early age that the woods would be his home. When it came time for college, he longed to head north to the University of Maine, but his parents kept him close to home. He graduated from Old Dominion University in Virginia with a degree in biology but finally got his way when he was accepted at the University of New Hampshire to gain a master's in wildlife ecology. Here, Fair's thesis involved the white-tailed deer, and during his research, he used an experimental tranquilizer drug mixture. Upon his graduation in 1976, Fair had a desire to work, not with loons in New Hampshire but with grizzly bears in the Rocky Mountains out west, and his background in the new drug helped make it happen after having filled out 99 different job applications. And that's what he did for the first years of his wildlife career, "the only Yankee trapping grizzlies in Yellowstone," and subsequently working for two deer seasons in Utah. But the call of northern New England was a strong one, and he came back east to work for the LPC in the summer beginning in 1978, working in the North Country on Lake Umbagog. Interestingly, "it was not because of loons at first" that Fair returned to New Hampshire. "I did it for the latitude," the northerly climate and setting more to his liking. He and his wife, Kathy, also a biologist, first lived in a tiny Fish and Game trailer, she "putting up with a lot" that first year until they eventually built a home of their own. He became friends with Scott Sutcliffe, who knew at his departure that Fair "got it" and understood the LPC mission and would do a great job. As for Jeff Fair, he accepted the directorship with gusto, recalling, "I was just old enough to be wise about some things and young enough to kick some ass." Fair also knew that the LPC was well-positioned for the future, commenting that "Scott Sutcliffe got all that in line. I could see why that was working and I just carried it on.... Scott's work is what this was built on. He was such a great guy." Fair, of course, worked hand in hand with LPC founder Rawson Wood, even if the two men had little in common except for loons. Wood moved in higher social circles with ease and was a master at fundraisers and like events, while the young Fair didn't even own a suit and was a bit on the wild side, preferring the outdoors to social events and board meetings. Fair recalled that Wood was "a hard cookie for the first couple of years," which involved 80-hour work weeks, as well as a co-directorship of NALF, which involved no extra pay. While Fair may have rubbed some of the New Hampshire Audubon board members the wrong way, he noted that "Rawson saved the day. I'm a field biologist. I respected the truth, and he saw that." In the end, Rawson Wood, as he did with his predecessor, treated Jeff Fair like a son and saw to it that the LPC had the support it needed to get the job done.

The hallmarks of Jeff Fair's 10-year tenure with the LPC were many. His philosophy was a simple and straightforward one, based on a cooperative approach. As he later recalled, "I would cooperate in strategy, but would not compromise in principle." To that end, he gained the trust of a wide range of people. Fair was a hunter and fisherman, an outdoorsman, so he worked well with both individual hunters and anglers, as well as Fish and Game officers. It was a world he knew and respected, and by his easygoing manner and fair approach, he could gain their support for loon conservation efforts. When a hunter was blamed by a local news editor for a loon death on Pea Porridge Pond in Madison in September 1986, Fair wrote a letter to the newspaper that not only corrected the account (the loon was not shot) but also defended hunters as folks who "enjoy having loons around" and referred to them in general as "one of the most important and effective conservation forces on the continent today," many of them "volunteers in our field programs." Fair's methods eventually became dubbed the "velvet glove" approach, an iron fist of reason and science wrapped in a soft velvet glove when it came to working with the public at all levels. Whether friend or perceived foe to the loon, Fair expected everyone from volunteers on up to be respectful in their dealings with those they came in contact with while helping the loons in the hopes of converting them to the cause. If that failed, then, and only then in some cases, the iron fist, the heavy-handed approach, might be brought to bear. For instance, the LPC had a long-standing $100 reward for information that led to the arrest and conviction of someone who killed a loon or destroyed a nest, but they'd much rather spend that money educating people to prevent such occurrences.

Fair's approach was also applied to the forces at work on Lake Umbagog, a significant nesting site for loons in northern New Hampshire and Maine. The biggest problem here was the entity, Union Water Power Company at the time, that controlled the dam and thus water levels in the lake, which helped produce the power for its customers. It was Jeff Fair who sat down at the table in 1983 with Bill Grove, a power company engineer, whose wife really liked loons, as well as a New Hampshire state engineer and the director of New Hampshire Fish and Game. It was a tense meeting due to past disputes, and the New Hampshire engineer thought that nothing could be worked out between "environmentalists" (Fair and the LPC) and the power company due to the unpredictable nature of estimating future water levels. However, Grove surprisingly disagreed and joined Fair in hammering out a verbal agreement on water levels in the lake and how and when the fluctuations might occur so as not to destroy loon nesting sites. The provisions were formalized in Federal Energy Regulatory Commission License No. 3133, issued in August of that year. Though New Hampshire Audubon officials were aghast that Fair would even sit down with the enemy, that agreement would last for years and directly contributed to continued loon breeding success on the lake. As a result, every year the power company was notified by the LPC when the first loon nested on the lake and when the last hatching occurred, and during the time in between, minimum changes in the water level would be enacted. It was one of Fair's major achievements, and he and successive LPC biologists continued to work with Grove and his successors over the years.

By the LPC's fifth year of existence, it was clearly evident that loon nest failures were a major problem. Fair not only greatly increased the use of nesting rafts but also put protocols in place to make them more likely to be used by loons and increase reproductive success. As Fair would later write, the use of these rafts was "the most successful program of its kind in North America" and was "a means of circumventing common loon nest losses due to shoreline predations and drought or flood conditions." However, he and the other LPC biologists knew, after some years of experience, that they had to be used only in the right circumstances and not just placed willy-nilly. Now, the conditions under which they would be used required that there had to be an already established nesting pair of loons that had lost their nest repeatedly to shoreline predation, mostly raccoons at this time, or water level fluctuations. Their use was also contingent on a safe area within the territory for placement, as floating an island in the wrong place at best left them unused (a waste of time, manpower and monetary resources) but also could trap a pair of loons into sure nest failure. For instance, an island placed, say, in a cove that is quiet in early May in Lake Winnipesaukee (before the summer season is underway) might attract a pair of loons, but this same area within a month might see heavy boat traffic, prompting the loons to abandon the island. As Fair acknowledged, these rafts "are not the solution to human disturbance problems. Here, education is the most powerful management tool." Finally, Fair also found that these rafts, built with the help of LPC volunteers, gave shoreline residents "something to own, bringing them in in the effort to save loons in a personal way." Indeed, one of the traditions he developed after successfully placing a raft with the LPC team after a long day's work was to pass around a flask containing a bit of Yukon Jack whiskey and raise a toast to the hoped-for success of the raft. It was one of those traditions, "family stuff" as Fair put it, that developed an "underlying connection amongst everyone in the LPC." While the science was most certainly correct, the toasts didn't hurt. In 1990, by the end of Fair's tenure, some 35 rafts were floated that summer, with 71 percent (25) in use, producing 23 chicks, of which 18 survived to fledge—22 percent of all surviving chicks on New Hampshire waters in what was a very successful year. Just 10 years prior, that number was at 17 percent.

In addition to the raft program, the LPC also started in 1983 its first annual Loon Census, where biologists and volunteers alike counted the loons for one hour on July 16 on 134 lakes and ponds across the state. While such a census could not be an exact count of the number of loons in New Hampshire (loons can be difficult to spot sometimes), it was useful in providing a snapshot of sorts on the state of the loon. It is an important initiative and tool that is still used to this day, a loon version of the National Audubon Society's annual Christmas Bird Count. During the annual Loon Census in 2022, 458 volunteers counted 462 adult loons, 80 chicks and 4 juvenile loons on 114 bodies of water, a third of all of those monitored by the LPC. If you want to be a part of this effort in the future, check out the LPC website for information on how you can join in and contribute.

Among other interesting loon events, of which there were many during the Fair years, are the following:

In 1981, the loons returned early to New Hampshire's inland waters, with 3 spotted on Sunrise Lake in Middleton on March 12 and 20 on Lake Winnipesaukee four days later. That summer, two canoeists were reported for stealing loon eggs. It is unknown what they intended to do with them.

In 1984, loon chicks were hatched on Loon Island off Meredith Neck in Lake Winnipesaukee for the first time in LPC history. That same year, the National Wildlife Federation gave its President's Award to the LPC for its efforts to save loons.

In 1986, Rawson Wood formed the Loon Preservation Policy Committee to assist the LPC in its decision-making processes.

In June 1988, two loons were deliberately shot on Lake Winnipesaukee, the first surviving, subsequently rehabilitated and released on the lake.

The summer of 1988 also saw the rising problems on Squam Lake when it came to territorial disputes. During this time, a group of floaters, loons seeking a territory of their own, terrorized the established pairs on the lake for weeks on end. Infamously known as the "gang of 10," these adult loons harassed and harried loon families and were suspects in the killing of 2 loon chicks.

In 1989, the future site of the LPC headquarters and Lake Winnipesaukee field station was designated to be built in the coming years at the newly established Fredrick and Paula Anna Markus Wildlife Sanctuary, a 200-acre site on the northernmost part of the lake in Moultonborough. The Markus Foundation was a major supporter of the LPC since 1976. Also in this year, eight loons, a record high, were recorded on Lake Winnipesaukee at the Winter Harbor Seaplane base in Wolfeboro.

The year 1989 was also bittersweet for the LPC; after 14 years of guiding and growing the organization he had founded and fought for, Rawson Wood stepped down as LPC chairman. While the chairpersons that came after him would serve honorably, none has had the same impact or served such a long tenure. However, this did not mean that Wood's work on behalf of New Hampshire loons was over. For more than a decade afterward, he continued to advocate for loons and raise funds for the LPC, all while approaching the age of 100.

By 1990, a record high of 100 lakes in New Hampshire had 324 paired loons, a record, and an overall record of 495 loons were counted in the state. In terms of reproduction success, the year saw a record 106 chicks hatched, up from just 57 in 1976 and a record low of 45 in 1977. Notably, Lake Winnipesaukee remained a big concern—while 10 chicks hatched on the lake, only 3 survived.

In the summer of 1991, an unusual bilevel loon nesting site was discovered on Kingswood Lake in Brookfield. The first nest was located on the shoreline and contained one egg, but when the water level suddenly decreased due to weather and climate conditions, the nest was left high and dry well away from the water. The loon pair hastily built a second nest at the water's edge below this nest, and here a second egg was deposited. For a two-week period, the pair alternated their incubation efforts on both nests, but both were eventually abandoned and neither egg developed, climate change and loon "indecision" being the culprits for this tragic turn of events.

Another event of import occurred on Squam Lake, "one of our largest and most inviolate lakes," according to the LPC. A dredge and fill operation in one loon territory resulted in material in the water that promoted and accelerated an algal bloom, thereby threatening them. That same summer, a large amount of #2 fuel oil leaked into the lake from an underground heating oil tank on Center Harbor Neck. While the spill was quickly cleaned up, the potential for loon harm was great. Should loons come into contact with oil, the natural oils in their plumage can break down, destroying their buoyancy capabilities and insulation from the cold. Further harm is caused when the oiled loon preens itself, causing it to become poisoned after ingesting the oil. While the Squam Lake loons in these instances caught a break, these events highlighted both the importance of environmental regulations on our lakes as well as the thin line that sometimes separates human activities from affecting loons.

Some notable personnel hires were also made by the LPC during this period that would have long-term positive effects on the organization and the loon population in New Hampshire and beyond. The first of these individuals brought aboard was Linda "Lin" O'Bara. A native of Massachusetts who moved to Laconia in the late 1970s, she holds an associate's degree in accounting. With a background in secretarial and bookkeeping work as well, O'Bara interviewed for a part-time position as director of the North American Loon Fund (NALF), which had been started by Rawson Wood and Scott Sutcliffe. With Wood and Jeff Fair running this groundbreaking organization, additional help was needed. As O'Bara laughingly recalled, "Rawson Wood interviewed me and made me take a typing test. He was very sweet, and NALF was desperate." In her position, which she held for 18 years, she at first helped sell the vinyl record recordings of loons, the proceeds of which were distributed as grant money for loon research projects. O'Bara wore many different hats during her time with NALF and was critical to its success, receiving grant requests and sending them to the grant committee for review, as well as organizing the yearly NALF conference (held in different states) with a team of volunteers and serving as the overall hub for incoming information that she passed on to Wood, Sutcliffe and Fair. As she recalled, "I am most proud of being the person that could connect different researchers with each other. I enjoyed being a part of that connection." O'Bara also helped create loon educational materials for classrooms, produced the NALF newsletter and, with a small staff of two, continued to sell loon-related products. As for Rawson Wood, O'Bara recalled that he "was so generous with his time and money. He expected certain things—he was the boss—but he was always fair and considerate. He was so down to earth, and in the summertime loved to buy pints of strawberries for everyone." Of her years at NALF, O'Bara recalled it as "a lifetime opportunity....We did a lot of good." The North American Loon Fund eventually closed its operation several years after Lin O'Bara's departure in 2000, primarily because its mission to help establish organizations for loon conservation in other states had been fulfilled. However, O'Bara's work with loons was not yet ended—after working for the Concord SPCA for 10 years, she worked for the LPC from 2010 to 2021 as the head of membership development. To this day, she still does volunteer work for the LPC, and though few in the public may realize the important work done by this kind and unassuming woman, those in the loon world hold her in high esteem.

Two other key hires during Jeff Fair's tenure were Linda Egli Johnson and Betsy McCoy. Johnson, who is today the LPC's longest-serving employee, was, and is, a dynamo who has worn all manner of hats and performed many different duties during her long career, both administrative and fieldwork related, and there is no denying the impact she has had on the LPC. McCoy has also had a long career with the LPC, starting out as field biologist, subsequently rising to the position of senior biologist before becoming LPC director. While she would leave the LPC for a period of time, she has recently (2022) returned.

During the early years of the LPC, when its staff was small and largely part-time, the director of the LPC was tasked with not only budgetary matters but also finding enough field biologists, whether graduates with degrees or interns working toward one, to do the loon fieldwork required

LPC biologists Linda Egli Johnson (*left*) and Betsy McCoy with a loon taxidermy specimen, 1988. *Photo by Phyllis Morrissette, Courtesy LPC.*

on many of New Hampshire's bodies of water, especially the big lakes. It was not always an easy task. The work is interesting, and the loon cause is an attractive one, but the work is hard, the hours long and the conditions challenging. Housing can usually be arranged, but the more remote the location, the harder it is to cover. Early on, Lake Umbagog was a tough lake for Jeff Fair to find coverage—he himself loved the wildness and isolation of northern New Hampshire, but such a locale was not to everyone's liking. Enter 1968 Dartmouth College graduate Jack Noon. Though Texas born, "to my everlasting shame," Noon had deep roots in New Hampshire, his ancestors having settled such towns as Eaton, Atkinson and Dover while his grandparents had had a home in East Sutton since 1945. On his graduation with a BA in English, Noon taught school in Greece and Alaska before returning to New Hampshire in 1971. He would subsequently teach for the newly established Dartmouth Outward Bound Term program, strict academic learning combined with wilderness encounters, which was conducted at the recently renovated Ravine Lodge on the slope of Mount Moosilauke in the wilds of the Second College Grant location.

Noon took to the wilderness living like a loon to water and even built a log cabin on the Dead Diamond River. Noon met LPC director Jeff Fair while he and his wife were working in the North Country, and later, when the Fairs were building a house of their own with Noon's expert help, "Jeff made the mistake of telling me he was having a hard time finding a biologist" up there. And the rest, as they say, is history. Noon would work on Lake Umbagog and the smaller lakes in the area for the next five years from 1987 to 1991. Here, Noon learned about the loons while bringing his wilderness experience to bear "making the rounds. I loved visiting the remote ponds especially. Loon[s] were once rare but were now expanding into new territories. I would identify myself as the 'loon guy' and worked with locals, paddling around in a canoe or a battered aluminum jon boat." Being new to loon science, Noon took direction from Fair and other LPC biologists but quickly made a name for himself. As he recalled years later, "I took pleasure in seeing new loon pairs, along with ospreys and eagles." While Noon was an excellent outdoorsman, it was his observational and writing skills that have stood the test of time. To this day, his field notes, their thoroughness and well-thought-out composition, are held up as examples for new field biologists to emulate during their initial training by the LPC's Senior Biologist John Cooley Jr. Turns out, a Dartmouth College English degree and loons do indeed go well together! Jack Noon, in addition to his teaching career and loon fieldwork, is an author and historian. In 1990, he authored *The Squam Lakes and Their*

Loons and is a noted expert on New Hampshire's fishing history. His 2022 work *Rambles Through New Hampshire, Early and Late* documents his time with the LPC in Coos County.

Finally, no account of the Fair years is complete without comment on his writing and communication skills. Jeff Fair was, and still is, an outstanding writer, and his writings in many different areas, combined with the connections of Rawson Wood, gave the LPC a high degree of visibility and publicity in the 1980s. Loons were being written about in every publication imaginable, from small local newspapers to the *Union Leader* (the only statewide newspaper) and the *Wall Street Journal* and a wide variety of magazines, even *Sports Illustrated*. While Fair did not write all these articles, he was always a good interview and was adept at explaining the plight of the loons in terms that regular people could understand. Too, as I have alluded to, Fair was not averse, in addition to his many other duties, to writing in to local newspapers to add colorful commentary or to working with local organizations that affected loons. Two examples suffice to highlight his efforts, one humorous and one serious. In 1989, when a small local paper in Meredith ran an article about the annual Loon Census with the headline "Loon Census Shows Fewer Chickens," Fair responded to correct the "foul error," stating that the LPC has never monitored the chicken population of New Hampshire. Funny stuff. In 1990, in the wake of a floatplane incident on Bearcamp Pond in Sandwich that "accidentally but avoidably" disturbed a loon nesting site, where tempers flared on both sides in the aftermath, Fair subsequently worked with local aviation authorities. In the spring, he began sending maps to the Laconia Airport manager identifying lakes and ponds where there were nesting loons and critical nesting sites, asking pilots to respect these areas and limit traffic so that disruptions could be prevented. Of course, as any longtime LPC member knows, it was his immensely readable pieces in the LPC's newsletter that really engaged its members and kept them in the know. The newsletter got a sporadic start in 1979 but became a regular publication late the following year. The message from the director in each issue became a regular feature, and Fair took full advantage of this simple but valuable tool, a tradition that continues to this day.

As far as publicity goes, it didn't hurt the LPC and its cause that the Hollywood movie *On Golden Pond* was filmed on Squam Lake and featured megastars Katharine Hepburn and Henry Fonda. Loons were part of the 1981 release's central theme, and the LPC was involved in the movie. Cast members stayed at the Squam Lake family compound of LPC volunteer Johanna "Hansi" Mead and her husband, architect William Mead, and the

Summer Week

May 25, 1989   **SCENIC NEW HAMPSHIRE**   VOLUME 17 NUMBER 1

Loons Making Comeback In N.H.

Scenic New Hampshire newspaper featuring the loon's comeback in New Hampshire, May 1989. Wide publicity of the LPC's work was highlighted in local publications like this throughout New Hampshire during this time. *Courtesy LPC.*

film was shot on their property. Interestingly, the dead loon depicted in the movie came from the LPC's freezer at its headquarters in Meredith. One of the most unusual items on display at the Loon Center is an oversized model of a loon that was used in the filming of the movie, an integral prop, its hinged neck controlled by divers underwater, as real loons make for unpredictable cast members.

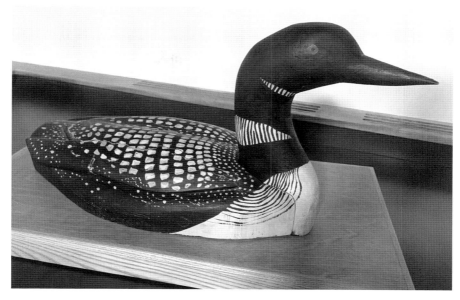

The original loon prop used in the movie *On Golden Pond* is now part of the LPC's collection and is on display at the Visitor's Center in Moultonborough. *Author photo.*

By 1991, Jeff Fair had served the LPC well for 10 years, but he knew his time was up. As the LPC's work grew in scope, Fair felt more and more like he was chained to a desk and missed the work of a field biologist. Then again, his inner compass continued to point him toward an even more northerly climate. Despite his departure, Fair has never really stopped working with loons. As we will see, as a volunteer he worked on the first banding project for New Hampshire loons and worked heavily with loons in neighboring Maine. Fair would eventually make his way northward to Alaska, where he has worked with yellow-billed loons as well as many other animals. His ties to the LPC were so strong that Rawson Wood even monetarily contributed to Fair's loon work in Alaska. Jeff Fair now makes his home in Palmer, Alaska, and, not surprisingly, has authored two books about bears. For many years, he worked for one of the LPC's partners in loon preservation, the Biodiversity Research Institute in Portland, Maine, and still writes for the institute today, his blog articles both evocative and eloquent. From time to time, Fair returns to New Hampshire to pay family, and his old friends at the LPC, a visit, and when he does, it's a cause for celebration.

BETSY McCOY, 1991–94

With the departure of Fair, the LPC did not have to look too far to find a new director, as a talented and dedicated biologist, Betsy McCoy, was waiting in the wings. Not only did she have the necessary qualifications as a biologist, having done fieldwork for six years, but she had also previously served as a full-time program assistant in 1987 and as acting director in the summer of 1988 when Jeff Fair took a sabbatical. As McCoy is passionate about the cause and its grassroots efforts, her selection was an important one; she was the first woman to occupy the position of LPC director. This was a big deal at a time, as both McCoy and Linda Egli Johnson recalled, that whenever they were working with loons in the field, any conversations with those in the public from outside the LPC were always directed toward the male biologists, even though these men often had less experience and were not actually in charge. During her tenure, McCoy continued the path that the LPC had forged from the very beginning, with evolving loon science being its guide in continuing to grow New Hampshire's loon population. As for her relationship with Rawson Wood, McCoy recalled that while he was gruff at times, he was also a "grandfather figure" and that his commitment to the cause of loons was absolute and he was never too busy to do what needed to be done and fully supported her efforts.

Under McCoy's leadership, many exciting changes occurred, and new loon initiatives were put into place in just three short years. Some of these had to do with the LPC's operating infrastructure. Betsy McCoy, along with Linda Egli Johnson, ushered in the computer age at the LPC, designing the organization's first database and entering in all the required data. McCoy and her team also oversaw the LPC's move from its old headquarters in Meredith to its new and current location at the Loon Center on Lees Mill Road in Moultonborough, located on the land of the Frederick and Paula Anna Markus Wildlife Sanctuary. As with any move of this type, there were many logistical and construction challenges to be met, but the results were worth it—a dedicated building, with room for growth, on a beautiful point of land whose trails could be enjoyed by both the public at large and the LPC staff. Construction began in June 1992, at the height of the loon nesting season, and by the following year, the LPC finally had a home all its own.

As for on-the-water accomplishments, the LPC also began several new programs. One of these combatted an age-old problem, that of loons becoming entangled in discarded monofilament fishing line. This line, a

Welcome sign on the grounds of the new home for the Loon Center in Moultonborough. *Author photo.*

seemingly innocuous byproduct of recreational fishing, was described in this manner by the LPC: "it lies in wait as a deadly trap." Such line could get entangled around a loon's feet or wing feathers, hindering or stopping altogether their ability to fly or dive for food. Worse, it can, and does, get wrapped around a loon's beak, making it impossible for them to ingest any food. The resultant effect is that a loon starves to death. The Berkley Company instituted a recycling program for this line in 1990, coming up with the slogan "Recycle when you respool," and in the first two years recycled 700,000 miles of fishing line. The LPC was now a part of this initiative, with recycling containers strategically placed on lakes around the state.

Perhaps the most exciting project the LPC was involved with during this time was the beginning of its loon banding efforts. Of course, many types of birds had been banded by conservation groups across the country for years, but banding loons was a different matter altogether, as they are extremely difficult to catch on the open water. Dr. Judith McIntyre, a pioneering loon biologist at Syracuse University, was the first to devise a method of catching loons in the 1980s. A young biologist named Dave Evers, a graduate from

Michigan State University (1984) with a bachelor's in wildlife management and a master's in ecology from Western Michigan University (1992), refined McIntyre's method and, in 1993, in cooperation with the LPC and including Jeff Fair as a volunteer, led a team on Lake Umbagog to band the first New Hampshire loons. The lake was chosen because it had a stable loon population. The idea was simple: catch the birds at night; take a blood sample and two secondary wing feather samples, each of which could be tested for potential toxins; place uniquely colored bands on one foot and the U.S. Fish and Wildlife Service numbered band on the other; and send them on their way. The banding, sampling and data recording process itself takes relatively little time—it's the capture that is the tricky part. As Jeff Fair related, Evers "pieced together two other techniques involving spotlighting, recorded loon calls and oversized landing nets, added a twist of his own, and to date has orchestrated the capture and release unharmed of thousands of loons." Among the loons banded on that first expedition over 30 years ago was the Sweat Meadows female, the oldest known loon in New Hampshire and one of the oldest known in the world as of 2023. Today, the LPC conducts nighttime banding expeditions on lakes all across the state, these efforts and their results to be discussed later on in detail.

As to other loon events, the nesting raft program was now an established program, and LPC personnel were hard at work in the spring constructing and placing them in their chosen area. The 1992 breeding season was a challenging one due to cold weather conditions, which delayed loon nesting for about two weeks on average, but despite this the loon population grew once again, doing so for the 12th straight year and achieving record results. The final accounting for the year showed 336 paired adults (a record) and an overall total of 415 adult loons (also a record). With 89 chicks fledged, that resulted in an overall loon population in the state (including juveniles) of 504 loons, also a record. Interestingly, the chick survival rate dipped to 67 percent, the lowest in years, but was still not deemed an alarming drop. Though uncertain, these hard-fought gains resulted in loon numbers that had probably not been seen on New Hampshire lakes and ponds for at least 40 years. One of the 7 new nesting pairs in the state was recorded on Newfound Lake in Bristol, which, "according to very reliable volunteer information," had not had a known nesting since 1945.

The 1992 numbers also highlight the causes of known loon mortality and the changing times. Human disturbances were seventh on the list, while unknown causes and egg disappearances caused the greatest losses. Interestingly, raccoon predation, once the number one cause of

Sweats Meadow territorial pair on the Androscoggin River in Errol. The oldest known loon in New England is the female at left. *Courtesy Nordel Gagnon.*

loon mortality, had slid to fifth on the list. This likely coincided with the occurrence of a raccoon rabies epizootic (a large-scale animal disease outbreak), which was first documented in Rumney in April and would, within two years, greatly reduce raccoon numbers from the Lakes Region southward. Nearly 40 percent of raccoons were afflicted with rabies within several years of the outbreak, and raccoon predation, while still an ever-present possibility, would never again require the efforts that the LPC exerted in its early years. On the other hand, avian predation, whether gulls, eagles or crows, was number two on the list of loon losses and the first among known causes. While rafts greatly reduced predation from land mammals, birds could still steal eggs from the nests on these islands. However, this same year, Jeff Fair and other loon biologists touted a new invention, that of avian guards, erected over these rafts to provide not only protection from birds swooping down to raid a nest but also the added benefit of offering shade to nesting loons. It was a win all the way around, and such avian guards were adopted in succeeding years.

In 1993, the loons were late in their return to New Hampshire, once again due to the weather, but this did not hinder their success. Some 348 loons were recorded during the annual Loon Census in July, a lower number than normal (the rainy day likely limiting sightings), but by the end of the breeding season, there were 112 lakes with a territorial pair, up from the previous record of 100. The following year's Loon Census counted more loons, 477 in all, showing that the loon population overall was constant during Betsy McCoy's tenure.

In 1994, Betsy McCoy stepped down as LPC director, though she would continue on as senior biologist until departing the organization in the spring of 1996, only to return some years later.

THE INTERIM YEARS, 1994–97

For the next several years, two LPC directors would serve for short periods of time, Jim Boyle (1994–95) and Lisa Sutherland (1995–97). During this time, the LPC continued with its established activities, such as placing rafts, monitoring nesting sites and rescuing loons in distress. Significant organizational events during this time include development of the LPC's first website, which went live in 1995. That same year, the LPC also aligned itself with another partner, the Society for the Protection of New Hampshire Forests, its New Hampshire Living Landscape agenda, particularly the strategic land protection component, closely matching the LPC's five-year goal plan to protect loon habitats. Finally, the LPC formalized its forward-looking approach by finalizing a five-year plan in 1995 that identified key actions and initiatives that would be taken to increase the loon population. Future results would demonstrate that this plan, along with a growing membership and increased grant funding, had a positive effect, and subsequent revisions to this plan have been made over the years.

The year 1995 was also an important one for furthering loon knowledge. On Dublin Pond that summer, a loon was observed acting oddly and lingering close to shore. The bird had previously been captured in someone's front yard in western New Hampshire, rehabilitated in Keene and released on Dublin Pond. The bird was once again captured by the LPC and was examined by veterinarian Lee Pearson, aided by Tufts veterinarian student Priscilla Pettit. The bird was found to have parasites, the first ever to be found in a New Hampshire loon. This newly discovered threat to loons was a wake-up call to biologists, and as shall be discussed later, such parasites, possibly caused by black flies or malaria-infected mosquitos, are a possible indicator of yet another climate change effect.

As to the bodily mysteries of the loon, 1995 saw a partnership further developed with Dr. Mark Pokras at the Cummings School of Veterinary Medicine of Tufts University in North Grafton, Massachusetts. With the aid of the university and grant funding from NALF, the LPC was able to have a summer intern, Priscilla Pettit, work right at the LPC's Loon Center headquarters and perform necropsies on New Hampshire loons, avoiding the necessity of having to send these bird carcasses out of state, as was done previously, and the resultant long wait to find out causes of death. Pettit also served as the New Hampshire coordinator for Pokras's six-year-long loon mortality study. By this time, there were many scientists working to find the root causes of loon declines, and the ability to perform these examinations at the LPC's headquarters was a great leap forward in gaining timely knowledge. Two years later, the LPC would develop its own wet lab with the help of Mark Pokras so that its personnel could perform egg analysis and loon necropsies. Few visitors to the Loon Center today likely realize that some of the latest discoveries in loon science could be in the making in the rooms below the visitor center and gift shop in this small New Hampshire town.

Beginning in 1996, the directorship of Lisa Sutherland would strengthen both the LPC's financial status and its relationship with the public at large.

Even New Hampshire brewers joined in the loon excitement generated by the LPC in the 1980s and 1990s. This now defunct craft brewery was not the only beer-maker to feature a loon brew among its offerings. *Author collection.*

While she was not a biologist, Sutherland did come from a marketing background and, as Linda Egli Johnson noted, turned the LPC's Loon's Feather gift shop into a professional and much more appealing retail operation. The shop had gotten its start in the LPC's cramped quarters in the Humiston Building in Meredith, but in its new location in the Loon Center, it was turned into a destination shopping place for all things loon and remains so to this day. Now, some 7,000 folks visit yearly, while many more can now shop online year-round at https://loon.org/shop/.

An event with far-reaching loon implications occurred in January 1996. It took place over 150 miles away from New Hampshire, and few in our state likely gave the event much thought beyond a potential rise in home heating oil prices. On January 19, 1996, the tanker barge *North Cape* grounded off the coast of Rhode Island, resulting in an ocean oil spill of 828,000 gallons of home heating oil in Block Island Sound. As a result of this environmental disaster, millions of sea creatures were affected, including lobsters, fish, clams, crabs and mussels, as well as over 2,000 marine birds. Of these oiled birds, 402 that died were loons. Compared to the millions of fish lost, this number seems small, but when we recall that the already threatened loon has a low reproductive rate, the loss of this many loons would have a significant effect on New England's loon population in the future. In the nearly $8 million 1999 settlement the barge owners subsequently reached with the government, $3 million was allocated toward protecting and securing lands around northern New England lakes to provide a buffer zone for loon habitats. How many of the loons that died in this event were New Hampshire birds is unknown, but the area of the oil spill was the wintering grounds for loons from New York, Vermont and New Hampshire, as well as Maine. The fact that loon numbers were down for 1996 and 1997 in New Hampshire may have been due in part to this disaster. While all the loon settlement money for this event would be spent on Maine lands, the LPC learned from this catastrophe, and when, not if, such an event happened again, the organization would see to it that New Hampshire loons were not forgotten in the aftermath.

A sad but inevitable event took place on Squam Lake in the summer of 1996 when the first death of a banded loon occurred. This was one of the River Bend territorial birds; it was attacked by an invading loon looking for a new territory. The resident loon sustained two puncture wounds in the belly and was found dead two weeks later. Though uncertain, it is believed that the surviving member of this pair mated with the invader. And so continued the loon circle of life and death on this heavily contested lake. As will be discussed, Squam was, and is, a virtual loon battleground, and incidents like these were becoming more common. In 1997, of the 60 unmated loons, floaters counted on all of New Hampshire's lakes, 10 were present on Squam Lake, more than any other body of water.

Finally, among the new personnel hired by the LPC during this period, one of the most important was Katherine "Kate" M. Taylor. A native of Minnesota, Taylor was hired in 1995 as a field biologist for the Monadnock Region, then one of the fastest-growing loon field territories, She graduated that same year from the University of Massachusetts with a bachelor's degree in biology and anthropology, with a focus on genetics. Her Environmental Protection Agency internship and work with aquatic contaminants on the Quabbin Reservoir in Massachusetts would bring valuable experience and insight. Taylor responded to an advertisement she had seen for an LPC position, but, as she laughingly recalled, "I knew very little about loons, nothing more than the average person, but I really loved wildlife. I called Betsy McCoy, and she took a chance on me. Once I was hired, I read all I could about loons, and Betsy was great….She really prepared me and really walked me through what the job entailed." That year, Taylor found that she loved everything about the work, and it was fortunate for the LPC that she did. The following year, with the departure of McCoy, Taylor was back in a larger role as the LPC's senior biologist, working across the state. That first summer, Taylor "felt the weight of making sure I did things right. I remember Jeff [Fair] called and offered to be a support for me, welcoming me into the community…another link in the chain…and offering his encouragement. He became a tremendous mentor to me." In fact, Kate Taylor would have a large influence on the LPC. Because of her extensive lab work experience, as she recalled, "I had a background for protocols and methodology and reworked the Loon Rangers Bible [the guide used by field biologists] into a more formal document. I wanted our team to realize that we were collecting real and significant data about loons that mattered. The LPC already had a great dataset that was a luxury and the best in the world, but I wanted interns and everyone to know where the data was going and how it was being used. That data set informed what we were doing." Interestingly, Taylor never cared for the traditional moniker, Loon Rangers, often given to interns and field biologists, especially by the media, feeling that it downplayed the scientific work that she and her team of biologists were performing. Taylor was also a part of the LPC's increasing efforts to rescue sick and injured loons, and she made it a "huge" priority, not just for her staff but herself as well. She recalled that most such calls always came at the end of the day, but "I just went crazy and did it. It was heartbreaking work at times. This is a labor of love, working with loons." She remembered one time around the Fourth of July when a pair of sick loons were recovered from Balch Pond in Wakefield, on the New Hampshire–Maine border. One adult was found acting strangely and had to be put down due to lead poisoning. The very next day, another call came to the LPC from the same pond; a second lead-poisoned adult loon was discovered and subsequently euthanized. I asked Taylor about the emotional difficulties of working with loons, especially in such trying circumstances. As Taylor so hauntingly put it, "You're holding them when they're put down. It's an intimate act, a solemn event. As scientists, we're supposed to look at loons from the population level, not individual loons. But you know those loons, you know those lakes, you've been out there repeatedly, and you become very involved." Reading the LPC newsletters and the articles Kate Taylor wrote during her tenure, both her scientific acumen and passion for her work are readily apparent.

The results of the 1996 and 1997 loon seasons at the end of this interim period were revealing as the LPC headed toward the new millennium. The numbers tell the story: in 1996, 538 loons were counted, of which 398 were territorial paired birds, 50 were adult floaters without a territory and 88 were surviving chicks, with 2 immature birds also counted. Also, in 1996, 44 rafts were floated, of which 27 hatched chicks, 24.1 percent of the total productivity, all great numbers. However, the 1997 season saw some trends that pointed to new realities the LPC would have to confront head-on. That year, a like number of rafts, 42, were floated, but their overall use and productivity was down to 15 surviving chicks, just 15 percent of the total chicks produced in New Hampshire (99) that year. Of greater concern were the leading causes of mortality among loons in 1997. With increased boat traffic on our lakes, boat trauma became the second leading cause of death, accounting for 20 percent of all losses. However, in 1997, the number one cause of loon deaths, 55 percent overall, was lead poisoning. This number brought into focus the loons' greatest danger in our state, but the lead problem did not just rise to the forefront in a single year. As time had passed since the LPC was established, the organization, now armed with greater scientific knowledge and a greater ability to perform necropsies on deceased loons in its own facilities, finally revealed, for all to see, a problem that had been growing for years.

The new leadership of the LPC would have the lead issue and many more loon problems to deal with in the coming decades. However, as it always had done in the past, under new and steady leadership and with continued initiatives and advances in knowledge, the LPC would confront these challenges. It would be a roller-coaster ride of sorts, with the highs interrupted by alarming lows, but in the end, the loon population of the Granite State under LPC's stewardship would rebound and grow.

4

THE LOON PRESERVATION
COMMITTEE EXPANDS ITS MISSION,
1997–PRESENT

In August 1997, a new era was ushered in when Harry Vogel was named the next director of the LPC. As Vogel was already a highly respected loon biologist with a great amount of experience, he and the LPC were the perfect match. Here follows a look at some important and interesting aspects of the LPC's work, including population trends, challenges, successes, incidents, operations and notable personnel who joined the LPC during this period, divided up into five-year segments. However, it should be remembered that this concise summation brushes the surface of the day-to-day work of the LPC and its staff in furthering the cause of Granite State loons. There is much behind-the-scenes work, whether it be raft construction or repairs, contaminant testing, fielding calls from the public, grant writing, legislative research and testimony, equipment repair and maintenance and countless other things big and small, that occur daily outside the public eye. While I do here include loon population numbers in several different categories, for the LPC it is, and always has been, the number of territorial pairs of loons, those with breeding potential, that is the most important. Floaters, or unpaired adults, are not breeding and are not contributing to current population growth (though they could in the future if they become paired), while chicks that have survived to fledge will, if all goes well, soon leave the state. According to Vogel, only a third of these birds will return as adults.

1998–2002

The summer of 1998 was a difficult start for Vogel and his team, as heavy rains in June, right at the height of the breeding season, led to major loon nest failures throughout the state. However, 1998 was also an important year. The work of the LPC was once again gaining recognition, not only within the conservation community but also the public at large. That year, the U.S. Fish and Wildlife Service (USFWS), based out of Concord, gave a special citation to the organization recognizing its loon conservation efforts. To this day, that federal agency is a valued partner of the LPC in its work. One unique form of recognition came from the Business and Industry Association of New Hampshire, which cited loon populations on New Hampshire lakes and ponds as a key indicator of the quality of life in New Hampshire. This made perfect sense and still does today; loons, by their very presence, enhance the New Hampshire experience that many residents hold dear. Hearing or sighting a loon just adds a nice touch to our daily lives, something that, as we have seen, was taken for granted in the past. But no more. In fact, it is not uncommon even today for the LPC to field calls from local realtors throughout the state who want to know if there are loons on the lakes where the houses they are selling are located. The presence of loons is a real selling point to those who move here for the lake life experience, and so, the LPC has added to that value.

It was also a year of action: the lead poisoning issue, due to ingested fishing tackle, had become known as the leading cause of loon mortality, and something needed to be done to tackle the problem. It was during 1998's legislative session at the New Hampshire statehouse that LPC biologists, for the first time, testified at committee hearings in support of a bill that would restrict the use of lead fishing sinkers and jigs in New Hampshire. Their testimony was based on the scientific loon mortality data that had been collected by both the LPC and Dr. Mark Pokras and his team at Tufts University. Three years later, in 2000, a first-in-the-nation bill (NH Rev. Statute 211:13b) was passed restricting the use of small lead sinkers and jigs on lakes and ponds. While this bill would have only a small impact, its importance lies in the fact that it set the groundwork for more significant legislation in the coming years. In the meantime, the LPC would continue its fieldwork and necropsies to build up even more scientific data to support more effective measures, and lead poisoning would continue to be a primary concern.

Also, it was in 1998 that the LPC continued its partnership with Dr. David Evers and his Maine-based Biodiversity Research Institute (BRI) to expand loon banding operations in the state. This time, the focus on these efforts was to examine mercury toxicity levels in New Hampshire's loons, especially in the Monadnock Region, but soon expanded statewide.

In 1999, Harry Vogel and LPC senior biologist Kate Taylor presented the New Hampshire state loon report at a loon symposium given at a meeting of the American Ornithologists Union in Minneapolis, Minnesota, discussing the trends of the state's population overall. While the 1999 population showed a continued increase with 200 territorial pairs on 123 lakes, with 95 chicks fledging, they also noted the decline in the number of nesting pairs compared to territorial pairs, as well as in the number of surviving chicks. Vogel and Taylor also warned that the data from the previous four years "suggests that loon populations in New Hampshire may be levelling off or even beginning to decline after 20 years of relatively steady growth." Their words would prove to be prophetic.

Weather conditions continued to pose challenges to the loon population in New Hampshire during this period, and it was becoming increasingly clear that climate change effects would be the norm, with weather patterns all over the place. In the spring of 2000, snow and heavy rain in late April grounded many loons, including a large "asylum," as a group of loons are called, 45 in number, on the Moore Reservoir, an impoundment on the Connecticut River that lies in Littleton and Dalton, New Hampshire, as well as Waterford and Concord in Vermont. The following year, in the spring of 2001, a late thaw on our inland lakes meant that the loons were late in returning, with 60 in breeding plumage spotted off the Isles of Shoals' Seavey and White Islands as late as May 17. The following winter of 2001–02 was very warm, with loons lingering well into December on Lake Winnipesaukee, Squam Lake and Newfound Lake, with one loon on the last of these lakes into February.

As to happenings on some of our big lakes, there were the normal raft placements that were now part of the LPC's important seasonal activities. On average, about 44 were floated on a yearly basis, accounting for about 25 percent of the surviving chicks hatched on New Hampshire lakes. Rescues of injured or sick loons in distress are also yearly challenges for the LPC's field biologists, some successful, many heartbreaking failures for reasons beyond LPC control. One interesting incident that demonstrated the stark effect that loon losses can have on a given territory was observed on Lake Winnipesaukee, close to the LPC's headquarters, beginning in the fall of 1996. That year, two loons from the Whaleback Island territory on Lake Winnipesaukee were killed by a boat strike. The mother loon was killed instantly, while one of her chicks was discovered the next day, so badly wounded that it had to be euthanized. The male stayed on the territory and cared for the remaining chick, but in the spring of 1997, he did not return and the territory was vacant. The territory would have no loons in 1998 either, though the territorial pair from neighboring Greens Basin did make their way over there and hatched two chicks, which afterward spent their time back in their home territory. One of these chicks died to sibling rivalry, while the other was tangled in fishing line but successfully rescued. Loons would return to this territory in subsequent years, but this was a close-to-home example for the LPC of how human influences could have long-term consequences.

The biggest surprise during this period—and it was not a good one—was the decline of the population on Lake Umbagog, previously the most stable of New Hampshire's large lake loon populations. In 2000, only 47 percent of the chicks hatched on the lake survived to fledge, compared to 69 percent on lakes in the surrounding area and even slightly lower than Squam Lake. However, despite this number, Umbagog still held the highest concentration of breeding loons in the state, with 31 territorial pairs. In 2001, things took a turn for the worst when the adult population on the lake declined by 22 percent, leaving eight territories vacant. In 2002, things went from bad to worse when the breeding population declined yet again, with the loss of an additional 8 territorial pairs. While a loss of several territories on big lakes with multiple territories from year to year is the norm, this kind of loss, 44 percent in two years' time, was unprecedented. What in the world was going on at Lake Umbagog? Only one loon carcass was recovered for testing, and it did not provide the answer, nor was there any suspected problem on their wintering grounds (where hundreds of loons gather), as there were no mortalities like this anywhere else in the region. The LPC scrambled to account for this loss, increasing monitoring of the lake and gaining funds to test for possible contaminants or some specific lake disease. Whether the population would ever recover was an open question.

The Lake Umbagog problem was the primary cause for a decrease in New Hampshire's loon population, and the numbers tell the story. The total New Hampshire population at the end of the 2002 season stood at 634 loons, including 199 territorial pairs, 117 adult floaters, 116 surviving chicks and 3 immature loons. Those numbers were slightly down from 2001 and down from a count of 675 loons overall in 2000. However, there were good things happening elsewhere in the state; in 2000, four new territories were occupied on Lake Winnipesaukee, with an additional territory in Paugus Bay added

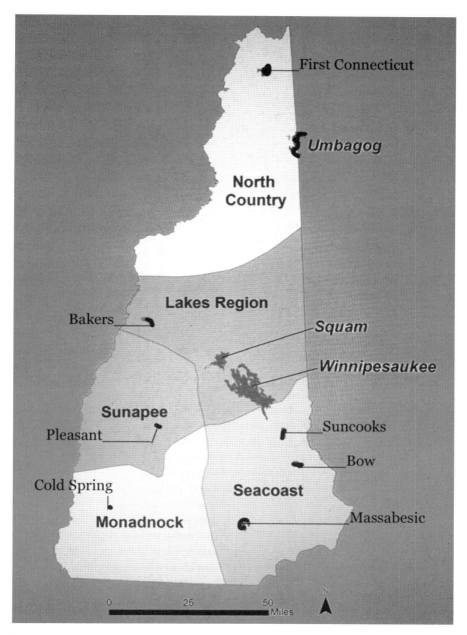

LPC map with author additions of some of the lakes and ponds mentioned. *Courtesy LPC.*

in 2001, while Pearl Lake (Lisbon), Bolster Pond (Sullivan), Canaan Street Lake (Canaan), Island Pond (Washington), Pleasant Lake (New London) and Clement Pond (Hopkinton) each gained a territorial pair in 2001.

Finally, in 2002 the LPC gained a victory on the mercury front when the state legislature passed the New Hampshire Clean Power Act (HB 284). This law, the first of its kind in the nation in recognizing CO_2 as a pollutant, sought the reduction of four harmful pollutants from the emissions from coal-fired power plants. It was formulated with the help of data gathered by the LPC, proving yet again that what is good for loons is also good for humans.

2003–07

The first year of this time span proved to be an eventful one. On April 27, 2003, the tanker barge *Bouchard 120* hit a rock ledge in Buzzards Bay off the coast of Massachusetts, a prime wintering area for New Hampshire loons. With a significant gash in its thin hull, this barge leaked 98,000 gallons of oil into Massachusetts and Rhode Island waters, creating yet another environmental disaster. As with the *North Cape* disaster, the marine impact was significant and, for loons, was made greater because it came during the spring migration period when there was a higher concentration of birds in the area than usual. In addition, the #6 fuel oil that was leaked is the most toxic fuel of its kind to sea creatures and birds, its viscous state adding to its deadly nature. Indeed, according to then senior LPC biologist Kate Taylor, the survival rate for birds covered in this oil is less than 6 percent. In the first days and weeks, 200 common loons and 35 red-throated loons were collected as mortalities, with others expected to die in the coming weeks and months at sites away from the ocean oil spill. Eventually, it was determined that 500 common loons died as a result of this spill, these coming from all across New England and New York. The LPC, at the behest of the U.S. Fish and Wildlife Service, was tasked with developing protocols for taking blood and feather samples from the oiled birds, with Taylor working on this project. From these samples, genetic testing would be employed to discover the breeding sites of the deceased loons. However, it did not take long to figure out that some of these were New Hampshire loons. The first oiled loon in New Hampshire was discovered, deceased, in early May on Pawtuckaway Lake in Nottingham. Later in the month, the banded female loon on the Rattlesnake territory on Squam Lake was seen to have a large oil spot on her breast. The compromised bird was subsequently ousted from her territory by another female and was never sighted again. A similar event happened up in Errol on Lake Umbagog: an oiled loon was tracked for a time and then soon disappeared. Later that summer, in July, an oiled loon was reported on Milton Pond in Milton. This bird was captured, and despite being cleaned and receiving medical treatment, it died some three months after being compromised. As with other disasters of this type, the barge owners settled with the government to cover the cost of the environmental effects, with $13.3 million set aside for loon recovery projects. However, the payout, as is typical, would be a long time in coming.

The year 2003 also saw the LPC still working to figure out what was causing the loon decline on Lake Umbagog. To that end, the LPC partnered with BRI, the USFWS, the U.S. Geological Survey (USGS) and the operator of the Errol Dam on the lake, Florida Power and Light-Maine Hydro (which funded the project), under the direction of senior biologist William Hanson to surgically implant satellite transmitters on two loons (with another loon implanted in 2004) to see what their winter destination might be and whether that might give insight into Umbagog's decline. Interestingly, all of these loons wintered in Maine waters. One of the loons, according to Jeff Fair, migrated to the Blue Hill Bay area, while the other winged much farther south to an area off Old Orchard Beach. The loon implanted in 2004 migrated to Muscongus Bay off Pemaquid Point. These efforts proved once and for all that whatever may have been causing the summer loon decline on Lake Umbagog, it was not due to something that happened on their wintering ground. Though two additional loon pairs did return to the lake for the 2003 season, Umbagog's loon count still remained at pre-1985 levels.

On the organizational front, 2003 saw the development of the Loon Recovery Initiative. This plan included not only the LPC but also state and federal agencies like New Hampshire Fish and Game and the USFWS, as well as other private nonprofit groups, all dedicated to conserving New Hampshire's loon population. This collaborative initiative was comprehensive in its approach, more so than ever before, a far loon's cry from the days when the LPC was the sole organization in the state dedicated to loons.

The effects of climate change, too, would continue to be a focus for the LPC. As nature writer Susan Story Gault commented in the LPC's Fall 2003 newsletter, "The changes we have already seen have occurred in less than the span of a person's lifetime; the speed of climate change is a major concern."

In 2004, the LPC scored another legislative victory on the lead front with the passage of a new statute that forbid the sale of lead sinkers and fishing jigs weighing one ounce or less. This law strengthened a previous bill that made it illegal to use this lead fishing tackle but still allowed for its sale. Once again, the LPC provided the data on lead's harmful effects on loons, having conducted many necropsies on the long and tortuous road to get this law passed.

The next year was notable for the addition of biologist John Cooley Jr., who has been in charge of all field operations since he was first hired to assist senior biologist Kate Taylor. She would later recall of Cooley that "we [the LPC] needed more statistical horsepower, and that was John. He had the analytical skills but also has a kind way about him, and our success at the LPC was in the quality of people on our team."

The year 2005 was a good one for New Hampshire's loon population. Though the total number of territorial paired birds was slightly down, coming in at 408 loons versus 418 in 2004, the number that nested, 152 pairs (75 percent of all loon pairs), was a record; 95 of these nesting pairs hatched 142 chicks, of which 112 survived to fledge. Overall, 511 loons were recorded in New Hampshire, the first increase in the loon population in five years. Of the 74 nesting attempts that failed, 17 failed due to predator activity, mostly mammals like the fisher, raccoon or mink, while 3 fell prey to either gulls or crows and 5 failed due to unknown predators. Other causes for nest failure included human disturbance (10), water level fluctuations due to weather and storm activity (16) by intruder loons (3). The rest of the failures were due to unknown causes. This same year also saw 45 rafts floated, with half of them used, resulting in 21 chicks being hatched, comprising 15 percent of all chicks hatched in New Hampshire. This number was lower than in previous years, though yearly variances are common for a wide variety of reasons.

The winter of 2005–06 was an unusual one, the first time ever since records started being kept, going back 119 years, that Lake Winnipesaukee did not completely freeze over. As LPC director Harry Vogel warned at the time, "Another symptom of global climate change is the increased variability of our weather....It's also apparent in the lack of 'normal' springs and summers in New Hampshire. Our loons have had a number of poor reproductive years as a result of weather events during their critical nesting period. Loons might be providing us with one of the first signs, an early warning, of the impacts of global climate change in New Hampshire."

As time has gone on, Vogel's warning has become a heightened concern: the only certainty about the weather is its uncertainty, with loons playing the part of the canary in a coal mine. In 2006, there were heavy spring rains for the third year in a row, and resultant flooding either delayed or prevented loons from nesting altogether. While there was a record 218 territorial pairs on New Hampshire lakes that summer, only 140 of them nested, while the number of chicks that survived (104) was down nearly 20 percent from the preceding five-year average. However, the year was not a total washout—there were 10 new territorial pairs on lakes where loon activity had been either absent or irregular.

That year also saw an important step in the organizational history of the LPC. Since its inception, it has operated under New Hampshire Audubon auspices, even though it has always been financially independent from its parent organization. Now, the LPC's policy board would serve as a true board after coming to terms with New Hampshire Audubon.

The climate change problem showed real lake effects on Lake Winnipesaukee in the winter of 2006–07 when loons were discovered stranded on the ice in the Broads by snowmobilers Judy and Scott Ellis of Gilford in mid-February. New Hampshire Fish and Game conservation officer Mike Eastman subsequently went to investigate and found 4 loons alive. These were gathered up and transferred to LPC custody. The birds were found to be in good health and were subsequently successfully released on the ocean at Portsmouth. This was a nice victory, but happiness turned to sorrow when, the following day, 17 more loons were found on the ice at the Broads, again by the Ellises. All but 1 were dead, and the Ellises described the area as a bird graveyard, commenting, "It was heartbreaking to see them. They had their beaks tucked under their wings like they were trying to stay warm." The lone survivor was subsequently taken to Maria Colby for rehabilitation and was later released into the ocean on the seacoast. Later that same week, 2 more dead loons were discovered on the ice north of Rattlesnake Island. These loons were spotted because an eagle was seen to be scavenging the carcasses, possibly after having predated the stranded and helpless birds. This event, with 18 dead loons representing about 3 percent of New Hampshire's entire loon population, was unprecedented in the history of the LPC. So, how did it happen? It likely resulted from the record warm temperatures that occurred in December and January— climate change rearing its head—that "lured" the loons into staying on the lake longer than they normally would. But when cold weather struck suddenly in early February, the lake quickly froze over. This problem was compounded by the fact that, as necropsies of the dead loons would show, they were in the process of the annual molting of their wing feathers, making them unable to fly off the lake. But what about the 5 loons that did survive?

The tragic result of climate change was starkly demonstrated in the Winnipesaukee die-off of February 2007. Here, LPC senior biologist Harry Vogel is retrieving 1 of the 18 loons that died after the lake suddenly froze over. *Courtesy LPC.*

They were likely latecomers to the lake, it being speculated that they were flying overhead, likely blown off course, and were possibly "decoyed" into landing, as expert Dave Evers suggested, by the already dead loons that dotted the clear ice. Despite this tragedy, it was later determined, according to biologist John Cooley Jr., that these loons were likely migrants passing through the area from somewhere outside New Hampshire or came from "a scattered set of lakes," as this Lake Winnipesaukee die-off turned out not to have a localized impact. Instead, the results for the 2007 loon season were similar to 2006, with a total of 528 loons counted overall in New Hampshire, the same as the previous year. As will be seen, winter stranding events like this would become the norm, though, thus far, none has matched the scope of this mass stranding.

Finally, 2007 was the year that the focused Squam Lake Loon Study program was developed by the LPC. Based on the challenges that continued to face this LPC legacy lake, the lake was more closely monitored and increased research activities began. This work's focus included banding efforts and necropsies on deceased loons, as well as the collection of inviable eggs for testing.

2008–12

This period got off to a difficult start in the winter of 2007–08, when loons were found stranded and iced in on Silver Lake in Madison in December, as well as on Duncan Lake in Ossipee and on Lake Winnipesaukee's Salmon Meadow Cove in Moultonborough. This was perhaps a harbinger of things to come, as 2008 proved to be, as characterized by the LPC, "a dismal year for nesting." It was the fifth consecutive year of nesting declines, even though a record 57 nesting islands were floated, half of which were used by the loons.

To the good for the year, there were new territorial pairs on Cold Spring Pond in Stoddard and on Upper Moose Pond in Pittsburg. However, the lead poisoning issue continued to rear its ugly head, and no matter what the public, and legislators, might think, the problem was not going away. In the space of a week in late June 2008, individual beached loons were discovered on Deering Reservoir in Deering, Pleasant Lake in New London and Sand Pond in Marlow. All of these birds died, the loss on Pleasant Lake a particularly tough pill to swallow for local residents and loon activists Kittie and John Wilson. Despite its lethargy, the loon on this lake held on for a week and evaded capture. By the time it was finally netted, with the help of the Wilsons, the loon had suffered for an extended period and died while being transported to a veterinarian office.

In 2008, the work on Squam and its focused study program began to receive data that would confirm some of the problems on the lake. In 2007–08, 13 loons were banded, and 13 inviable eggs were also collected and tested. Results showed that there were high levels of man-made contaminants, including PFOS, a chemical compound used in many consumer goods. While PFOS is now recognized as a global pollutant, in 2008 it was just coming to the fore. Also discovered were high levels of PBDE, a flame-retardant chemical, as well as PCBs, a highly carcinogenic chemical that was once used in many industrial and consumer products before it was banned in 1979. It was somewhat of a shock that despite being banned for nearly three decades, this substance was still present and causing harm to New Hampshire loons. These results clearly demonstrated, yet again, that loons are the Granite State's sentinel species, their eggs harboring not only the hazardous chemicals of our past mistakes but also the new ones that we continue to make.

On the personnel front, 2008 also saw some notable news for the LPC. The intrepid Rawson Wood turned 100 years old in September, and his birthday was celebrated by all. Though he had slowed down a bit, understandably, he still kept in touch with the LPC from a distance and was anxious to know of its yearly successes. Sadly, the end of this year also saw the departure of Kate Taylor, though it was not unexpected. Taylor was by now a resident of Maine and for the previous few years had begun to ramp down her time with the LPC, working for BRI, the LPC's partner in its banding operations, in her home locale. Years later, reflecting on her time with the LPC, Taylor fondly recalled her "foundational" relationship with Betsy McCoy, Linda Egli Johnson and Harry Vogel, stating that "there was something about working in that grassroots organization, the feelings of camaraderie and friendship. It was a special time." When asked about her greatest achievement, Taylor cited the lead initiatives that the LPC was working on, stating that "it was a concerted effort and we got a lot done with lead. I felt so honored to be a part of that organization." To this day, Taylor remains a friend to many of her former LPC colleagues and is still remembered for her accomplishments. While Taylor was a loss, two important additions were made in 2008 that would have long-lasting effects. Wisconsin native Tiffany Grade began her career working on Squam Lake in the summer of 2008 while a student at the University of Wisconsin–Madison pursuing a bachelor's in wildlife ecology. She has yet to leave that lake, being appointed the Squam Lake biologist on a full-time basis in 2012. Finally, it was also in 2008 that Plymouth State University student Chris "Biff" Conrod began his work with the LPC. Though many in the public today know this biologist for his witty and insightful LoonCam blog posts, he got his start working as a field program coordinator.

The numbers for 2008 showed a record 247 territorial pairs of loons in New Hampshire, up from 224 the previous year. However, only 7 chicks fledged on New Hampshire's largest lakes, with only 2 surviving on Squam Lake, 4 on Lake Winnipesaukee and just 1 on Lake Umbagog. This last number was concerning, as it was the lowest count since 1980.

LPC founder Rawson Wood in his later years. Note the loon tie-tack. *Courtesy LPC.*

In 2009, the LPC developed its Loon Recovery Plan to specifically address the drastic declines on New Hampshire's three largest lakes and increase chick survival rates. This coincided with a year in which there was a record number of nest failures, 94 in all, due in part to the fact that it was a very rainy summer. While this did serve to keep people off the lakes—one factor in a 12 percent increase in the number (109) of surviving chicks from the previous year—it also resulted in below-normal temperatures, which may have affected the incubation process. As the LPC would later sum up the season, with rain events it was all about the timing and intensity of these events, rather than just the number of rainy days overall.

The 2010 season began with the earliest ice-out on record, which meant that loons began their nesting season earlier than normal. The first loon chicks hatched this year in the state came on June 6–7 on Pleasant Lake in New London, named Percy and Poppy by local residents.

One feel-good story in 2010 was experienced, finally, on Leavitt Bay in Freedom. A territorial pair of loons claimed the bay as their own in 2006 but had four straight years of nest failures. These failures came about from a wide variety of reasons: in 2006 their nest was flooded; in 2007 a picknicker's dog scared them away; in 2008 their nesting likely failed due to human disturbance, as a discarded flip-flop was found in the abandoned nest; and in 2009, a combination of boat wakes and rising water levels soaked the nest despite valiant attempts to save it by LPC field biologist Tori Kentner. However, for the first time in about 50 years, loon chicks, two of them, were successfully hatched on the bay in 2010 and survived to fledge. This was such a big success that news of the event even made its way to Jeff Fair in Alaska.

While 2010 was a rebound year overall for loon productivity, with a record 275 territorial pairs, three of the four largest lakes in the state, as the LPC put it, "scraped the bottom of the barrel." Lake Winnipesaukee produced 3 chicks, Squam Lake 2 and only 1 chick survived on Lake Massabesic. The failures on these lakes were due to human causes, eagle predation, the presence of invading loons and, in one case, all three factors (and more) combined. On Lake Winnipesaukee, the field biologist on Robert's Cove witnessed in the space of a half an hour a loon nest attacked by an eagle, a crow and an invading loon in the territory. However, while the nest survived these attacks, it ultimately failed several weeks later due to its proximity to an active campsite on a beach that was exposed to large waves.

The "normal" loon rescues also took place in 2010, some with a happy ending, but most without. One beached loon was found on Merrymeeting

Lake in New Durham, recovering from a fight with another loon a few days prior. It was subsequently rehabilitated by Kappy Sprenger and released on Danforth Pond in Freedom. Not so lucky were the lead-poisoned loons on Granite Lake in Nelson, Squam Lake and Lake Umbagog. While all such losses are bitter blows, these losses were all galling for their circumstances. The affected loon on Granite Lake was a female that was banded in 2009, part of the first successful nesting pair on the lake in over 20 years. She was seen to be acting lethargically, the classic sign of lead poisoning, and was subsequently captured, tested and euthanized. Within a few weeks of her death, her chick was killed by a rogue loon. The loss on Umbagog was a male that had been banded in Potter Cove and was known to be at least 19 years old, one of the oldest known loons in the state. And on Squam Lake, the Great Island territory male was banded and tested during routine fieldwork, it being discovered that he had lead poisoning. The bird was not able to be captured until a week later, when he was driven ashore by an invading loon that killed his chick. A necropsy would reveal that the lead fishing jig he had ingested was large enough to make it legally permissible, a loophole in the law. So, there were three dead adult loons due to lead and two dead chicks, five birds in all. As senior biologist John Cooley Jr. wrote, these cases "robbed the recovering population of key adult players and probably contributed to the immediate loss of the young chicks they were raising, not to mention the chicks they might have produced in future seasons.…Each instance casts such a long shadow on the viability of the whole population." That shadow, sadly, still exists today.

As had been the case in the recent past, the 2011 season started out rainy, though there were no major rain events until Tropical Storm Irene hit northern New England on August 28. It was also a bad year for black flies, but despite these challenges, the year was a good one. A record number of chicks were hatched, of which 148 fledged, a record high by 11 birds. Bow Lake in Strafford had 6 chicks that fledged, the best year since 1976, while Lake Massabesic fledged 5 chicks. There were also some new territorial pairs in places where none had been for quite some time. This included Baptist Pond in Springfield (the first since the late 1980s), Ogontz Lake in Lyman (the first nesting success since the 1980s) and Spectacle Pond in Groton, where dam repairs that stabilized the water levels resulted in 2 chicks being fledged for the first time in a decade. Additionally, Little Island Pond in Pelham had its first ever nesting pair this year. Small Sawyer Pond in the ghost town of Livermore, off the Kancamagus Highway, also had a pair, though one of the adults here was found dead in the aftermath of Tropical

Storm Irene in late August. On the other hand, Lake Umbagog achieved almost no breeding success, the 14 loon pairs on the lake fledging but 1 chick. Lake Winnipesaukee's 26 territorial pairs fledged 7 chicks—a number that was subpar compared to the rest of the state. The continued stewardship of New Hampshire loons by the LPC also resulted in some statewide publicity and recognition when Governor John Lynch set aside a day for the first ever Loon Appreciation Day in 2011.

In 2012, the LPC's 2009 Loon Recovery Plan showed real advances in its third year of implementation, as demonstrated by the year's results. A record number of rafts, 91, were floated this year, including those on Lake Umbagog put in place by the U.S. Fish and Wildlife Service. This was a 63 percent increase over those floated from 2005 to 2009. In fact, this effort was a major part of the most intensive nest management program in the last 30 years. Additional action included correspondence to 71 dam owners on all impounded lakes in the state to alert them to the risk that fluctuating water levels pose to loon nests. Over 40 of these dams were owned and operated by New Hampshire state agencies. Volunteer Dana Duxbury-Fox, the leader of this dam initiative, and LPC staff met with the officials in charge of these dam sites and helped formulate management guidelines that would meet the needs of breeding loons. These efforts were not only a success but also indicative of the devotion and dedication of LPC volunteers.

The weather that year was mild, with no major storms or heatwaves, and it was hoped that the nesting season would be a banner one. Several lakes had their first nesting pair of loons in 2012, including Sawyer Lake in Gilmanton and Franklin Pierce Lake in Hillsborough and Antrim. Sadly, both nests failed, the one on Sawyer Lake due to human disturbance, as the nest was right on a public beach. Several interesting loon events took place on Lake Winnisquam in the Lakes Region. A new territorial pair set up house in a new southern territory on the lake, though the nest and the egg within would be abandoned. On the north end of Winnisquam, however, an unusual and rare event took place. The territorial pair here hadn't nested since 2008, but this year they hatched two chicks in August. However, soon after the chicks were born, a group of rogue loons, as many as nine in number, began harassing the parents in an aggressive manner. Eventually, the female of the pair was displaced and one of the chicks went missing. The male loon continued to care for his remaining chick and was eventually joined by a second adult female. At first, the new female largely kept her distance, though when she did approach the chick, the male warded her off. By this time, the chick was struggling to stay alive, being attacked by an eagle and beaching itself. It would often return frequently back on the nesting raft where it hatched. But an unusual turn of events occurred: by late August, it was clear that the new female had taken over the role of mother, as both she and the chick's father were observed feeding the chick in September. This example of a "collective or non-pair member brooding" was termed by the LPC "an exciting discovery." This adoptive behavior, the first time it was observed in New Hampshire, had only been observed a few times before elsewhere in the United States and was yet another loon secret revealed.

A tragic and senseless act of violence resulted in the death of one loon on Back Lake in Pittsburg in August. It started out strangely, with a loon being reported on the water's edge, actually being hand-fed small fish by local residents. Now, this behavior is highly usual, and the LPC didn't know what to make of it. When it was subsequently reported that the loon had beached itself, the NH Fish and Game and an LPC biologist worked together to pick up the loon and transport it for medical care. An examination showed that the bird had over 20 pieces of buckshot in its head, neck and one wing. Rehabilitator Kappy Sprenger tried to nurse the bird back to health, but it was not to be, and it was subsequently euthanized. Who would do such a thing? While the perpetrator was never discovered, the shooting of this bird was no accident; it took place outside the duck hunting season when a loon might be mistaken for a merganser or some other waterfowl. This shooting event, as Harry Vogel would later state, "became national news," but the "outrage" surrounding the death was out of proportion to the real problem for loons in New Hampshire. As Vogel wrote to LPC members, "I find it odd that one shot loon can engender national outrage, when we have lost **30 times** more loons to lead fishing tackle than to shot in New Hampshire with, apparently less concern. No one put their gunsights on those 120 lead-killed loons, but they are just as dead as that unfortunate Back Lake bird." This was a sobering thought, as three loons died due to lead poisoning in New Hampshire in 2012.

By the end of this five-year period in 2012, New Hampshire's loon population stood at 280 territorial pairs, with 170 chicks hatched and 134 fledged, all substantial increases from the pre–Loon Recovery Plan years from 2005 to 2009. However, despite the mild weather, there were 99 nest failures, most due to unknown causes. Clearly, the plan developed by the LPC and implemented by its dedicated biologists and volunteers was working, though work remained to be done.

Finally, 2012 marks the year when the LPC became a fully independent nonprofit after coming to an agreement with New Hampshire Audubon on some organizational sticking points. While some historic connections remain between the two conservation powerhouses, the LPC now had full control of its direction in all aspects of its work. It was a long time in coming, but the change would allow the LPC to operate to the utmost of its ability without administrative distractions.

2013–17

The first year of this period saw a major legislative victory for the LPC and all loon lovers when Democratic governor Maggie Hassan signed into law a new measure (SB89) that closed some of the loopholes regarding previously passed lead fishing tackle restrictions, which would go into effect in 2016. The law was sponsored by Republican senator Jeanie Forrester and was passed on a bipartisan basis. The LPC had learned long before that for any environmental bill such as this, it was critical to gain Republican support. To that end, the LPC provided the hard-won loon mortality data to prove the need for the bill, and as Harry Vogel jubilantly stated at the time, "We have convinced our legislature to finish the job and unreservedly choose loons over lead fishing tackle." One major player in this effort by the LPC was lawyer Sheridan Brown of Concord, who mobilized strong support for the bill among legislators. While Brown had been retained by the LPC for his expertise, he went above and beyond and logged many extra hours of work in driving this effort to a successful conclusion. The bill was a long time coming, previous bills having been rejected due to skepticism, and it is fair to say that the current bill was passed on the back of way too many dead loons and the resultant loss to New Hampshire's future loon population. Squam Lakes biologist Tiffany Grade worked tirelessly on this lead bill as well, along with Harry Vogel and Dr. Mark Pokras, as to the facts surrounding the need for such a bill. During earlier, failed efforts, the LPC was even accused by those opposed to the bill of photoshopping the pictures and X-rays of loons that served as visual evidence. Many legislators simply refused to believe that lead poisoning could have a population-level effect on New Hampshire's loons—after all, it was just, by their reckoning, a small number of birds. Tiffany Grade and the LPC would not be denied, and all had a personal stake in this effort, having handled loons that were either dead or dying from lead. Grade herself had experienced her first poisoned loon on Squam in 2010 and saw the devastating after-effects. As she later recalled, "I was really upset. I take my loons personally and I didn't want that loon to die in vain, and so I helped to put the science together on lead legislation." It was a hard lesson for New Hampshire to learn, but common sense finally prevailed.

Climate change yet again raised its ugly head in 2013 when New Hampshire had the 10th wettest June and the 10th hottest July since the late 1800s. These factors were contributors to the 98 failed nests in the state for the year, and though the number of territorial loon pairs and pairs that nested was strong, the number of chicks that survived per territorial pair was down nearly 10 percent from the pre–Loon Recovery Plan days. Interestingly, while predation and flooding were the two major causes of nest failures, failures due to human disturbance were way down, a tribute to the LPC's initiatives regarding public education and outreach, as well as continually expanding efforts to rope off and placing signage in sensitive nesting areas.

Other notable events in the 2013 season included five ponds—Ashuelot Pond (Washington), Bear Brook Pond (Errol), Big Island Pond (Derry), Pleasant Pond (Henniker) and Streeter Pond (Sugar Hill)—that had first-time nesting pairs, two of which (Bear Brook and Big Island Ponds) also had their first successful hatches. Of course, as you know by now, long-established and successful nesting pairs are sometimes broken up, and when it happens it is a sad occasion. This occurred on Cold Spring Pond in Stoddard, where a female loon resided that had been banded in 1998 on Long Pond in Lempster six miles away. This female successfully nested on Cold Spring Pond in 2013 but then late in the season went back to Long Pond, where she lost a battle with the resident female there.

The 40th year of the LPC's fieldwork in recovering New Hampshire's loon population was marked in 2014. No other organization in the world has worked to save loons longer than the LPC has, and as Harry Vogel commented, "We've learned a thing or two about how to help loons survive and thrive." The year got off to a rough start when three loons died in a single week in mid-May. One of these loons, the male of the State Park Territory on Lake Wentworth in Wolfeboro, died from lead poisoning. He had been banded in 2009. The two other loons were killed by gunshot; one was found in Dover, in an open field near the Cocheco River, wounded in the leg. The bird was gathered and given medical attention, but it was determined that the bullet could not be extracted. It was hoped the bird would heal, and it was subsequently released on Long Pond in Henniker. However, the wound proved to be too severe, and it died several days after being released. The day after the Dover loon was recovered, another loon was discovered on the shore of Lake Winnipesaukee in Gilford. It was dead, and though not at first apparent, examination showed that its body had a large bullet lodged inside, causing internal bleeding. While mortalities from gunshots are rather rare, when they do occur it is a shocking example of human brutality.

This 40th anniversary year also saw a major event happen when loons nested on Lake Sunapee, a first since the LPC began its work in 1975. The pair actually nested twice, but both attempts were failures for unknown reasons. There were also first-time nesting pairs on nine other bodies of water: Gloriette Lake (Dixville), Tewksbury Pond (Grafton), Shellcamp Pond (Gilmanton), Adder Pond (Andover), Mirror Lake (Whitefield), Smith Pond (Washington), Long Pond (Northwood), Meetinghouse Pond (Marlboro) and Cook's Inlet (Madison). In addition, loons continued to repopulate New Hampshire waters, with first-time pairs recorded on Gilmore Pond (Jaffrey), as well as the previously mentioned ponds in Dixville, Andover and Marlboro. Finally, bodies of water that had their first successful nesting pairs included Ossipee Lake (Ossipee), Kezar Lake (Sutton) and Thorndike Pond (Jaffrey), as well as the previously mentioned Adder Pond, Mirror Lake, Shellcamp Pond and Cook's Inlet locations.

Many of today's loon aficionados may not realize it, but the LPC's livestreamed LoonCam got its start in 2014 filming nesting loons on a Lakes Region lake. Using a system designed and operated by Bill Gassman since the beginning, this live feed first ran in June and July, running 24-7 as it still does today. The first year featured a hatching success and was a huge hit with both biologists and the public at large. The project was started with funding from the Loon Recovery Plan and since its inception has been a valuable source of scientific data. In order to protect nesting loons, their behavior is usually observed from afar by biologists, and of course, no one previously knew just what New Hampshire loons were doing on their nests at night. Now we know because of the LoonCam. The LPC was not the first organization to livestream loons, with earlier efforts taking place in Minnesota and Alaska, but its technology is the best in operation today and is now a spring and summer viewing tradition.

Finally, this year also saw an increase in the banding work done, with 17 loons banded on 20 nights on 14 lakes. In addition, 10 previously banded loons were recaptured, all birds having feather and blood samples taken in order to gather genetic and contaminants data. Interestingly, of the by now over 300 loons that have been banded in the state since the early 1990s, nearly 100 were re-sighted in 2014.

The year 2015 proved to be like 2014, with 289 territorial pairs, of which 211 nested, hatching 234 chicks, with 174 surviving to mid-August. However, nest failures were down significantly, and the chick survival rate was higher. For the second year in a row, against all odds, Lake Winnipesaukee was the leader, a fascinating turn of events, as New Hampshire's big lakes simply have more challenges to face. Lake Sunapee was also a big win for the LPC, as for the first time in 40 years, chicks were hatched and successfully fledged on the lake, in this case 2 of them, by a pair that nested on a raft built and floated by LPC volunteers. This year also saw first-time nesters on Kilton Pond in Grafton.

The year brought a potential new threat to the forefront when a dead loon on Lake Umbagog was found. This in and of itself was not necessarily a surprise, but after a necropsy was conducted at the University of New Hampshire, there was shock in the world of loon biologists. The bird was found to have been infected with malarial parasites. The presence of this tropical disease in a northern New England loon was a surprise to all and perhaps represented yet another climate change effect.

On the conservation front, Bow Lake, which has long been a successful loon habitat, got a major boost in 2015 from local landowners Hammond Brown and Liza Evans, the owners of two islands on the north end of the lake that were the location of a new loon territory. They worked with the Bear-Paw Regional Greenway, a local land trust organization, to place conservation easements on the islands. This type of commitment by local landowners has been a key factor in preserving loon habitats throughout the state.

The winter of 2015–16 was yet another record-breaker in terms of warm weather, and as a result, many of New Hampshire's lakes failed to freeze over, leaving some birds stranded during their winter wing feather molting period. Overall, 14 loons were rescued during the winter season, including 5 on Lake Sunapee and 1 between Ellacoya State Park and Lock Island on Lake Winnipesaukee. Interestingly, in both cases, skate-sailors were integral in discovering and helping these stranded loons, winter sports enthusiasts on the ice being frequent partners with the LPC in rescue efforts as part of its grassroots efforts. Four of the Lake Sunapee loons were treated and released into the ocean near Searsport, Maine. While it is often the case that once loons are rescued, treated, banded and released into the ocean, they have future fates that are unknown, a gratifying exception occurred in 2016. A loon that was rescued on Martin Meadow Pond in Lancaster in 2014 and treated for a mild case of lead poisoning before its release was spotted on the same pond, successfully hatching two chicks. As senior biologist John Cooley Jr. noted, "In this one case, at least, the rescue and treatment and travail for the loon has paid off," and as a result, this one rescued bird has helped grow the New Hampshire loon population.

Personnel-wise, the LPC gained a valuable addition in 2016 when biologist Caroline Hughes joined the staff. She had graduated from the College of the Holy Cross in Worcester, Massachusetts, with a bachelor's in environmental conservation the year prior and had served several internships on Squam Lake in past summers. It was during this time she came into contact with Squam Lakes Project biologist Tiffany Grade and was "fascinated with the idea of working with loons, even if she 'knew nothing about loons growing up.'"

The 2016 season was warm and dry, with no major storm events, and the season was a modest success in terms of numbers. Black flies were a huge problem this summer, for both humans and loons, and likely caused some abandoned nests. In terms of pure numbers, this year was the "absolute worst" for nest failures, with 112 such events, but the overall failure rate was just average when compared to previous years. A record 100 rafts were floated, with 47 being used to hatch 43 chicks.

The 2016–17 winter season was a more normal one compared to the previous winter, resulting in fewer loon rescue attempts. One unusual event happened in Ossipee when local resident Kaitlyn Gallup found a loon by the roadside, its feet trapped in the ice and snow. How it got there is anyone's guess, but Gallup did signal duty by thawing the loon's feet and sticking by its side for a few hours until LPC and NH Fish and Game personnel could retrieve the bird. It was subsequently taken to Avian Haven in Freedom, Maine, a facility that takes in loons and other rescue birds at all times of the day and night.

In 2017, the LoonCam saw its fourth year of operation by Bill Gassman, but with a twist. This year was the first that it was live-streamed via YouTube, reaching worldwide audiences in all 50 states and 201 countries. Who knew that New Hampshire loons would be so famous? The loon chat conversations, monitored by Gassman, that accompany the live feed are also enlightening and a place where loon fans from all over can get together to talk about their favorite bird, while the accompanying blog posts by biologist Chris "Biff" Conrod offer additional information and commentary about LoonCam events. In all, nearly half a million viewers, six times more than in 2016, looked at the LoonCam, the average viewer watching for 17 minutes.

Regarding Squam Lake, this was a year that the LPC expanded "the circle of concern" for the lake. By 2017, the LPC, with Squam Lakes biologist Tiffany Grade leading the way, had identified a number of contaminants and three potential source sites for them on this important lake, submitting a report to the New Hampshire Department of Environmental Services detailing their findings based on sediment samples. The LPC would soon find out that "contamination in a lake ecosystem manifesting itself in a top-level predator [loons] but which is not clearly from a factory pipe or other point source falls through the established programs of DES." In other words, this type of situation affecting loons had fallen through the cracks, and there was no money from the state to address the issue. This is yet another case of loons serving as an early warning indicator for humans— chemical contaminants in the water might be found not only in the fish that loons eat but also those that anglers catch and eat. As a result of this research and report by the LPC, there is now a circle of organizations, including the DES, EPA and the NH Geological Survey, working with the LPC to figure out what is happening on Squam Lake.

The final year of this period was a tough one, with 2017 experiencing the fourth-wettest spring in the last 100 years. This resulted in not only many washed-out nests, but many other normally used sites were now unsuitable as well, many on lakes that offered no other nesting options. However, the loon numbers still speak to the LPC's overall success with the implementation of its Loon Recovery Plan. In 2017, it recorded 296 territorial pairs, up 28 percent from the 2005–09 numbers, and 168 chicks hatched, with 126 surviving into mid-August, when the monitoring period typically ends. Predictably, nest failures were high, with 107 recorded, that being 37 percent higher than the pre–Loon Recovery Plan numbers. Even though not all such failures are due to flooding, and many in the general public may want to deny climate change, LPC biologists know that it is already here and having an effect. To combat this, 100 rafts were floated, one of the main tools in the loon recovery toolbox.

2018–23

The loon season started slowly in 2018 due to the long and cold weather, with ice-out coming in late April. However, May was hotter and less rainy than in recent years, though stormy weather early in the month resulted in what the LPC termed a "noted fall out of migrating waterbirds on large lakes throughout western New Hampshire." One near victim of this was a loon that ended up in a small pond in a commercial area of Littleton. Unable to fly out due to the small size of the pond, the loon tried to escape by land and ended up in a parking lot near Route 3. Local photographer Lorraine Virge discovered the loon and with help from the police corralled the loon and called the LPC. After being examined by a veterinarian and found healthy, the loon was released by LPC on Echo Lake in Franconia, an early success story.

This year also marked several accomplishments in the fight against lead poisoning, the leading cause of death among New Hampshire loons. In January 2018, the LPC published an important scientific paper titled "Population-Level Effects of Lead Fishing Tackle on Loons" in the *Journal of Wildlife Management*. Backed by years of scientific data, the paper was well-received, and within a year it had become one of the journal's most widely read articles, thereby spreading word of the issue across the wildlife community, many of them the ones making decisions. Also that winter, the idea of the Lead Tackle Buyback Program came up during a Loons and Lead Working Group meeting at the Concord headquarters of NH Fish and Game, and a pilot program was launched that summer. The effort started small, with two tackle shops, AJ's in Meredith and the Tackle Shop in Newbury. Anglers who brought in one ounce or more of lead tackle could exchange it for a $10 gift certificate to buy non-lead gear. This program was a direct result of the successful legislative issues that the LPC had pioneered in 2013, with attorney Sheridan Brown and LPC biologists Harry Vogel and Tiffany Grade leading the way. It also came on the heels of the loss of eight loons that died from lead poisoning in 2017. The program was a success, resulting in 20 pounds of lead jigs and sinkers being turned in. The program was also a valuable public educational tool, the results so promising that LPC donors enthusiastically donated over $100,000 to fund expanded efforts in the coming years. Overall, the Lead Tackle Buyback Program was yet another one of those grassroots approaches to loon conservation for which the LPC has been known, and it continues to grow every year.

Overall, 2018 turned out to be a good year for loons, with 309 territorial pairs counted (a record), 226 of them nesting, producing 224 chicks, of which 157 survived into mid-August. Bodies of water that gained loons for the first time in years included Pool Pond in Rindge and Great Pond in Kingston, showing that the recovering loon population is continuing to expand into "suitable but unoccupied habitat," as characterized by the LPC.

One exciting experimental program was undertaken this year by biologist Caroline Hughes, her research being conducted while studying for a master of science degree at Antioch University New England. This involved equipping the covers on three nesting rafts with UV-blocking shade material that, it was believed, would reduce the heat stress loons feel while sitting on a raft during the time they are incubating. The ambient temperatures collected using iButton temperature loggers were compared to the current rafts normally used by the LPC, as well as rafts with no cover at all. As expected, the results showed that this fabric did indeed succeed in lowering temps by nearly 10 degrees in the hot month of July, when loons are more vulnerable, over the current raft covers in use. This made for cooler loons, which in turn led to a greater probability of nesting success. This was a great example of what LPC director Harry Vogel termed "a venerable tradition at LPC of bringing best science to bear on an issue."

Despite the successes of 2018, the year ended on a tragic yet interesting note, when the banded female loon from Squam Lake's Moon Island territory was found beached in Cape May, New Jersey, on November 30. This was an eye-opener, as New Hampshire loons are not generally known to migrate this far south, hundreds of miles farther than is thought to be the norm. Sadly, despite being cared for by a wildlife rehabilitator, the bird died within 12 hours of being recovered. The carcass was subsequently sent northward for testing by Dr. Mark Pokras, and the loon was found to have died from lead poisoning. For Squam Lakes biologist Tiffany Grade, this female loon "seemed like just the strong and experienced bird Moon Island needed to stabilize that territory." This loon was originally banded on the Heron Cover territory in 2009 and from that time to 2015 hatched seven chicks and fledged three of them, as well as fledging a chick in 2018. For Grade, with this female, "Moon Island looked set to be a stable, successful territory for years to come. The news from New Jersey ended those hopes."

The next year, 2019, proved to be a successful one, with a record of 313 territorial pairs counted, of which 221 nested, producing 193 chicks, of which 148 survived. While it is true that this year saw a record number of nest failures (114), with a record number of inviable eggs collected, as Harry Vogel explained, some of these numbers are due simply to a larger loon population overall, as well as expanded efforts by the LPC and its network of volunteers to collect more data. The year was also one of milestones, including the launching of its 2,000th nesting raft, protecting its 1,800th pair of territorial loons and banding the 400th loon in New Hampshire, all reflective of 44 years of loon recovery work.

For the year, several bodies of water experienced nesting pairs of loons for the first time or the establishment of new territories on larger lakes. These include Arlington Mill Pond (Salem), Burns Pond (Whitefield), Hildreth Pond (Warren), Hanover Reservoir, Lake Sunapee North Territory and the Smith Cove and Back Bay territories on Lake Winnipesaukee. This last-named territory is highlighted in the last chapter, as the male loon that came to Back Bay, several hundred yards from my home, makes for an interesting case study. Several locations also saw the first-time use of a nesting raft, including Lake Sunapee North, Chalk Pond (New Durham), Lake Francis South Cove (Pittsburg) and Balch Pond Middle Territory (Wakefield). It was also a summer when three more loons were confirmed to have died from avian malaria, a sure sign of a warming climate. These came from Kezar Lake (Sutton), Squam Lake and South Pond (Stark).

The beginning of the COVID pandemic in 2020 brought changes to every aspect of society in New Hampshire and worldwide, and this included loon conservation efforts. For the first time, incoming summer field staff were trained remotely rather than in person, and events like the annual Loon Festival were canceled. Still, LPC biologists were out in the field monitoring, counting and rescuing loons, their job made even more difficult by the large influx of people seeking to get away from it all and out on the water where the loons are. As LPC director Harry Vogel wrote, "That means a lot of dusty tackle boxes—still full of old, now illegal lead fishing tackle—are being dug out of garages and their contents put on lines and into the water. Some of those lead sinkers and jigs will end up in our loons this summer, and that oversight will be lethal for those birds." As time would show, 2020 saw record boat sales and more people taking to the outdoors, whether on the water, along hiking trails or at state parks. Despite this invasion, loons held their own with the LPC's help. The year started out with extreme temperatures in the mid-90s in May and June, but a record number of territorial pairs, 321, were recorded, and the rest of the numbers were on par with recent years. This included 203 chicks being hatched with 156 surviving. The normal rescues also occurred, including 6 loons late in the year between December 18 and 21. Of those birds rescued on Webster Lake in Franklin, Angle Pond in Sandown, Townhouse Pond in Milton and Lake Kanasatka in Moultonborough, all iced in and unable to fly off their lakes, 5 were successfully treated and released back into the ocean. Two of the birds had major problems, one having fishhook fragments in its digestive tract and suffering from mild lead poisoning, while one had aspergillosis, a deadly fungal respiratory illness, and had to be euthanized.

On the organizational front, 2020 was also the year that the LPC completed its Spreading Our Wings Capital Campaign, renovating, modernizing and expanding the Loon Center in Moultonborough. This expansion included the Kittie and John Wilson Field Operations Center, named in honor of a couple dedicated to LPC and the loon cause for years, both on Pleasant Lake in New London, as well as on the ocean. The late Kittie Wilson was a beloved LPC member who was known for her outstanding loon photography (some of her photos appear in this book) and the use of these spectacular images, whether in the pages of the LPC newsletter or in calendars sold at the Loons Feather Gift Shop, to support the LPC's mission. Both she and her husband, John, were and are active in loon conservation efforts on their home lake and have monitored Pleasant Lake for years, so the naming of this new operations building was appropriate in every way. In addition, the laboratory facilities at the Loon Center were upgraded with new and additional equipment, all of which has added to the effectiveness of the LPC biologists' work of monitoring and studying New Hampshire's loon population on an ongoing basis.

The increasing popularity of wake boats on New Hampshire lakes was also a growing concern with many in the state, causing the passage of House Bill 137. This bill established a commission to study the effects of this kind of boat. Among those serving on this commission was LPC director Harry Vogel, who testified to the potential harm that could be caused by these boats to New Hampshire's threatened loon population. The evidence gathered clearly showed that wake boats generate larger and stronger waves than other boats used for, say, water skiing, but the major concern was the possible shoreline effects in terms of erosion, as well as disturbing loon nesting sites. Once again, the LPC was there to advocate for loons, making sure they were part of the narrative in the state's mission to balance the competing uses of publicly owned recreational bodies of water.

Finally, despite the cancellation of all in-person major events during 2020, the LPC did not stand pat and found other ways to educate the public about loons. These included YouTube loon talks and Thursday Night Nature Talks. Thankfully, Bill Gassman's annual LoonCam was in full operation, so this gave the public, many of them now stuck at home due to the pandemic, a chance to enjoy this by now highly anticipated yearly look into the lives of loons. I suspect that many loon lovers, like me, also viewed this footage to escape some of the harsh realities of life during COVID, perhaps serving as a bit of mental relaxation in an otherwise stressed-out world.

Though 2021 was yet another year affected by COVID, it also brought a resolution of sorts to the *Bouchard 120* oil spill, which affected New Hampshire loons. After 18 years, the LPC finally received the first installment (to be paid out over 5 years) of New Hampshire's share of the so-called B120 payment, $844,000 when all is said and done. That money has been used to greatly increase the number of nesting rafts that are placed each year, as well as for educational programs, rescue operations and the Lead Tackle Buyback Program. The reporting work and reports that are required for the use of these monies, as Linda Egli Johnson can attest, are exacting and exhausting at times, but the LPC is getting it done. The 104 rafts floated this year were part of the first year of the 5-year restoration project that will help offset the oil spill losses.

This was a year of extreme weather with heavy rain over Memorial Day that flooded several loon nests, while it was the third-hottest June on record, with no rainfall at all. As has now become the norm, an increasing number of severe heat and rain events occurred. Though a good number of territorial pairs of loons were counted this year, 326 (652 birds total), as well as record number, 229, of pairs that nested, it was the third-worst season ever since the LPC began for chick production, with 133 chicks surviving into August. Interestingly, while fewer nests had problems with predators, there were more human disturbance–related nest failures than usual, as well as those lost due to intruder loons and flooding or wave action, some of which was due to wake boat action.

The LPC's scientific research, which has continued to increase, reached a new milestone in 2021 when it released a groundbreaking report to the NH Department of Environmental Studies and the public in November detailing its findings on contaminants in loon eggs.

Several ponds had interesting loon action in 2021. There was the harrowing case of the male loon on Skatutakee Lake in Harrisville, which was swept downstream below the dam during heavy flooding in July. Locals Russ Cobb and Brett Thelen were quite "intrepid" and made a search for the missing loon, eventually finding it on the wooded bank of a stream several hundred yards from the lake. Despite this wild water ride, the loon would be fine and was released on his home lake after spending time with wildlife rehabilitator Maria Colby. Another feel-good story for the year was a nesting attempt on Loon Pond in Gilmanton, the first time this had happened in over 50 years or more. Loons, indeed, continue to reclaim their ancestral waters all over New Hampshire, and it just seems fitting when they do so on their namesake ponds.

As the LPC would later comment, the year 2022 started "with a bang." The previous fall and early winter had been warmer than usual, but a cold snap in January, as biologist Caroline Hughes characterized it, "came as a shock not only to us humans, who had grown accustomed to the above-freezing temperatures, but also to a group of 10 loons on Lake Winnipesaukee long past the time when they should have migrated." Nordic skiers on the lake had discovered the loons in a small spot of open water, and the LPC was soon notified. Would this be a repeat of the 2007 die-off, when 22 loons became iced in, with 18 dying? LPC senior biologist John Cooley Jr. skied out to the area where the loons were located daily from January 16 to 20, and the situation was concerning—feathers were all over the place, indicating that the loons were probably molting their primary feathers and would thus be unable to fly. Too, the loons looked lethargic, perhaps an indicator they may not have been getting enough food. By January 21, with the open water now even more narrowed down, rescue attempts were begun. The first attempt, with John Cooley and LPC staff, accompanied by members of the Tuftonboro Fire Department, NH Fish and Game and several of the Nordic skaters who had originally found the loons, failed. The next day, Cooley tried again and found the loons' situation even more untenable, with now just 15 feet of open water after overnight freezing temperatures. However, this also meant that attempts to capture these loons would be less difficult. The subsequent rescue, using gill and long-handled nets, took five hours, but it was a success. For this day, it was an all-hands-on-deck situation for everyone at the LPC, many of them out on the ice. Once captured, the loons were carefully placed in boxes and placed on an ice-sled for the mile-long trip back to shore. They were then transported to the Loon Center in Moultonborough, where the center's conference room/library was turned into a triage center. Here, the loons were banded (3 were already banded birds) and blood samples were taken. Everyone pitched in on this long day, with non-field staff toting supplies to and from the lake, serving coffee and aiding in holding the birds while samples were taken. Once samples were taken, the 10 loons, now referred to as the "Winni 10," were then taken to a veterinarian in Concord, where, working with wildlife rehabilitator Maria Colby, the birds were X-rayed and then taken to Colby's facility. Here she fed and observed them, with donors supplying 30 pounds of fish to keep the loons fed. During their 36-hour stay with Colby, the birds were observed to make sure they could do all the things a loon should do—swim, dive and catch food—with one loon treated for lead poisoning. After this time, all the loons were ready for release and taken to the seacoast at Odiorne Point in Rye for the event, which took place with the help of LPC staff. This was an extremely perilous and complex rescue operation, and it was a rare occurrence where all the loons survived to be released. The blood tests would later confirm that all were male loons, but the reasons why they didn't migrate earlier to their ocean home remain a mystery. It's entirely possible that the warm winter in the preceding months had tricked the loons into staying way too long. Then again, the fact that they were all male led to some interesting speculation. Did these loons, as Hughes comments, "take a gamble and stay around long after other loons had left for the ocean" in order to return to their breeding grounds even earlier than other males? Like I've stated before, loons seldom give up their secrets easily, and this is one of those cases.

In hindsight, the Lake Winnipesaukee rescue seemed to have set the bar high for success in the 2022 season. While COVID did catch up with some of the LPC staff, the Loon Center remained open and field activities continued at their regular, hectic pace. No matter how difficult things were, the results, in a summer that saw relatively stable weather, were record-breaking. The final tally of 345 territorial pairs (690 loons) was a record, as were the nesting pairs (236), number of chicks hatched (244) and surviving

The "Winni 10," a group of loons that became stranded on Lake Winnipesaukee in January 2022. With the aid of the LPC and many other local partners, all were saved under very difficult conditions. *Courtesy Harry Vogel and the LPC.*

chicks (177). The survival rate of chicks per territorial pair, most critically, came in at .50 percent, 12 percent over the previous five-year average. You will recall that number, .48 percent, that is needed for the New Hampshire loon population to remain viable. While many years have been close to this figure, it was a victory to exceed that number in 2022.

Too, the B120 funds now in hand really paid off as well in 2022, with 141 rafts floated (most having the UV-blocking shade covers developed by Caroline Hughes), a 48 percent increase, while the Lead Tackle Buyback Program, now ending its fifth year, had 10 retail partners in the endeavor. The lead initiative also resulted in lead tackle being collected in the Lakes Region during eight hazardous waste collection days, all done with the partnership of the Lakes Region Planning Commission. Other notable lead initiatives include the work done with 27 lake associations across the state to educate members about the dangers lead poses to their loons. The Newfound Lake Region Association took the program even one step further, its Lake Host collecting lead tackle from anglers right at the boat launch and handing out lead-free replacements. The LPC did not stop here, though— despite staffing challenges, it gave 141 loon presentations throughout the state, each of them detailing the lead dangers to loons. The LPC's efforts are working, even if there is work yet to be done. From 2016 to 2021, according to the LPC's data, lead tackle mortality rates have decreased by 27.6 percent since the current lead law went into effect in 2016 and have declined 57.4 percent from the peak years of 1996–2000.

Finally, the year 2022 was a record one in terms of rescue, with 34 loons rescued overall by the end of the summer, with more to come. That number would have been closer to the previous five-year average, but the Winni 10 birds changed that in a hurry. In fact, the rescues were so prevalent that each loon region in the state had at least one rescue. These included a five-day-old chick rescued on Lake Waukewan in Meredith in July, the bird subsequently rehabilitated by Kappy Sprenger and released in Maine, as well as a stranded loon found by the side of Route 103B near Newbury in June, which was subsequently released on Mountainview Lake in Sunapee after being banded. And these were just in the summertime. In early December, climate change was in play yet again with warm early winter temperatures, leaving many lakes, including Lake Winnipesaukee, open and ice free. However, when temperatures started to drop, the rescues began again. These included rescues on Kezar Lake in Sutton, Partridge Pond in Littleton and Loon Pond in Gilmanton, with many more lakes being closely observed through the remainder of the year. Indeed, by Christmas there were still a number of loons remaining on Lake Winnipesaukee, and the frigid temperatures that weekend were of great concern. Luckily, high winds that battered the region kept the lake's waters moving just enough to prevent a freeze-up. On December 26, I observed what was probably the lone remaining loon in Wolfeboro Bay floating among the debris in the water near the town docks. As you shall see, I knew this banded loon well and told him it was time to get gone and off to the ocean. Maybe he listened, or maybe he had already made up his mind—either way, I did not see him again for the rest of the year, and I hoped he made his migration safely.

Sadly, 2022 was also a record year for collected mortalities (31 adults, 1 immature bird and 18 chicks). While a higher loon population means there will be more mortalities, some of these losses were preventable. These include at least 5 that died due to lead poisoning and 3 adults killed due to boat strikes. These boat strike losses were made even worse because each of their chicks perished afterward. As senior biologist John Cooley Jr. notes, "It takes two loon parents to raise a chick." Any boater out on New Hampshire lakes who also loves loons should take this sobering fact into account.

As already mentioned, the winter of 2022–23 was a mild one once again, and Lake Winnipesaukee and other large lakes would not freeze up until February arrived. As had by now become the norm, the frigid temperatures resulted in a quick freeze-up and numerous loons stranded in one week. On February 6, one iced-in loon was successfully rescued on Newfound Lake, while on February 8 seven loons were discovered on Lake Winnipesaukee. Once again, the call went out to the LPC, and senior biologist John Cooley Jr. was on the scene by about 2:00 p.m. Assistance was given by the three members of the Tuftonboro Fire Department, who came equipped with an airboat. The loons consisted of four adults and three juveniles, and the rescue took hours because the loons kept diving away and resurfacing. As darkness fell, spotlights were used, and eventually, by 7:30 p.m., six loons had been recovered. It is believed that one of the loons dove under the ice and likely drowned, as it was never seen to surface. The other loons would be banded and cared for before being released into the ocean a few days later. All in a day's work.

At the conclusion of the 2022 field season, the LPC had grown New Hampshire's loon population, and for now, it is in a good place. As a result of 47 years of fieldwork and scientific discoveries, there are now 690 breeding loons in the state.

As I write these words, the 2023 loon season has wound down. The annual Loon Census in July counted 489 loon adults and chicks, and the

LPC monitored 338 lakes and ponds during the season. While the LPC has not yet issued its year-end official report, the year was a challenging one in terms of climate change effects on loons, with high levels of rainfall making for difficult conditions and failed nesting attempts. As Harry Vogel commented, "Flooding was the big story in 2023," with a record wet July that had more flash-flood warnings than ever before. There were approximately 343 paired adults in New Hampshire this year, which was about level with 2022 numbers, but their nesting success was abysmal, coming in at chick survival rate per territorial pair of about .39 percent, far below last year and well below the .48 percent survival rate that is the baseline for loon success in New Hampshire. While 94 failed eggs were collected for future study, the year was a good one in terms of lead poisoning deaths, with only 1 recorded.

As for Squam Lake, where the LPC first got its start, biologist Tiffany Grade reported in August 2023,

> Squam had a lower rate of nesting than usual this year, so we were starting off from a deficit in that regard. My guess is that the wet spring we had starting in June was a contributing factor to this. There were several pairs that were showing interest in nesting, but then never went on the nest and there were no other evident reasons to account for their failure to nest. We ended up with seven nesting pairs and four nests that hatched five chicks between them. Sadly, we lost two chicks from one family as a result of a loon intrusion and the eviction of the male from the territory. Three chicks are still doing well on Squam—two of them at nearly nine weeks old at this point. We also had a very late hatch, so the other chick is three weeks old now but so far doing well! Fingers crossed! But, even if these chicks fledge, it is another challenging year for Squam's loons. Overall productivity is slightly lower but basically on par with the average since the declines in Squam's loon population between 2005 and 2007—and, sadly, that average is half the average pre-decline breeding success rate, as well as half the statewide average.

While loon results from season to season are unpredictable, what we do know is that the LPC has achieved great success, something that every nature- or bird-lover, every Granite State resident or seasonal visitor, should appreciate. But this work can't be taken for granted. So, should you see an LPC biologist while you're out and about this summer, give them your thanks and, if you want to help them even more in their continued mission to bring more loons back to New Hampshire, consider making a donation at https://loon.org/donations/. Whether big or small, every bit helps the LPC in its mission. You'll be glad you did every time you hear the haunting cry of the loons on your local lake.

5

KEEPERS OF THE LOONS

The Women and Men of Today's LPC and Working Partnerships

Today, there is a small cadre of dedicated individuals of the LPC working year-round to protect and grow New Hampshire's loon population. Chances are, if you've been out somewhere on a lake or pond that has loons, you've seen them hard at work, whether it be floating rafts or placing warning signs in nesting areas, taking water samples or even rescuing a loon stuck in the ice or tangled in fishing line. Their work is hard and challenging, and while the public is mostly sympathetic to LPC efforts, there are those who are still resistant to them. Oh, the stories every biologist could tell in this regard! Still, any such difficulties are more than offset by the grassroots volunteers with whom they collaborate every season. Without these individuals, the LPC's efforts would be greatly reduced. And last but certainly not least, there are the chairpersons and board of trustee members, past and present, who help to guide the LPC in its overall mission. It truly is a team effort, and in times of great need or crisis, everyone pitches in to do their part, even if they're not trained biologists. With this in mind, let's take a look at the women and men who run the day-to-day operations of the LPC.

The LPC's longest-term employee today is special assistant/newsletter coordinator Linda Egli Johnson. She was born "a Jersey girl" but spent vacations in Maine and had some familiarity with New Hampshire. She graduated with a bachelor's in wildlife management from the University of New Hampshire in 1983 and moved to Meredith with her future husband, Carl Johnson Jr. As Johnson, a friendly and upbeat person who "has an artistic side," fondly recalled, "Full-time, year-round jobs in wildlife management were hard to come by in the Lakes Region at the time. I reached out to LPC director Jeff Fair. He had already hired his seasonal staff, but he encouraged me to apply for an upcoming vacancy as shop/office manager. He emphasized the importance of all positions to LPC's mission and that my degree would be an asset. I was hired in March of 1986, and the rest is history! As office manager I had to maintain LPC's donor base on index cards and type each thank-you letter individually. I had never taken a typing course. (Jeff gave me a very entertaining typing test when I applied for the job, apparently required by Rawson Wood.) And Jeff's donor thank-you letters were long—typically two pages. It would reach the point that I would type the letters from memory. It's no wonder I developed carpal tunnel syndrome!" However, it wasn't just all about office work for Johnson or, indeed, for any of the staff, especially early on. She vividly recalled the loon rescues that took place in an era when there were no wildlife rehabilitators in the state, stating, "We would bring loons to the vet and monitor them in our bathtub at home." Johnson's responsibilities at the LPC have been many and varied over the years, and to this day she is still a dynamo. She added, "My LPC duties have covered the spectrum over the past 37 years: shop/office manager, bookkeeper, events coordinator, newsletter designer/editor, graphic designer, some seasonal loon monitoring and summer and winter loon rescues. I serve on the Finance and Facilities Committee and oversee LPC's annual audit. I entered all of LPC's biological field data into its first computerized database." When asked to summarize her time at the LPC, Johnson was unequivocal in her response: "Why am I still here 37 years later? First and foremost—the loons. Second—the people. The LPC has more than tripled the state population since I started, and I am proud of that. I feel blessed to live in a place where I can hear a loon tremolo overhead while working in the garden or catch sight of one peering for fish in the bay as I drive to and from work. A place symbolized by the loon's mournful cry on a moonlit night. Where people care deeply about the preservation of a species that brings so much beauty and mystery into our lives." As you can tell, if you've never read an LPC newsletter, Johnson is also a talented writer. As to the people, Johnson also commented, "I am inspired daily by the network of staff, volunteers, members and work colleagues who make up the LPC family. I have met so many wonderful people who have devoted their time and talent to LPC's mission. I am so grateful for the amazing people who stepped up to chair our Board of Trustees. It requires a tremendous amount of time and dedication." Linda Egli Johnson also notes her whole family involvement with loons. Her late father-in-law, longtime New Hampshire state senator Carl R. Johnson (1922–2010), was a great friend to the loons and the LPC and sponsored two pioneering bills that restricted the use of lead fishing tackle, one of the greatest threats to loon survival, while her husband, Carl Jr., and children, Eliot and Tim, played integral roles in LPC's annual events throughout the years. She summed up the Johnson family's loon involvement thus: "Our children were born into the LPC family and have grown up embracing the camaraderie that typifies a grassroots, nonprofit organization. They have been blessed with an extended family that has taught them the value of service above self, and the importance of preserving our natural world." In summing up Johnson's many contributions to the LPC over the years, Betsy McCoy stated, "Linda's been here through thick and thin and is the institutional memory of the LPC." Indeed, Johnson's loon career has been a long and important one and is not yet over. LPC director Harry Vogel said of Johnson simply and unequivocally that "Linda and her family are the heart and soul of the LPC."

LPC director Harry Vogel, a native of Canada, holds a bachelor's degree in environment and resource studies and biology from the University of Waterloo in Ontario (1990). He wrote his undergraduate thesis on the subject of the conservation biology of the common loon. In 1995, Vogel earned a master's in zoology from the University of Guelph, Ontario, his thesis studying the variations in loon calls. His field experience included work as a project biologist and coordinator for the Canadian Lakes Loon Survey of Birds Canada, as well as a research assistant working on a study of wolves at the Algonquin Provincial Park. It was here that he gained his first substantive loon experience, and it is a favorite place he has returned to many times over the years, "a place of reflective calm." To put it succinctly, Vogel knows loons well. In addition, by 1993 Vogel was also a trustee of the North American Loon Fund, which was started by Rawson Wood, so he already had some familiarity with the LPC. As if this experience wasn't enough, he also had the support of former LPC members, including Jeff Fair, who believed that Vogel had not only great loon experience that would benefit the LPC but he also had the right temperament for the job. The director of the LPC has many responsibilities beyond that of fieldwork, which includes fundraising and budgetary matters, as well as, at that time, coordinating with the New Hampshire Audubon Society and its board. Though the LPC raised funds on its own and was largely autonomous, it was still under the umbrella of its parent organization, and disagreements

A loon parent dumping a chick off its back on an unidentified pond, 2018. *Courtesy MooseMan Nature Photography.*

A pair of loon chicks on an unidentified pond in western New Hampshire, 2016. *Courtesy MooseMan Nature Photography.*

Early morning view of a loon parent and its chicks on an unidentified pond in western New Hampshire, 2017. *Courtesy MooseMan Nature Photography.*

Top: A loon parent bringing a fish to a newborn chick while still on the nest, Cold Spring Pond, Stoddard, 2013. The other parent is still incubating a second egg, which will soon hatch. *Courtesy Brian J. Reilly.*

Middle: A 10½-week-old chick getting close to its parent, in hopes that its parent will feed it, even though the chick can now feed on its own. Cold Spring Pond, Stoddard, 2011. *Courtesy Brian J. Reilly.*

Bottom: An adult loon taking off on Bolster Pond, Sullivan, 2012. The splashes show how the loon paddles across the water to get airborne. *Courtesy Brian J. Reilly.*

Top: A loon flying high over Pleasant Lake, New London. *Photo by Kittie Wilson, courtesy John Wilson.*

Middle: A loon parent holding a chick on its back while it naps. Middle territory, an unidentified pond in western New Hampshire. *Courtesy MooseMan Nature Photography.*

Bottom: A loon in a "vulture" posture on Pleasant Lake, New London. This is an aggressive display made when loons feel threatened by an intruder loon or another perceived imminent threat like humans. *Photo by Kittie Wilson, courtesy John Wilson.*

A loon in the process of swapping incubation duties with its partner and leaving the nest. Cold Spring Pond, Stoddard, 2013. *Courtesy Brian J. Reilly*.

A loon chick with its parents, Pleasant Lake, New London. *Photo by Kittie Wilson, courtesy John Wilson.*

A loon chick spreading its wings as a parent looks on, Pleasant Lake, New London. *Photo by Kittie Wilson, courtesy John Wilson.*

A loon chick swallowing a fish brought to it by its parent, Pleasant Lake, New London. *Photo by Kittie Wilson, courtesy John Wilson.*

LPC senior biologist John Cooley Jr. netting a loon and saving it from being iced-in on Lower Baker Pond, Wentworth/Orford, December 2021. *Courtesy Cathy Eastburn.*

The first loon chick, just a few hours old, hatched in modern times on Upper Baker Pond, and its parent on a nesting raft. Orford, June 24, 2023. *Courtesy Cathy Eastburn.*

The Back Bay loon, off the Wolfeboro town docks, December 2022. Note the banded leg. *Author photo.*

The Back Bay loon, off the Wolfeboro town docks, December 2022. This bird's banded legs, visible here, identify it as the same loon that was banded on Little Sebago Lake in Maine in 2005. *Author photo.*

A loon desperately trying to save its flooded nest and the eggs within due to heavy rains and flooding on Lower Baker Pond, Orford/Wentworth, June 2020. These efforts would fail. *Courtesy Cathy Eastburn.*

A social gathering of the three territorial loon pairs on the Suncooks, Upper Suncook Lake, Barnstead, August 2023. *Author photo*.

Loon parent feeding its eager, and quickly growing, loon chick on Lake Massabesic, Auburn. *Courtesy John M. Rockwood*.

Loon in breeding plumage, Lower Suncook Lake, Barnstead, August 2022. *Author photo.*

A loon family, Lake Massabesic, Auburn. *Courtesy John M. Rockwood.*

"Loon Waterdrops," Bow Lake, Strafford, July 2009. This bird was one of the Bennett Island pair. *Courtesy Jon Winslow.*

A loon catching a perch, Bow Lake, Strafford, September 2013. This bird was one of the Kooaukee Island pair. *Courtesy Jon Winslow.*

A loon parent protecting its chicks, Bow Lake, Strafford, June 2012. This loon was one of the Blueberry Island pair. *Courtesy Jon Winslow.*

A loon parent, one of the Blueberry Island territorial pair, crouching low and spreading its wings to protect its chicks, Bow Lake, Strafford, June 2012. *Courtesy Jon Winslow.*

A loon chick foraging underwater for food, Lake Massabesic, Auburn. Note the legs acting as paddles and the wings folded tightly to the body. *Courtesy John M. Rockwood.*

Above: It took a lot of people and equipment to successfully rescue the "Winni 10" loons, January 22, 2022. *From left to right*: LPC biologists Tiffany Grade, Linda Egli Johnson, Caroline Hughes, John Cooley Jr. and Harry Vogel. *Courtesy LPC.*

Opposite, top: A loon turning its eggs with its bill. This process is done several times each day so that the egg may be evenly incubated. Lower Baker Pond, Orford/Wentworth, 2022. *Courtesy Cathy Eastburn.*

Opposite, bottom: The eye of a loon. This view shows its distinctive red iris, which is present during the breeding season. Lower Baker Pond, Orford/Wentworth, 2022. *Courtesy Cathy Eastburn.*

The author having a loon encounter on Upper Suncook Lake, Barnstead, August 2023. *Courtesy David Wemmer.*

Two loons having a close encounter during a social gathering on Upper Suncook Lake, Barnstead, August 2023. *Courtesy David Wemmer.*

sometimes rose to the surface. However, Vogel was perfectly equipped to deal with whatever came his way, and the mild-mannered Canadian has guided his LPC team through all the highs and lows they have experienced since that time. Vogel stated his goal from the outset of his directorship: "I regard loons as ambassadors with the ability to promote a greater appreciation and understanding of the natural world. I have dedicated myself to studying them and working for their preservation." While it has not been easy, the numbers tell the full story, and today the LPC continues as the premier loon conservation organization, not just in New Hampshire but the entire country. Granite Staters should be well-satisfied with Vogel's leadership and all that his team has accomplished.

The LPC's senior biologist is John H. Cooley Jr. A native of Rochester, New York, Cooley came to loons, like many have done, in a roundabout way. He graduated from Middlebury College in Middlebury, Vermont, with a bachelor's in physics in 1991. An active outdoorsman, Cooley was on his college's cross-country ski team and even tried out for the 1994 Olympics. He came to New Hampshire through the AmeriCorps program, where he performed trail work in the White Mountains, as well as a variety of other work, including wildlife surveys. He would subsequently work for the Sandwich Range Conservation Association and, after settling in the area, taught school in Tamworth. He would then go on to teach at a bilingual Quaker school in Costa Rica for a year. On returning to New Hampshire, Cooley enrolled at Antioch University in Keene, where he earned a master's in environmental studies, graduating in 2005. That same year, he was hired by the LPC's then senior biologist Kate Taylor. From the start, Cooley has had a great influence on the LPC and its operations. Not only does Cooley have an analytical mind, but he also enjoys the work. Whether it be raft building, equipment maintenance, banding operations or necropsies, to name just a few, Cooley is involved in all of it. Cooley also draws on his teaching background and is excellent, and patient, when it comes to teaching others anything loon related. Without a doubt, John Cooley is the LPC expert when it comes to loon rescue techniques, balancing the organized and thoughtful approach that is needed for planning out such operations with a certain amount of fearlessness when it comes to going out on the ice in the wintertime. I witnessed one such rescue operation on Loon Pond in Gilmanton in December 2022, what Cooley called a 3 on a scale of 1 to 10, and it was impressive to see his determination and persistence, two qualities that always come in handy when it comes to dealing with loons. In any event, there are many loons that are alive because of Cooley today, though he would downplay such credit and be the first to emphasize that any such rescues are a team effort.

Director of development and membership management Betsy McCoy got her start as a young biologist, hired by LPC director Jeff Fair. She would have an impact on the LPC that is continuing to this day. The daughter of a navy service family, McCoy spent much time in Newport, Rhode Island, but knew she wanted to go to college in northern New England because she was an avid skier. Her college choices came down to the University of New Hampshire and the University of Vermont, but the former won out and so would New Hampshire's loons. McCoy not only loved the beautiful UNH campus but also preferred the focus of its wildlife program to that of Vermont, which was more fisheries based. Betsy McCoy subsequently graduated with a bachelor's degree in wildlife management in 1986 from UNH but had worked the previous summer as a field biologist. She heard about the LPC through the university's job postings and laughingly recalled her very first day at work, taking a wild truck ride with Jeff Fair to her first lake destination. McCoy would later state that Jeff Fair "was the single greatest influence on my career." McCoy's subsequent career was indeed a groundbreaking one, but those first summers she worked as a field biologist in southern New Hampshire and was involved in raft-building and related activities.

In the spring of 1987, she became a full-time LPC biologist working as a program assistant and, like many at the LPC, wore many different hats and excelled at all of them. In 1988, when Fair took a summer sabbatical, McCoy served as the acting director, subsequently becoming assistant director in 1989. In addition to fieldwork, she also wrote many informative and interesting articles for the LPC newsletter, these today serving as an archival record of what was happening with loons and the LPC across the state. In 1991, with Fair's departure, Betsy McCoy became the fourth director in the history of the LPC and the first of only two women to occupy this position as of this writing. Though she would step down from the position in 1994, the LPC was well-positioned for the future. On looking back at her loon career, McCoy thoughtfully stated, "My greatest skill was probably in being a bridge between Jeff [Fair] and what would come next with Harry [Vogel]." After stepping down, McCoy served as senior biologist from 1994 through early 1996, departing before the summer season began. She would subsequently work for several years as a wildlife consultant, doing avian surveys and drafting management plans for New Hampshire Audubon, the Army Corps of Engineers, NH Fish and Game and the U.S. Fish and

Wildlife Service. In 2006, she took a position at Plymouth State University, also gaining a master's in education there in 2013. In May 2022, McCoy returned to the LPC, accepting her current position in the wake of the retirement of Lin O'Bara. Today, she works closely with Linda Egli Johnson and is passionate about her "stewardship" of both the LPC's members and trustees. She commented, "The LPC is truly a grassroots organization, and I'm so proud of the fact that the LPC has maintained such a strong network of supporters and volunteers all these years." While the LPC does receive some significant donations, McCoy is amazed at the commitment of those who have donated year after year at all levels. "I am humbled every day at the support we receive, and we are committed to being sure that every dollar donated is spent responsibly."

Squam Lakes biologist Tiffany Grade is a native of Wisconsin. Her parents had a lake house, and some of her earliest memories are of loons; she was "absolutely hooked" and loved going out in the family canoe. The affable Grade looks every bit the biologist today, so you might not believe that her first degree was a bachelor's in history and English, with a specialty in medieval studies, from the University of Wisconsin–Madison. As she explained, "I got sidetracked by a favorite English teacher," and she would subsequently go on to study history at Cambridge University in England and there gained a master's before attending Notre Dame University, where she earned a master's and doctorate in medieval history. Very impressive, but how did she go from ancient England to loons? As she explained, "I could see birds receding out of my life, and that was just not OK, so I started over." Grade went back to the University of Wisconsin and earned a bachelor's in wildlife ecology. During the last several years of her studies, she ended up on Squam Lake as a summer biologist starting in 2008. The rest, as they say (and she would know more than most), is history. Grade returned to Squam Lake in the summer of 2009, laughingly recalling that "I kept coming back to the LPC, hoping maybe I could infiltrate and get a job there." Grade, in the meantime, was working on her master's in conservation biology at Wisconsin, and "fate intervened." She had originally chosen as her thesis topic the subject of human disturbance of loons, but after her first experience with a loon dying from lead poisoning, she switched her thesis topic to studying lead mortality in New Hampshire loons. She graduated in December 2011 and came aboard full time at the LPC in February 2012. Grade has been working on Squam ever since and is passionate about the lake and its loons. She recalled her first lead-poisoned loon on Squam vividly as an "absolutely horrible situation," and it has motivated her ever since.

While the job of any biologist in the field of loon conservation is a difficult one that is often filled with tragic events, Grade's role as the Squam Lakes Project biologist is particularly challenging based on the unpredictability of that lake and the many factors that affect the loon population there. However, it is clear after speaking with Grade that she has the needed knowledge, determination and persistence, and if anyone can get to the bottom of the troubles on Squam, it will be her. To say that Grade has bonded with her loons is an understatement—she referred to her favorite loon on Squam as a "spitfire" and an "amazing" bird.

Caroline Hughes is the LPC's volunteer and outreach biologist and is a native of New Hampshire, born in Manchester. As she recalled, "I knew nothing about loons growing up" but was interested in environmental issues. Hughes attended the College of the Holy Cross in Worcester, Massachusetts, graduating in 2015 with a bachelor's in environmental studies. During her summers, she performed an internship on Squam Lake. It was during this time that Hughes encountered the LPC Squam Lakes biologist Tiffany Grade, and she recalled, "I was fascinated talking to Tiffany during some banding work" and was subsequently hooked on loons. Hughes wanted to stick around in New Hampshire and did some work for the Blue Ocean Society in Portsmouth and also Squam Lake Association, managing its intern group. However, Hughes "was interested in getting back to hands-on work" and subsequently joined the LPC in 2016. Originally slated for the position of field biologist on Lake Winnipesaukee, Hughes instead became the LPC's field program coordinator when that position became available, her prior experience making her the perfect fit. She worked full time in the summers and pursued her master's in environmental studies at Antioch College, with a concentration on conservation biology. I've had the chance to see Hughes at work in the field, and it's easy to see her dedication, talent and gentle and calming way in working with loons. She's also a great public ambassador for the LPC in her role as outreach biologist. Her people skills are evident, and as she said, "I really do love interacting with the public and teaching. We [the LPC] can't do this work on our own, and I like hearing other people's experiences." In her role, Caroline Hughes maintains a volunteer list that runs anywhere from 700 to 1,000 people and through the seasonal field biologists works on getting many rafts floated, more now than ever, and enjoys working with "a lot of kind volunteers." For Hughes, hers is "a dream job," and some aspects of her work, like successfully releasing a rescued or rehabilitated loon, "never gets old." She is also proud that the loon numbers in New Hampshire are growing and that her outreach work is helping to make it happen. However, there are hard parts of a biologist's job, the ones the public rarely sees, that can be difficult. As Hughes reflected, "The decision to euthanize a sick loon is difficult, even when you know it's the right thing to do." Caroline Hughes is sometimes asked, Why loons? What is so important about a few birds? Her passionate, and reasoned, reply is simple: "It's important to remember that every species has an intrinsic value. Loons are an 'umbrella species' for our ecosystem, and the impacts on them have a much broader implication." That, in a nutshell, is the underlying philosophy of the LPC mission.

Database technician Joan Plevich is a native of southern Pennsylvania, a resident of Mechanicsburg, doing her work for the LPC remotely on a part-time basis. She is truly one of the unseen faces of the LPC, yet her job is an important one. She manages the LPC's vast historic database, the oldest loon database in the world. It is her job to update all of the field data gathered by LPC biologists on a yearly basis for each New Hampshire body of water that has loons, those that no longer have loons or ones that have newly acquired loons. All of this carefully gathered and hard-won data serves no purpose if it can't be organized and accessed, and that's what Plevich has done for over 20 years now. She designed the current database through an AmeriCorps program. So, how does a Pennsylvanian end up managing a New Hampshire loon database? As Joan tells it, "I came to LPC in the summer of 1999 from my home in southern Pennsylvania to do volunteer work in exchange for some time out on the lakes to see the loons. I have always loved the loons since the time I first watched *On Golden Pond* back in the early '80s. It was so fitting then that during the summer of 2000 I became the Loon Ranger for Squam Lake, which is the setting for the movie. We don't have resident loons in southern Pennsylvania, so it was quite the treat to spend so much time with them in New Hampshire. I then took on the task starting in 2001 of creating a database for all of LPC's data. It would house historical data as well as being a means of having the biologists enter the data at the end of each field season." The initial work with AmeriCorps lasted a year, but it would take another 3 years to complete, Plevich going over 25 years' worth of field data to check for accuracy and make sure it conformed to current protocols. The data Plevich manages informs the LPC's fieldwork decisions and ongoing research activities—it's that important. She also started doing this same work for Maine-based BRI (which includes more wildlife than loons) several years later but keeps the two data sets separate, as they are proprietary databases. As she is gatekeeper of the LPC's loon data, no one gets access to this data without approval from LPC biologists. In requesting the varied lake data cited in this book, it was quickly evident that Plevich is not just a data-entry person but someone who knows loons and has a great recall of the numbers for not just the many different lakes but also specific information about territorial and banded pairs. While she doesn't get up to New Hampshire as often as she'd like, Joan Plevich still has fond memories of her earlier loon experiences.

Holly Heath is the development and membership manager for the LPC, an important position that she has held since 2022. Prior to that, she held the position of development assistant. She is a native of Center Harbor and lives in Moultonborough. Her job entails LPC membership renewals and the logistics surrounding annual fundraisers and appeals to donors initiatives that take place throughout the year. Heath holds a bachelor's degree in theater from Northeastern University in Boston, and as she recalled, "I did the 'city girl' thing in Boston and LA, then came home." She has worked for nonprofits since her graduation, mostly in the cultural field, so, as she laughingly stated, working for the LPC "stretches the STEM side of my brain." Heath enjoys the variety in her job and the small, close-knit group that she works with and has made a difference by streamlining aspects of their work to make it more efficient. However, when crisis comes—such as when 10 loons end up in the LPC's conference room—Heath pitches in wherever she can, taking calls or serving hot soup or cocoa to field staff. Sometimes, when no biologists are around, she even must field phone calls about loons, humorously recalling the time that a man called, yelling at her and wanting to know what the LPC was going to do about the loons eating all the fish. Never a dull moment! As Heath says, her work is important, behind-the-scenes stuff because "it allows fieldwork for the mission of loon conservation."

Last but not least, two local women operate the public-facing Loon Center and the Loon's Feather Gift Shop. Kirsten Knell, who lives just a stone's throw away from the center, has recently become the Loon Center manager and, as she succinctly put it, "I love loons and I like working close to home." She first worked with the LPC in 1994 as a part-time members assistant, bringing her office experience in the insurance industry to the LPC after she and her husband made Moultonborough their year-round home in 1993. As Linda Egli Johnson said, "Some may argue that she was hired for her baking skills." During the LPC's recent capital campaign, Knell was invaluable in directing daily activities, as Johnson recalled, "our person in hard-hat on the ground." As manager, Knell does the gift shop ordering as part of her many duties, fulfilling online orders and serving as ambassador to the many public visitors who make the Loon Center their destination, as well as being tasked with taking care of logistics for any special events that may be held there and assisting in loon rescue operations when needed.

Bette Ruyffelaert, hired in 2004, serves as the assistant Loon Center manager and in-season assists in running the daily operations of the public-facing operations. Due to her residence on Wakondah Pond, she has an "intimate knowledge of loons" and has even taken part in a banding operation, humorously stating that "I'll hold their head and leave the back end to others." She is a Massachusetts native who first encountered loons when at her family's vacation home in Maine on Sebec Lake and recalled that "I heard a loon let loose on the lake" with its wild calls, and wondered "what the heck is making that noise." She was taken out to see a loon the very next day, and "that was that, I fell in love with loons." She loves the camaraderie of those with whom she works, and speaking of the "new challenges" that they face every year, is proud that the loon numbers in New Hampshire continue to climb. Ruyffelaert is also the longtime organizer of the annual Loon Festival but, like everyone else at the LPC, helps with whatever else may need doing, whether it's fundraising and mailing activities, arranging logistics for professional events and conferences or even helping out with a loon that is brought to the center. In the off-season, you can find Ruyffelaert in Punta Gorda, Florida, where she works with the Peace River Wildlife Center, which does similar work to the LPC. There, she has worked with loons, "not ones from New Hampshire," as well as turtles, owls and other animals.

The LPC has developed working relationships with a wide variety of individual professionals, academic institutions, local and regional nonprofit organizations and state and federal agencies in pursuit of its loon conservation mission. It is true that the LPC is the only organization in the state that works on loon conservation, 24-7, 365 days a year, and if you've ever wondered why you can't get a New Hampshire license plate with a picture of a loon on it (moose plates are available), it's because the state does not fund the LPC's loon conservation efforts. These efforts are funded by the LPC, using grant money and private donor funding, and virtually any loon matters the state does encounter, it usually sends the LPC's way. However, no work such as this can truly be accomplished by one organization alone, and throughout its history, the LPC has taken a cooperative approach, dating back to the days of the North American Loon Fund. This cooperative approach has been a winning strategy for New Hampshire's loons. The following is an account of some of these partners in loon preservation.

Bill Gassman, LPC LoonCam Operator

Few may know the story of the man behind the LPC's famed LoonCam operations, he who designed the system from the start and still operates the LoonCam today. Moultonborough resident Bill Gassman was "freshly retired," having worked on local economy and ecology issues, when he partnered up with the LPC in late 2013. As he humorously recalled, "I knew nothing about loons at first," but that is no longer the case. He has now spent more time than most biologists observing loon behavior in real-time situations. Gassman worked with LPC senior biologist John Cooley Jr. "to get the technology figured out." Once biologist Caroline Hughes came aboard, "she spent a lot of time figuring out the early problems." One of his and the LPC's major concerns is privacy: "We don't want to surveil people. There is one LoonCam site that is no longer used because the people nearby 'partied hardy' and made so much noise the microphones had to be muted." As Gassman asserted, "We're past most of the problems now." Gassman's work in preparing the equipment prior to the set-up day is extensive, usually beginning in February, with much testing to be done and de-bugging the system. This process takes many hours to complete each season. Once the set-up day comes, it's about eight hours' worth of work to get the system in place and operational. Interestingly, the camera is remotely monitored. Bill Gassman does this work all on his own, and occasionally, when something goes wrong, it's Gassman who has to take the trip to the camera to rectify things. While he does admit that "the commitment is a bit challenging family-wise," Gassman also said, "It's a privilege to work with the LPC. It's an honor really, and I get to play with some expensive toys." Gassman does more than monitor the footage; he is also the online chat moderator for the event. He added, "The community is a huge part of it and many are birders from other bird camera operations." Not only do participants get a chance to talk and ask questions about loons and their behavior, but it also serves as a fundraising platform. The switch to YouTube was Gassman's idea and has expanded the visibility of the LoonCam greatly. He had to really talk the LPC's Board of Trustees into going to this new platform, and even though the chat messaging was a bit crazy at first, things soon calmed down, and regular LoonCam viewers learned how to act appropriately. Indeed, the LPC has worked hard on the LoonCam platform, and as Gassman related, "Harry [Vogel] has marching orders to make things perfect and I take that challenge personally. I'm a fanatic about quality because ours is the best LoonCam on the network." He, like many viewers, can recall many memorable LoonCam moments, his favorites including a shot of loons on their nest in May after it had snowed, as well as those shots that show the parents training their chick. For both Gassman and LoonCam viewers, there can be difficult moments to watch, but when bad things happen, the LPC lets nature take its course and does not intervene. While Bill Gassman has been operating the LoonCam for 10 years now, how much longer this "retiree" may be doing so is open to question, and as he admitted, "It's going to be tough to let it go." Until then, LoonCam viewers, and the LPC, will continue to reap the benefits of his expertise and dedication.

Wildlife Rehabilitators

For the LPC, rescuing and recovering sick and wounded loons has from the very beginning been an integral part of its work. However, the treatment of loons to get them back into the wild is a specialized and difficult process that requires trained professionals. This is where a wildlife rehabilitator comes in. The folks who do this work are not only specialists but also some of the kindest people you will ever meet.

Martha "Kappy" Sprenger of Bridgeton, Maine, is a Colorado native who has long worked with the LPC. As a child, she had an interest in birds and wildlife: "I think I was born a rehabber.…I'd bring animals home as a kid, but pretty much everything died." She got her start as an avian rehabilitator in California and at one time was dealing with 1,000 birds a year there. The first bird she ever rehabbed was a California scrub jay in July 1985, while her first waterbird was a gull with a broken wing. Sprenger also dealt with many loons on the West Coast, first in dealing with a California oil spill, probably the 1988 Shell Oil Martinez spill. Sprenger also humorously recalled that the first loon she rescued, a red-throated loon, had landed on a field, mistaking it for a lake. This occurred while she was out on a date, heading to a party. As you may have guessed, the date was put on hold and she never made the party. She would later move to Maine, where her parents lived and she had spent her summers, and continued her avian rehabilitation career. She first worked for Avian Haven in Freedom, Maine, which was established in 1999, but now works independently and has her own facilities for rehabbing loons. Sprenger believes this the best situation for rescue loons to be in: "I work alone.…It's quiet here. Loons are smart and know what's going on around them. They get used to me, and they can trust me to a point. They learn and sense how to work with me. I'm totally comfortable with fish-eating birds."

As a rehabilitator, Sprenger has done it all, from removing hooks to cleaning and bathing them to restore the waterproofing to their feathers. Sprenger, an octogenarian who is a tough, yet kindly, bird herself, has learned many things about loons from her experiences. When approaching them, she makes a "certain noise" to keep them calm and laughingly recalled that she no longer wears a favorite black and white checkered shirt because it would set them off. She has also been known to use a stuffed animal adult loon to help calm chicks in her care, having worked with chicks since 2002. Sprenger is available day and night as a rehabilitator, with the attitude that "the people who bring you animals were ones who were first taking care of them and needed help." Over the years, Sprenger has handled close to 200 loons in all, some from Lake Winnipesaukee or Squam Lake and from many other places in Maine and New Hampshire. During the course of her work, she has had two back surgeries—one for lifting a large loon—and two rotator cuff surgeries. The work is not easy, but for her "it's absolutely wonderful" for a recovered loon to show its abilities, even if only for a few minutes before it swims off. As recently as September 2022, she had five loons in her care at once, wayward migrants brought down by foggy conditions. As to her relationship with the LPC, she said it is a "wonderful organization and John [Cooley] in particular a great resource." When I asked Sprenger how she does it, how she deals with the loons and other birds in her care that don't make it, she offered a unique yet fitting philosophy: "In my mind, everything brought to me is already dead. If I save it, it's a win. If they die, at least they were being cared for in a safe place. That's how I've gotten through everything. Otherwise, emotionally, it could shred you." It's a philosophy that has worked well for her and the loons in her care.

In New Hampshire, Maria Colby is probably the best-known wildlife rehabilitator in the state. She has been featured on such popular television shows as Channel 9's *New Hampshire Chronicle* as well as the show *North Woods Law* on the Animal Planet channel. And for good reason—she's very good at what she does. Colby is a native of the Boston area and moved to New Hampshire in 1974. She was originally in the medical profession and was going to nursing school at the time. She has an undergraduate degree in microbiology in addition to a master's in environmental science from Antioch University. In 1988, she joined the nonprofit animal rescue group Wings of Dawn (now Wings Wildlife) in Henniker. Despite its original name, the organization handles all manner of birds and mammals, with Colby as director and a staff of six, as well as many volunteers. From the beginning of her wildlife rehabilitation career, Colby has worked with the LPC, recalling

SAVING OUR NEW HAMPSHIRE LOONS

that the first loons she treated were lead poisoned—"It was not good." She also laughingly recalled that before John Cooley Jr. joined the LPC, "I was the one that had to do the rescues in many cases. The ones found on land or along the road were easy," but when it came to going out on the ice for winter rescues, Colby admitted, "I'm not that crazy." Colby has a "very close relation with the LPC.…I enjoy working with the girls [Caroline Hughes and Tiffany Grade]. We girls have to stick together!" The way it works between her and the LPC these days is simple: "Any loon in distress, John texts me or I text him, and we work together.…It does take a village to save the wildlife. Their well-being is also dependent on people letting us know something's not right." Colby has learned much about loons over the years, and having seen her in action, she has a strong yet calming presence with the loons in her care. As she stated, "Loons are their own crazy, unique beings. You have to be prepared for them and you have to be smarter than the animal you're dealing with. It's extra rewarding to help them when they're in harm's way." While Maria Colby is concerned for the future of New Hampshire's loons, she is all in when it comes to helping them, stating, "I love doing it, and when I hear that a loon we handled has returned and nested, what more could you ask for?" Colby, in addition to her rehabilitation work at Wings, has also taught at New England College in Henniker, passing on some of the knowledge she has gained over the years. How many loons she has helped rescue and rehab she can't recall, but there is no doubt that her efforts have played a major part in sustaining New Hampshire's loon population.

Avian Haven Wild Bird Rehabilitation Center in Freedom, Maine, is another organization the LPC has worked with over the years. Founded in 1999 by Marc Payne and Diane Winn, it treats nearly 4,000 birds a year and is one of the largest avian rehabilitation groups in New England. It has extensive facilities, including an enclosed outdoor pond and an aquatic center with pools that can accommodate loons and smaller water birds. A number of loons rescued from eastern New Hampshire lakes have made their recovery here, as have many Maine loons.

VETERINARIAN PRACTICES

Local veterinarians have been vital partners with the LPC when it comes to handling rescued loons in need of medical assistance. They take in loons at any hour, day or night, often on an emergency basis, performing X-rays and providing what is often life-saving care. Because the loon is such an unusual bird, such care is not provided by most veterinarians. Dr. Lindy North and Dr. Kelly Keenan of the Meadow Pond Animal Hospital in Moultonborough have been stalwart partners for many years with the LPC, often the go-to veterinarians since they are close to the Loon Center. They have also supported the LPC's own scientific efforts by supplying the examining table as an outright donation when their wet lab was established. In Concord, the veterinarians at the VCA Capital Area Veterinary Emergency and Specialty (CAVES) practice have also been a valuable asset, often working in close relationship with wildlife rehabilitator Maria Colby. In the summer of 2023, the staff at the Hopkinton Animal Hospital successfully treated a loon tangled in fishing line that was rescued from Townhouse Pond in Milton by LPC personnel and subsequently returned to its home waters. These named veterinary practices are just a few of the many such organizations that have partnered with the LPC to help New Hampshire's loons over the years.

STATE AGENCIES

The LPC is issued permits yearly by the NH Department of Fish and Game to monitor, research and conduct management to help loons in New Hampshire. The men and women of the Fish and Game Department working in the field are important partners with the LPC. It is often their conservation officers who first encounter sick, injured or stranded loons, or they are notified of such loons by New Hampshire citizens and are first responders. Once such a loon is discovered, conservation officers reach out to the LPC for assistance and guidance, so some incidents are a joint effort. The Department of Environmental Services (DES) is also another partner in several different areas, including dam maintenance and management, as well as possible lake contaminants that affect loon habitats, contracting with the LPC for PFAS testing.

FEDERAL AGENCIES

The major partner here is the U.S. Fish and Wildlife Service, part of the Department of the Interior, which has in-state offices and is responsible for administering the Lake Umbagog National Wildlife Refuge, which was established in 1992. This lake is a major loon habitat in New Hampshire and Maine and has been the site of much work since the LPC was founded. When it comes to oil spills that have affected loons, the LPC has worked with the National Oceanic and Atmospheric Administration (NOAA), part of the Department of Commerce. The LPC has worked with other government agencies on a limited basis, including the National Aeronautics and Space Administration (NASA) regarding satellite data. Who knew that NASA and loons would have something in common?

LOCAL GOVERNMENT AGENCIES

Police and fire department officials in towns throughout the state have helped play a part in loon rescue operations, sometimes—as was the case in early 2023 with the Tuftonboro Fire Department—providing the equipment that makes such operations safer for all involved. The LPC also works with town governing bodies on local initiatives, such as the possible installation of boat ramps, conservation easements and other local development issues that can have an effect on loons.

LAKE ASSOCIATION ORGANIZATIONS

These organizations, starting with the Squam Lakes Association (the oldest such organization in the country), even before the LPC got its start, have long been partners for conserving loons on many lakes. Operated by local lake residents, many of whom are also LPC members, they have a vested interest in keeping their bodies of water as pristine as possible, balancing nature conservation and recreational uses. The LPC has worked with these groups on a whole host of issues, including raft placements and protecting nesting areas, conservation easements, water quality issues and other influences on loon populations. Many of these groups, like the Bow Lake Camp Owners Association (Strafford), led by loon advocate Herb Cilley for decades, and the Pleasant Lake Protective Association (New London), whose leaders include John Wilson and his late wife, Kittie Wilson, have played an active part in protecting loons that has led to sustained population growth. Not surprisingly, many of these organizations have an image of a loon as part of their logos. Indeed, many lake associations take their loon protective measures seriously and have information for members and residents posted on their websites, often referencing either the LPC directly or otherwise guiding residents on how to protect their lake's loon population. These include information on the dangers of using lead fishing tackle, as well as warning recreationists not to approach loons too closely. Organizations that go above and beyond to provide this important loon information to the public include the previously mentioned organizations working on Squam, Bow and Pleasant Lakes, as well as the Lake Kanasatka Watershed Association (Moultonborough), the Granite Lake Association (Nelson), the Halfmoon Lake Association (Alton-Barnstead), the Pawtuckaway Lake Improvement Association (Nottingham), the Lake Armington Association (Piermont), the Mascoma Lake Association (Enfield), the Lake Sunapee Protective Association (Sunapee), the Spofford Lake Association (Chesterfield), the Little Ossipee Lake Association (Ossipee), the Silver Lake Association of Madison, the Nippo Lake Association (Barrington) and the Winnisquam Watershed Association. It is safe to say that without the cooperation of these loon partners, the activities of the LPC would be severely curtailed on many bodies of water.

One final organization worthy of mention is the Rockywold Deephaven Camps on Squam Lake. This family retreat has been in operation since 1897, founded by teachers Mary Alice Ford and Alice Mable Bacon. This organization very much appreciates the loons on Squam, counting them as part of their cherished experiences, and each year helps the LPC on Squam in many ways.

ACADEMIC INSTITUTIONS

Not surprisingly, the University of New Hampshire has been a longtime partner, and many LPC personnel have gained their degrees here. Dr. James Haney of the university's Department of Biological Sciences is director of the UNH Center for Freshwater Biology and is a co-founder of the New Hampshire Lakes Lay Monitoring Program. He has been researching the subject of cyanobacteria toxins within lake food chains and their effects on loons and fish. Another University of New Hampshire partner is Dr. Inga Sidor, the senior veterinarian pathologist in the Department of Molecular,

Cellular and Biomedical Sciences, New Hampshire Veterinary Diagnostic Laboratory. She got her start at the Tufts University School of Veterinary Medicine and while there worked closely with Dr. Mark Pokras on his pioneering loon mortality study. She was also a veterinary intern at the LPC in the late 1990s. The LPC has worked with many colleges and universities over the years on a wide variety of matters that involve loon science. Summer interns working in the field have been employed from many schools across the country, as well as Plymouth State University and the University of New Hampshire, while individuals working on advanced degrees involving loon conservation issues have collaborated with the LPC during their research projects. Dr. Kerry Yurewicz, professor of ecology at Plymouth State, and her students were valuable partners in the study of crayfish on Squam Lake in 2013. Relationships with other institutions have been developed because of the expertise they can offer the LPC in terms of testing and ongoing loon research and data-gathering programs. The University of Vermont is also an important partner for the testing that Dr. Ellen Martinsen does at their laboratory to collect avian malaria data. Usually, whenever a loon necropsy is conducted by the LPC, tissue samples from deceased loons are sent to Martinsen for testing.

Dr. Mark Pokras, an associate professor emeritus at Tufts University's Cummings School of Veterinarian Medicine, has been a major partner with the LPC since the 1980s. Before the LPC built its own facilities, most New Hampshire loon necropsies were conducted by Pokras and his team at Tufts, and even today, Pokras will make regular appearances at the Loon Center to conduct necropsies alongside the LPC's biologists and has found grants to help Tufts veterinary students do summer research at the LPC for many years. Without a doubt, Pokras holds the world record for the number of loon necropsies, about 4,300 and counting, performed, and it's safe to say that few know the inner workings of a loon better than he. The story of this veterinarian is a fascinating one that is worth telling because of his work unraveling some of the mysteries of loon physiology, which has in turn led to a greater understanding of this secretive bird. His work not only revealed the lead poisoning problem, but his yearslong study of loon mortalities also demonstrated just how widespread and devastating its effect was on New Hampshire's loon population.

Pokras grew up in a family where, as he put it, "we had all sorts of animals," and has childhood memories of seeing loons but never dreamed they would become a specialty. His mother wished that one of her children would become a veterinarian and was "overjoyed" when he became one, but it took some time. Pokras first attended Cornell University, graduating with a bachelor's in ecology and systematics in 1971, and afterward taught at Stockton University in Galloway, New Jersey, from 1974 to 1980. It was during this time that he and his wife were doing ornithological, marine biology and environmental conservation work. Pokras recalled, "I first got my hands on one [a loon] in the mid-1970s in New Jersey while working an oil spill on the Delaware River. We rescued oiled loons, and one of the things that struck me then was that loons were almost impossible to rehabilitate. Why are they so different?" By the end of the 1970s, Pokras's career had taken a turn when he decided to become a veterinarian. As he recalled, he already had a career, and "I had to convince some doubters." And so, Pokras went back to school, gaining his doctorate in veterinarian medicine from Tufts University Cummings School of Veterinary Medicine in 1984. As he stated, "I went there specifically to build a career in wildlife ecology. One of the things I love about veterinary medicine is that it's OK to be a jack of all trades but a specialist in none. The ability to have a career where I can do different things during each day fits my personality and skills." Tufts was the only veterinary school in New England at the time, and thus its veterinarians were those tasked with working on regional recovery programs for various endangered species. As Pokras stated, "Tufts has had unbelievable resources and vet students who really want to learn. Vet students there will spoil you rotten as a professor, they're so hungry for knowledge." Pokras also has a unique take on the role of veterinarians, stating, "There's a T-shirt available at most vet schools that says 'Real doctors treat more than one species.' My license covers every species of animal on the planet but one [humans]! There's more room for intellectual breadth, though the downside is that we know so little about the majority of species…an infinite number of things we don't know." With these things in mind, it's perhaps natural that Pokras would circle back to loons while at Tufts. In the past, necropsies weren't performed on loons, but he found his past work and "interdisciplinary language was useful in bringing people of various disciplines together." Enter the LPC, which, because of Pokras's Loon Mortality Study, now had a partner in figuring out what was causing loon deaths. As Pokras firmly believes, "You can't understand the whole life-cycle of a species without knowing what makes them tick, why they die as well as how they live. I've always liked to take things apart since a young age and I've always had that fascination carry over to my medical pursuits with fish, animals, and birds." Because of the work of Pokras, the deadly harm of lead poisoning in loons was first documented in the 1980s and, as he told the LPC and anyone who was willing to listen: "If you ever get another dead loon, call me." And boy did they. Before Pokras's work, lead poisoning in birds was best known in waterfowl, raptors and captive birds, and what he discovered was alarming. Because of his necropsy expertise, Pokras discovered that, indeed, there was much more to the loon than meets the eye, and he has over the years published his significant findings in many journal articles. Pokras today, though retired, still serves as a consultant to the LPC and other wildlife organizations and agencies, and his expertise and experience are an invaluable resource. Speaking of the LPC, Pokras said, "The LPC has been doing loon conservation work for so long and so well, and they're continuing that today and I'm honored to be a part of it." Ever the seeker, Dr. Pokras stated that there are things "we still don't know about loons," but he is still doing loon necropsies and by this work continues to both teach a new generation of loon conservation biologists and veterinarians and further our knowledge of these mysterious birds.

Wildlife and Conservation Nonprofit Organizations and Consortiums

Several organizations in this category stand out for their collaboration with the LPC over the years. The first is Dr. David Evers and his Biodiversity Research Institute (BRI), which he founded in 1998 "to further progressive wildlife research and conservation." It was through Dr. Evers, as discussed previously, that loon banding efforts got their start in New Hampshire, and to this day, the LPC bands loons as sub-permittees under BRI's Master Permit. The LPC has also worked with BRI on issues related to mercury poisoning in loons, on which Dr. Evers is regarded as a leading expert. Personnel-wise, the two organizations also have a long history. Not only is former LPC senior biologist Kate Taylor now BRI's director of operations, but a number of other field biologists who have gotten their start at the LPC have migrated over to BRI as well.

The Squam Lakes Natural Science Center works with the LPC by hosting its fun and educational Loon Cruise from June to July, one of its many nature offerings. Each 90-minute cruise features a biologist who provides loon commentary, and a portion of the proceeds supports the work of the LPC. For more information, go to https://www.nhnature.org/programs/loon_cruise.php.

The Squam Lakes area residents and organizations have embraced loon conservation efforts from the start, so much so that even the local police department features them on their uniform. *Author collection.*

The Squam Lakes Conservation Society in Holderness is a local land trust nonprofit that includes in their lands many of the loon nesting sites on Squam. They have been an important partner in securing these lands in order to maintain the loon population on this lake.

Finally, there is the Northeast Loon Study Working Group (NELSWG), which was founded in 1994 and of which the LPC is a founding partner. This consortium of state, federal, academic and private conservation organizations was founded to proactively study the threats to common loons and to share data and coordinate strategies to protect the species. They have met annually to do this work, typically at the LPC's headquarters, a loon information "hub" so to speak, in Moultonborough. During these two-day sessions, loon experts from all over cooperatively share information in the belief that no one organization has all the answers to loon conservation issues. This organization may be seen to have its historical roots in the North American Loon Fund organization, established by LPC founder Rawson Wood, which worked to establish like organizations in other states but also served as a clearinghouse for the latest in loon conservation science.

6

LOON THREATS NOW
AND HOPES FOR THE FUTURE

The LPC has been successful in bringing the New Hampshire loon population back from the brink, but there are threats that it continues to face here even today. The LPC has been diligent in its pioneering research and educational outreach, and facing these continued threats is its priority. Those in the public, with the increasing numbers of loons, may grow complacent and believe that the loon's problems in the state are solved. After all, their numbers are growing, right? However, those who can appreciate the loon should remain concerned for the welfare of this sentinel species, for the battle continues and, indeed, has evolved as our environment has evolved. Due to the combination of a loon's long life expectancy and low reproductive rate, the loss of even a few loons due to these threats is a real blow to sustaining their population in New Hampshire. One of the complicating factors here, perhaps, is the fact that, worldwide, the common loon is classified as a "species of least concern," with a population according to the Partners in Flight Database of about 1.2 million birds, most of them in northern Canada. And therein lies the rub: as I stated at the outset, New Hampshire is now at the extreme southern limit of its breeding range. The question remains, in terms of numbers, how many loons can New Hampshire lakes and ponds reasonably sustain? The answer here is a complicated one. LPC data based on the calculations of noted biologist Judith McIntyre estimates that the carrying capacities of the state's bodies of water, when all possible territories are considered, would be about 618 pairs of loons. If only. That number is the ideal, and the LPC's Loon Recovery Plan numbers, which consider the stresses that loons face here and their degraded habitat, puts that carrying capacity number at 452 territorial pairs, far from the 345 territorial pairs that were counted in 2022. However, the LPC admits that the 452 number is conservative and that recent field observations support an estimate that 618 territorial pairs could be supported in the state. It's almost certain that, without the LPC's efforts, the bird would have disappeared forever here. We came close, once upon a time, to letting this happen. The LPC is doing the utmost to make sure it doesn't happen again and is striving with intensive loon management plans and scientific research to increase their numbers. What the limit may be for loon numbers in New Hampshire is yet to be seen. But as the history of the organization's grassroots approach has shown, they can't do it alone, and everyday folks who spend time on our lakes can make a difference in this effort. What can you do if you think you see a loon in distress? Check out the LPC's guidelines and reporting procedures at https://loon.org/distressedloons/#reporting for further information. You might just help to save a loon's life. As has been mentioned throughout this work, it is important to understand that the loss of even one loon is often magnified and results in multiple loon deaths, especially for a territorial pair with chicks. The death of one loon parent, for example, due to lead poisoning, may lead to the death of one of its chicks to loon intruders or predators because it usually takes both parents to successfully fledge a chick. Unfortunately, there are those who would like to see the loon's threatened status removed altogether. They point to the loon's growing numbers and recent success to support this change. This would be a mistake. It is only by the LPC's intensive management activities that the loon population has been recovered. Once the loon's threatened status is removed, many of the LPC's conservation activities, including championing shoreline restrictions, and even such activities as signing and roping off loon breeding areas, would end. A change in status would also ignore the growing threats of climate change and future effects that are only just now beginning to be understood.

Note that the threats listed here are only those that pertain to inland bodies of water, and not on the ocean, where additional threats include oil spill events, entanglement in fishing nets and emaciation syndrome, caused by cold weather conditions, which result in stressors in individual birds that lead to decreased feeding and subsequent malnourishment.

Dangers from Fishing Activities

The lead poisoning of loons is a critical issue—the single largest one by far—that has been affecting loons for decades, and the LPC has worked mightily since the 1980s to find a solution. Its extensive legislative efforts to get lead sinkers and fishing jigs banned by law have come into full effect since 2016 with more comprehensive and effective laws that better protect loons and have reduced mortality numbers. However, the lead poisoning issue is far from being solved, and the LPC has continued its efforts. This includes educational outreach, as well as the pioneering Lead Tackle Buyback Program begun in 2018. For details on how to participate in this program, please visit LPC's website at https://loon.org/loons-and-lead/.

Many may wonder, How do loons get lead poisoning? The answer is straightforward: loons can ingest lead sinkers or jigs in several different ways, the most common being the ingesting of fish that have such tackle attached to them after having broken an angler's line, the literal "one that got away." Or they can ingest such lead tackle directly after striking at an angler's line while they are trolling, the loon mistaking it for underwater prey. There is one final way in which loons can ingest lead sinkers, but LPC research has shown that it is a rare occurrence—that of loons ingesting discarded sinkers on the lake bottom, where loons periodically ingest the small stones that are used in their gizzards to grind up the prey that they swallow whole.

Once ingested, the lead gear is eroded in the gizzard and eventually makes its way into the loon's bloodstream. This process can take anywhere from two to four weeks and is almost always fatal, mainly because by the time a lead-poisoned loon is caught and taken in for care it is already too late. Mild cases, if caught in time, can be treated, but this kind of victory for the LPC is rare. Loons that are poisoned suffer weakness and tremors and become less coordinated, thereby more vulnerable to predators and attacks by intruding loons. Unable to feed properly, they become emaciated and lethargic, more vulnerable to disease and predators. It is a terrible way to die, and it is eminently preventable. Anglers who care about the full outdoors experience should know the law and replace their lead tackle and trade it in for legal gear. Information on this subject is readily available at https://fishleadfree. org/nh/, and the LPC has made this transition an easy one, with anglers receiving a $10 voucher for turning in one ounce or more of lead sinkers and jigs at participating tackle shops. As of this writing, 2023 marked the sixth year of the program, with 7 new tackle shops across the state joining the program, making for 17 in all. As the LPC's senior biologist John Cooley

Haunting portrait of a dying loon. This lead-poisoned loon was discovered on Pleasant Lake, New London, in 2008. Note the emaciated look and sunken eyes. By the time it was captured, this suffering bird was beyond help and died soon thereafter. *Photo by Kittie Wilson, courtesy John Wilson.*

Jr. has noted, the voucher is a good monetary incentive, and there's no reason not to switch to other sinker materials such as tungsten, as they can result in better fishing performance, or less expensive alternatives like tin, bismuth and steel. Additional problems surrounding the lead issue include the older tackle that is stored in many boathouses and garages around the state, occasionally brought out for summertime use. This was a big problem during the COVID years, when countless people were making their way into the great outdoors, but the LPC's vigorous outreach is making a dent in the problem. Another concern are those anglers coming here from other states that have no lead laws and may not be aware of their illegal nature here, but some dockside exchange programs, along with educational outreach, will help solve this issue over time.

While LPC biologist Harry Vogel's signal statement on this problem is "even one loon death from lead poisoning is too many," the fact that just one loon died in 2023 from lead ingestion proves that what the LPC is doing is working. However, the lead problem cannot yet be considered solved, and the LPC will continue to be vigilant with its public education and outreach efforts.

It is interesting to note that many folks are concerned about the fishing hooks that loons may swallow. However, hooks are not made of lead, and those that make their way into the gizzard are usually ground up there and pose no severe problems. However, they do cause problems when anglers hook loons by mistake, with these barbs imbedded in their mouth or body. Such hooks can impair a loon's abilities to feed, and so, in order to solve potential problems, anglers are advised simply to "reel-in" and move elsewhere if a loon is in the area and could be accidentally hooked. Some on

A loon with fishing line wrapped around its bill. The bird will soon starve to death if not rescued and freed from the line. The LPC takes many calls each year to help loons in distress like this one. *Photo by Don Polunci, courtesy the LPC.*

the water have failed to follow this simple rule, resulting in physical trauma for the loon and mental trauma for the angler involved. Another threat to loons is that of improperly discarded monofilament line. This hard-to-see line is a clear and present danger and can easily become entangled in a loon's wings, around their body and feet or, as is often tragically the case, wound around their bill. If the latter is the case, it impairs or impedes altogether a loon's ability to feed and can cause it to slowly starve to death, a terrible fate to suffer. Anglers are advised by the LPC to "recycle when you respool" and to carefully gather all discarded line, which can be put in recycling bins that are in place on many lakes. If no recycling bins are present, anglers should have a carry-in, carry-out approach and discard the line at home. It's a simple solution to what often becomes a deadly tragedy.

Finally, studies show that "near-shore fishing can impact nest establishment and nesting success." This includes the abandonment of nesting sites because of heavy fishing activities, as well as the potential for flushing loons off their nests, studies showing that near-shore fishing is a greater risk than most other boating activities in this regard.

Despite these kinds of threats from fishing activities, the LPC has worked diligently to educate New Hampshire anglers, and many of them are not only LPC members but also active supporters in the cause of loon conservation on the lakes in which they fish. They appreciate the beautiful natural setting in which they pursue their passion, and loons are part of that scenery and experience.

Boating

This threat category has several components that affect loons directly, as well as those that have effects on loon reproduction success. Loons and loon chicks are killed every year by being struck by motorized boats on bodies of water both big and small in New Hampshire. These may happen under a variety of circumstances—in some cases, boat operators, usually a tiny minority, may be malicious and purposefully chase down loons and other waterbirds as a form of sick sport. I've witnessed these actions myself on Lake Winnipesaukee toward geese and ducks, and I've no reason to believe that these same individuals would spare loons. However, the bigger problem may be sheer inattentiveness while out on the water or ignoring signs that the LPC has placed around nesting areas. In other cases, a boat operator may see a loon in their path and just assume that it will dive away safely, but this is not always the case. The LPC realizes that most boat operators are responsible citizens and advises all boaters to follow water speed limits, be aware of their surroundings and respect loon nesting and brooding areas.

Loons in the path of a speedboat on Lower Suncook Lake, Barnstead, August 2022. These loons dove away safely—but not all are so lucky, and some die every year from boat strikes. *Author photo.*

Motorboat wakes have also been documented to lead to nesting failures among loons. This includes direct impacts, such as washouts of nests if a boat is too close to shore, as well as disturbing loons and flushing them off their nests. This can result in reduced incubation time, which may result in inviable eggs, or leaving the eggs unprotected and more vulnerable to predators. Studies have shown that when loons are flushed off their nests early in the incubation process, when they have less investment in their eggs, there is a greater chance of a nest being abandoned altogether.

Canoers and kayakers can pose risks to nesting loons by flushing loons off their nests, resulting in greater exposure to predators, as well as reduced incubation times.

Finally, there are many boats on our lakes, whether they be pontoon boats, canoes, kayaks, personal watercraft, fishing boats or sailboats, that can disrupt loon families, including separating chicks from their parents or interrupting feeding activities or otherwise "taxing chicks" that can lead to tragedies. Oft-times these activities are unintentional or in the seemingly innocent attempt to get closer to loons in order to photograph them. The LPC advises boaters to always stay at least 150 feet away from loons to avoid such disruptions.

SHORELINE DEVELOPMENT

This issue is one of the most complex aspects of loon conservation, and the challenges are many. While New Hampshire loons have shown a remarkable ability to adapt to the presence of greater human activities, these issues have resulted in lower breeding success on New Hampshire's most developed lakes, including Lake Winnipesaukee. Heavily developed shorelines lead to less suitable nesting sites for loons, with studies showing that loons are less likely to nest in areas that are near roads or shoreline structures. This often causes territorial pairs, as has been documented around The Weirs and elsewhere, to choose alternate nesting sites, whether it be on or near public beaches or docks, that are much more likely to fail. The LPC's greatly expanded nesting raft program certainly helps combat this issue, but it is not the sole solution to the problem. The LPC's work with locals in establishing conservation easements is also another way to help solve this issue on some lakes, but some lakes are so developed already that this approach is less workable. Several other effects of increased shoreline development include a loss of vegetation and groundcover, often causing shoreline erosion or water runoff that can compromise the water clarity and quality, which is vital to a loon habitat. Finally, shoreline development also leads to an increase in those animals that predate loon eggs. Such wildlife influences make the news frequently in New Hampshire, such as when bears encroach on human places in search of food, but the same thing happens with loons. More people means more trash, which means more scavengers like raccoons make their way to lake shorelines, becoming opportunistic loon egg predators, thereby affecting loon reproduction rates.

Gunshot Deaths

It's hard to believe that anyone would shoot a loon in New Hampshire in this day and age, but it does happen from time to time. Not only is such killing illegal at all times of the year, but there's no reasonable explanation for such activity either. It has sometimes been asserted that a hunter might mistake a loon for a merganser, a diving duck that has a long bill like the loon. However, mergansers are much smaller than loons and have a completely different plumage color and pattern, and most loon deaths from this cause take place in the summer months, when duck hunting season has not yet begun. Thus, it is most certainly the case that most gun-shot loons are killed for malicious reasons only. Luckily, the numbers here are small, the last known gun-shot death taking place on Bradley Lake in Andover in 2016.

Climate Change

First and foremost, climate change is real, and it's here. It's happening for a variety of well-known reasons as we speak, and there's no denying it. Such threats were once projected for years into the future, but as LPC senior biologist John Cooley Jr. recently commented to me after yet another round of loon ice rescues, "It would seem that climate change impacts are happening right now." So, how does climate change manifest itself for New Hampshire loons? First, weather patterns both in New Hampshire and globally have changed dramatically, resulting in varied and unpredictable weather, with severe events happening on a much more frequent basis. The increasing number of heavy rain events in the spring and summer can not only wash away loon nests but also result in rising waters that flood nesting sites. Both events have an effect on reproduction success.

Summertime temperatures, too, are changing according to data gathered by the LPC: "The number of weeks during which the average or maximum temperature exceeded respective 30-year averages by more than 10 percent has increased over time on Squam Lake. Such temperature trends can have wide-ranging effects, including heat stress resulting in decreased incubation and increased egg predation." So, if you've thought that our summers in New Hampshire are warmer now than before, it's not your imagination. The effects of rising temperatures include heat-stressed loons (which the

LPC is mitigating using UV coverings on nesting rafts) and the possible increased presence of cyanotoxins from algae blooms, as well as increased exposure to parasites and tropical diseases (to be discussed further). If you recall, loons have already vanished from southern New England, due in part to climate change and warmer temperatures, and they're barely hanging on in Massachusetts. Southern New Hampshire is next in line, and though the LPC is working to minimize effects, the climate change problem will worsen. Here's one way to think about it: climate experts predict that such coastal cities as New Orleans or Miami could, within less than 100 years, be inundated by rising seas due to global warming, forcing residents to move elsewhere. For the loons of New Hampshire, this is already happening on an increasing basis on their home lakes, their nests being flooded out by weather events. It's a sobering thought.

Yet another aspect of our warming climate in New Hampshire is everyone's favorite outdoor pest, the black fly. Those who spend any time in the Granite State in the spring and summer months are well aware of "black fly season" and take measures to protect against them. Loons, too, can be severely bothered by these highly annoying insects. Black flies thrive in warm temperatures and wet conditions, which have occurred with greater frequency in recent years, and can be a problem for loons during their nesting season. Now, imagine you must sit outside on a hot, 80-degree day (or night) in a bed of grass on the shore of your favorite lake, hidden by surrounding vegetation, after a week of rainy weather. Oh, and you won't be allowed to use any insect repellant, and you can't use your hands to swat the black flies away. How long do you think you could last before you just up and left? Well, loons have this same problem while incubating their eggs and are sometimes forced to abandon their nests due to severe black fly infestations, this event leading to reproductive failure. Such abandonments have been noted on a number of lakes in the last 10 years, and it remains to be seen how prevalent this problem may be in the future.

Finally, one of the most distressing impacts of climate change is our warming winters here in New Hampshire and the effect on loon migration and potential deadly consequences. Loons will typically leave the lakes in the late fall, heading off to the ocean by late November. However, in the last 20 years, loons have increasingly lingered on inland waters well after the onset of winter. This is a problem, as loons molt their primary feathers by late January and are unable to fly for several weeks. New Hampshire's winter of 2022–23 was one of the warmest on record, and loons were on our lakes well into February, no longer an uncommon occurrence.

A loon being swarmed by black flies, Pleasant Lake, New London, May 2011. Such pests will sometimes cause loons to abandon their nests. *Photo by Kittie Wilson, courtesy John Wilson.*

Unfortunately, when the cold winter hits in New Hampshire, it hits hard, a lake often flash-freezing in a short time when the temperatures drop precipitously. When this happens, loons are trapped within a quickly shrinking area of open water. Unable to fly, their ability to feed impeded by the ice and contained in a small area that makes them vulnerable to eagle predation, loons, as you will read, often perish. The biologists at the LPC used to have a bit of downtime in fieldwork in the months from December through February, when loons were usually away from inland waters, but this is no longer the case. Now, these months are intermittently busy, biologists monitoring loons, with the help of many volunteers, that remain on lakes that could become iced in or performing rescue operations of iced-in loons, some of them, as in 2016, 2022 and early 2023 on Lake Winnipesaukee, complex operations.

CHEMICAL CONTAMINANTS

The LPC has done increasingly significant work on the contaminants found in New Hampshire lakes that affect loons. There is no room for doubt that all of these contaminants are detrimental to the health of animals, loons included, but as Dr. Mark Pokras commented, these contaminants are "wicked complicated" and "no one has a handle on them yet." The LPC's work has larger implications than just the loon population when we recall that these birds are a sentinel species, adverse effects on their population a warning sign of what may come for humans since we all share New Hampshire's water resources.

In November 2021, the LPC released to the NH Department of Environmental Services and NH Fish and Game, as well as the public, a paper documenting its scientific testing results on loon eggs. The research involved testing 81 failed loon eggs collected from 24 New Hampshire lakes, including Squam and Pleasant Lakes and Lake Sunapee, over the previous 10 years, 60 percent of which were found to have levels of contaminants "documented to cause negative health or reproductive effects in other bird species." The report also noted that these contaminants get magnified as they move up the food chain. For example, a fish that has consumed the bugs that have fed on contaminated sediment at the bottom of a lake will have a concentration of these contaminants at a much higher magnitude than its concentration in the water. Loons then eat these fish, resulting in increased health dangers.

The presence of these contaminants was no surprise to the LPC, but the concentration levels were, these including such toxic chemicals as DDT, PCBs and PFAS. The state had previously responded to earlier LPC contaminant reports by testing fish and, finding corroborating evidence of these contaminants, even advising anglers not to consume certain types of fish, including the perch often eaten by loons. This 2021 report went further, leading to the LPC's current contract with the DES for PFAS testing. While the NH DES has praised the LPC for its work, much remains to be done by the state. One state official commented to reporter Claire Potter on the release of this report, "Yes, there are some of these high levels [of contaminants] here and there. In general, we have extremely good water quality in New Hampshire." These kinds of comments are frustrating for biologists, as they ignore the underlying problem of contaminants, which have no place in our lakes. As the LPC's Squam Lakes biologist Tiffany Grade commented to me, "In some respects, yes, the water quality is good on Squam and other lakes, IF you just look at clarity, nutrient loading, water chemistry, etc. But, if you look at what our contaminant report demonstrates, there is reason for concern and it can't be shrugged off as good water quality." And this, in partnership with the state, is just what the LPC is currently working on in terms of research and ways to address the issue. In this regard, further testing has been done (results are not in as of this writing) on another 144 loon eggs collected over the last six years on 77 bodies of water. There are three goals for this testing, the first being to identify where hot spots are in the state. The second is to gain an understanding of how these chemicals move through the food web, with additional testing on fish. And third, from the LPC's perspective, is the goal of discovering how these contaminants affect loons. It is already known that eggshells are thinner than in the past and that eggs are also smaller. LPC research has already revealed that smaller and thinner eggs are correlated with higher contaminant levels, likely resulting in loon chicks that are smaller and less robust. While it is not yet clear that these factors have resulted in reproductive issues, further testing may prove this to be the case in the future.

As to these chemical contaminants listed in the LPC's report, some have been banned for years due to their harmful nature, while others are just now being studied.

DDT was a chemical used in insecticides beginning in the 1940s and used to control mosquitos. It was banned in 1972 due to its effects on humans (a possible carcinogen), as well as in birds, fish and other aquatic animals. In birds, it causes eggshell thinning and effects on embryos that result in a decreased reproductive rate and was a primary cause for the decline of the bald eagle, which was highly publicized. The LPC's 2021 egg contaminant report showed that this chemical was found in 100 percent of the eggs tested.

PCBs are a man-made organic chemical that was banned in 1979. It was used in a wide variety of products, from electronics and appliances to insulation materials, adhesives, tapes, plastic items, oil-based paints, motor oils and a range of other manufactured items. Though no longer widely used (some inadvertent uses are still allowed by the EPA), these chemicals remain in our environment because many of the items that contain them have ended up in landfills or illegal dump sites, the chemicals subsequently leaching into the soil and water. Their possible adverse health effects on animals include cancer and detriments to the immune, reproductive and nerve systems, to name just a few. For humans, PCBs may be carcinogenic, as well as causing neurological and other health effects. The LPC's 2021 egg contaminant report identified several potential hot spots for this chemical, including Squam Lake, Lake Francis (Clarksville) and Merrymeeting Lake (New Durham).

PFAS are a group of man-made chemicals that have been in use since the 1940s, used to waterproof clothing and make fabrics and carpets stain-resistant. They are also used in some cosmetics and firefighting foam, as well as products that are oil, water or grease resistant. Chemicals in the PFAS family include PFOA, PFOS, PFHxS and PFNA. Most of these chemicals do not break down over time, and all persist in the environment for long periods and can build up in the bloodstreams of people and animals. Though PFAS chemicals have been linked to harmful health effects in humans and animals, their full effect is not yet fully known and research is ongoing. They first reached public consciousness in New Hampshire in 2016 when two public water-drinking wells were found to contain a high level of one type of these chemicals in the town of Merrimack, which emanated from the Saint-Gobain factory in that town, a company that manufactures products using these chemicals. In the aftermath of this incident, studies showed that residents in that town had a higher rate of thyroid cancer than the national average and higher levels of three other types of cancers when compared to surrounding towns, but the state's own studies did not agree, and the regulation of these chemicals is still an ongoing debate. However, the LPC is still researching and gathering data on these chemicals and is sounding the alarm bell for loons and, by extension, everyone in New Hampshire. The LPC identified several potential hot spots for these chemicals in its 2021 report, including Canobie Lake (Salem), Arlington Mill Reservoir (Salem) and several territories on Lake Winnipesaukee.

Historically speaking, the first of the chemical contaminants to be studied by the LPC on a statewide basis, in partnership with Dr. David Evers and BRI, was the heavy metal mercury, which is the most prominent of the trace metals that have affected loons. Mercury exposure, caused by eating fish that contain mercury absorbed through the aquatic environment, can affect reproduction rates, including nest in-attentiveness and lethargy, according to BRI's data. Testing showed that New Hampshire and Maine loons were found to have the highest concentrations of mercury among all the loon populations in North America. Mercury's presence in our inland waters is due to two factors: the mercury emissions carried on the winds from in-state coal-fired plants and waste incinerators, as well as those from outside in neighboring states and beyond. The second source of mercury contaminants is from the sites of former chlor-alkali plants that were once used to make chlorinated organic chemicals.

While mercury power-plant emissions were being fought by other environmental groups across the country, the LPC gathered data in New

Hampshire to help determine the local impact in order to back proposed legislation. In all, 70 adult loons and 24 juvenile loons were banded, and early testing results demonstrated that 20 percent of eggs laid by loons in the state were at risk for contamination and that male loons were at the highest risk, somewhere in the range of 20 to 30 percent, for contamination. It was also shown that 20 percent of all juvenile loons, the potential future of our state's population, "had mercury levels that pose a risk to survival." This alone was sobering news.

Further statewide study on a number of lakes in 2000 was conducted, including Armington Lake in Piermont, Bearcamp Pond in Sandwich, Childs Bog and Silver Lake in Harrisville, Eastman Pond in Grantham, Fish Pond in Columbia, Gile Pond in Sutton, Horn Pond in Wakefield, Howe Reservoir in Dublin, Ivanhoe Lake in Wakefield, Millsfield and Moose Ponds in Millsfield, Pawtuckaway Lake in Nottingham, Pemigewasset Lake in Meredith, Pout Pond in Lyme, Sunset Lake in Alton, Walker Pond in Boscawen and Mendums Pond in Barrington. This last body of water was particularly concerning, as an abandoned loon egg found here that was subsequently tested showed a mercury level of 3.92 parts per million (ppm), the highest recorded level at that time of over 400 loon eggs tested from all over North America. It was yet another wake-up call, and with supporting data from the LPC, New Hampshire became the first state in the nation to pass a law regarding emissions from coal-fired power plants and incinerators, in 2002. A few years later, in 2005, another emissions measure (House Bill 1673-FN) was passed in the state, this time based in part on the collected data from loon blood and egg samples that demonstrated the high mercury levels in New Hampshire loons. It required an 80 percent reduction in mercury emissions from the state's five coal-burning plants—Merrimack Units 1 and 2 in Bow and Schiller Units 4, 5 and 6 in Portsmouth—by July 2013. As of early 2023, only one of these plants, the last coal-fired plant in New England, remains in use, one of the Merrimack units in Bow. Its owners are contracted to provide power to the grid through mid-2025, though it may be out of service after that time, as it currently has no contract commitments. One of the Schiller units in Portsmouth, plant no. 5, was converted to burning wood biomass in 2006, while the other two are no longer in daily operation but are available to serve as contributors to the power grid during peak period emergencies. Since the closure of these plants, as well as several others in western Massachusetts that affected southern New Hampshire loons, blood and egg mercury levels in loons in Hampshire have declined.

While the problem may never go away entirely, the LPC's efforts have had results, and mercury levels continue to be monitored.

As for former chlor-alkali plants, one site in Berlin on the Androscoggin River in operation from the 1890s into the 1960s was eventually razed, with debris buried on-site. In 1999, after the last building was demolished that same year, mercury was discovered in the river directly adjacent to the site. Now considered a Superfund Site by the Environmental Protection Agency (EPA), removal of the mercury was attempted, but the toxic metal remains, even though 135 pounds of mercury and mercury-contaminated debris were removed. As a result, the site continues to be monitored. The EPA advises, "The Androscoggin River is currently designated 'catch-and-release' from Berlin downstream to the Maine border. People who disregard this designation and eat fish caught in the river may be exposed to elevated levels of PCBs, mercury, and dioxin, all of which are toxic. Seven rare bird species are known to live or feed close to the Androscoggin River near the Site and could, therefore, be harmed by the contaminants being released from the site. These species include the bald eagle, peregrine falcon, common nighthawk, northern harrier, osprey, common loon, and Cooper's hawk."

Finally, regarding chemical contaminants, it is highly likely that environmental problems will continue to arise for both loons and humans far into the future. In interviewing Dr. Mark Pokras about various contaminants, I was struck by his comments that "there are so many chemicals and the EPA has had a hard time catching up since the 1970s. There is a lack of pre-market testing, and of the 2,000 new chemicals developed each year, the EPA tests only a fraction of them and is falling further behind every year."

Infections and Diseases

Loons, like humans, can be infected by a wide variety of diseases. The leading cause of death for infectious diseases in loons is *Aspergillosis fumigatus*, a fungal infection that was first discovered in a scaup duck in 1813 and in loons in 1866. This blue-green or grayish mold is found in the lungs, airways or air sacs of infected loons and is almost always fatal. LPC biologists can determine its presence in the body through X-rays and, once discovered, usually results in the bird being humanely euthanized to avoid needless suffering for a condition that can't be cured. About 6 percent of loon mortalities in New Hampshire are due to aspergillosis. It should be noted that this infection can also occur in conjunction with other stressors, like lead poisoning, which suppresses the loon's immune system, resulting in a response that can lead to death. Additionally, loons in captivity, according to studies, are extremely sensitive to this fungal disease, which is why they seldom survive for long outside the wild.

Salmonella, a bacterial infection, has also been found in loons but is not a leading cause of death in New Hampshire. Loons, like many animals in the wild, can also be affected by a number of parasites, including nematodes (roundworms) and those transmitted through the bloodstream by such insects as black flies, ticks and mosquitos. Of most concern in recent years are the loons that have been found infected with avian malaria. According to studies by Dr. Ellen Martinsen, Dr. Nina Schoch and Dr. Mark Pokras, loons in the Northeast have been infected with malaria from six different parasites, many of which have origins farther south. Of the 128 loon blood samples from New York, Vermont, Maine, New Hampshire and Massachusetts tested, 14 tested positive for malaria parasites. Half of these came from New Hampshire. This is interesting because it was in New Hampshire in 2015 that the first case of malaria in a loon, a new threat, was discovered in a dead bird recovered from Lake Umbagog. This loon was examined by Dr. Inga Sidor at the New Hampshire Veterinary Diagnostic Laboratory at the University of New Hampshire in Durham and suspected to have died of malaria, with tissue samples sent to Dr. Ellen Martinsen of the Smithsonian Conservation Biology Institute. The bird was confirmed to have two different malarial parasites in the brain, heart and lungs, possibly dying from a heart attack or cerebral paralysis. This discovery, especially so far north, was a complete shock and was yet another possible result of climate change. This loon was the first ever in the Northeast to have died from a tropical disease, with nature writer Derrick Z. Jackson terming this death "as haunting as their wailing cries in the middle of the night," while LPC senior biologist John Cooley Jr. stated that "you would have expected it [Lake Umbagog] to be a safe haven longer than you'd expect along the coast or in southern New Hampshire. It's sort of the last place you'd expect a mosquito-borne disease." How prevalent malaria may become in the loon population in New Hampshire is yet to be known, but sample collection is ongoing, and the disease remains a concern.

Another potential threat for New Hampshire loons is the avian influenza epizootic that has seen a global increase since 2020. This outbreak, the first significant avian flu outbreak since 2006, has occurred largely among domestic poultry flocks and first hit America in December 2021 when the virus was discovered in a wigeon duck in South Carolina. Wild aquatic birds like gulls and shorebirds and waterfowl like ducks, geese and swans are natural hosts for this disease, which infects the gastrointestinal and respiratory tracts. While most birds are asymptomatic, they can infect domestic poultry. How devastating this outbreak may become is not yet known, but avian flu is now found in 47 states and has, at a conservative estimate, killed tens of thousands of wild birds worldwide. Though most of these are seabirds that nest colonially, the LPC believes that the loon could be at risk and is on high alert.

THE WILD WEST ON SQUAM

Having discussed the varied threats to New Hampshire loons, it is important to understand that these do not occur in a vacuum and that multiple threats affect loons simultaneously on New Hampshire's lakes. However, when such events take place in quick succession and over a prolonged period, the ecological balance can be upset, resulting in chaos and turmoil for loon populations, which in turn affects reproductive success. Nowhere is this more apparent than on Squam Lake, where the LPC's Squam Lakes biologist Tiffany Grade has her hands full and, honestly, never knows what to expect from year to year. This lake is a legacy one for the LPC—it's where Rawson Wood had his summer home and first became interested in loon conservation—and, as Grade commented, it has "had the most awareness and eyes on it." It was here in 1976 that the first loon to be documented as dying from lead poisoning, anywhere in the world, was discovered. For the first 30 years of the LPC, Squam Lake was relatively stable. That all changed in 2004–05, when the lake had the largest single drop in its number of territorial pairs, from 16 to 9. After several years of further decline, only 1 chick was hatched on the lake in 2007. That same year, the LPC launched its Squam Lake Loon Initiative and began testing loon eggs for possible changes in the food web. All these tests came back negative. The factors on Squam over the years that were contributing causes to this decline include the improvement of the one public boat ramp on the lake in 2001. This created more boat traffic and greatly increased fishing activities, and as a result, loons suffered. The number of loon lead mortalities doubled, and boat strikes became more common, with three boat strike mortalities since 2008. These numbers might seem small, but remember that many deaths like these have multiple effects on loon chicks and long-term future reproductive success.

And then there was the contaminant issue that reared its ugly head. On the northern shore of the lake there is an old apple orchard that once had a barn and outbuildings. An older resident recalled that chemical spraying in this area was frequent, and the finding of DDT in the soil and sediments likely resulted from the past on-site storage of this now long-banned chemical and a recent "intense runoff event from tributaries to the lake," as Grade characterized it. Because of the nature of this contamination source, the NH Department of Environmental Sciences could offer no help, and the problem fell through the cracks. In all, crayfish testing by the LPC and Plymouth State and sediment testing by the LPC revealed three areas of the lake with elevated levels of contaminants, two with DDT and one with PCBS, dioxins and furans. Further searching for the source of contaminants around the lake by Grade and her team resulted in the finding that, off the many old dirt roads in the area, many of which were once treated with oil (which contained PCBs) to keep the dust down, there were some illegal dumping sites for things like old electronics. In effect, while Squam has all the appearance of a pristine lake, there is more there than meets the eye when it comes to long-term human impact. It is speculated perhaps that the steep decline in breeding success on Squam coincided with that runoff in the early 2000s. That this contaminant issue may come into play in some of the lake's loon territories was highlighted in 2022 by Grade in a comparison of the performance of the Moultonborough Bay and Sturtevant Cove territorial loons. Even though Sturtevant Cove had no nesting in 2022 (only the third failure in 10 years), the LPC and residents know that it is one of the most consistently productive on Squam and has been so for quite some time, hatching 10 chicks and fledging 6 of them in the past 10 years. The Moultonborough Bay territorial pairs, however, have had a poor rate of reproduction success, ranking near the bottom among all the lake's territories and producing but 1 chick in that same period. Grade looked at the contaminant levels found in inviable loon eggs gathered from failed nests in these territories since 2000, revealing that of the five contaminant categories tested for, those for Moultonborough Bay tested higher in four of them. While it is unknown if these contaminant levels are directly responsible for the differences in breeding success, they very possibly have played a part. Happily, in a year when Sturtevant Cove produced no chicks, Moultonborough Bay had a rare success, hatching its first chicks in 10 years, with 1 of them fledging successfully. It has been speculated that by 2008 the released contaminants had "mostly flushed through the Squam system" and that perhaps the food web was recovering. Forthcoming testing results may, hopefully, confirm this, and Moultonborough Bay could be one of the territories reaping the benefits of recovery.

So, these aforementioned factors—more people on the lake, increased lead poisonings from fishing activities and a rise in unseen and previously undetected contaminants—combined with advancing climate change factors, including avian malaria, resulted in what Grade has called "the perfect storm" and a situation of low-level chronic mortality. This proverbial storm has resulted, for loons, in "social chaos, a breakdown of the social order," also known as territorial destabilization. Think of it this way: when a parent loon dies from a boat strike or lead poisoning, this has several immediate results—its chick will almost certainly be killed by an intruding loon trying to take over the territory, both of which events decrease reproductive rates. Throw on top of that the possible effects from some of the newly discovered contaminants in the lake. Some biologists hypothesize that ingestion of these harmful chemicals by loons has led to increased or "hyper-aggressive" territorial behavior, resulting in a never-ending summertime battle for territory that seems to occur more on Squam than any other lake. Were these factors, for example, at play when that band of rogue loons, infamously known as the "gang of 10," way back in 1988, terrorized the lake? We can never know but, as Grade has commented on more recent events, "These factors cast a long shadow over the loon population on Squam." So, what gives her hope for the future? She cites two main factors: first that the people around Squam "care so much and are very invested" in their loons. The second is that the LPC is "doing the most focused research on Squam, and what we learn here we can apply elsewhere." As previously stated, the loon's importance as a sentinel species cannot be overlooked.

The Future

With all these threats and the varied factors in play, it is impossible to know the future of the loon in New Hampshire, and even among biologists there is a difference of opinion. Former Lake Winnipesaukee field biologist Ralph Kirshner, who worked in the first few years of the LPC's existence and wrote the first report for that lake, believes the future is bleak, stating that "I don't have any hope that in 20 years there will be loons breeding anywhere in the U.S.," primarily due to climate change.

Another early LPC biologist, Connie Manville Johnson, is pessimistic, but for a different reason. She said, "I think people are going to continue to be the problem. There's so much boat traffic [on Lake Winnipesaukee] and it's 100 times worse than when we started, and some shorelines are now packed solid with houses. It's terrible."

Wildlife rehabilitator Maria Colby, too, has her worries: "I see in the next 50 years there won't be any loons in New Hampshire….They can only tolerate so much," referencing not only climate change but also the development issues on many bodies of water.

However, not everyone is so pessimistic. Dr. Mark Pokras offers a perspective that most can relate to: "I go up and down on the question of loon survival in New England….I am hopeful because the inventory of scientific resources we have is keeping up with the threats."

Finally, there are the men and women of the LPC themselves. They, of course, believe in their mission of restoring and growing the loon population in New Hampshire. However, while they are not unaware of the difficulties they face, they are putting the power of science—in the form of contaminant research, banding efforts and improvements in rafting methods—and a grassroots and cooperative approach, working with local conservation groups, lake associations, dam operators, state and federal agencies and their large volunteer network to get the job done. And the numbers are growing. As LPC director Harry Vogel commented, "We don't know what would happen to the loon population [in New Hampshire] if our work went away, but our intensive management program is working well and we project that it will continue in this manner for the foreseeable future."

It is hard to disagree with Vogel, and having gotten to know a little something about the men and women of the LPC, I feel that the future of our loons is in excellent hands. Humans all over the world have offered a great amount of support to save such iconic species as the panda bear, the polar bear, whales, elephants, the bald eagle and many others. The loons right here in New Hampshire are well worthy of that same support. Objectively, we know that there are plenty of loons in far northern places, so they are not yet threatened with extinction as a species. But that reasoning isn't good enough for me, and I suspect that you who are reading this may feel the same. I want to experience loons, hear their wild calls and see them in all their varied plumage, right here where I live in New Hampshire, and I want my grandson, and his children too, to be able to do the same. The LPC is working hard to make my wishes, and those of countless others, a reality for years in the future, and that gives me hope.

7

UNRAVELING THE SECRETS
OF THE LOON

As one of the premier scientific organizations in the state, the LPC has worked diligently to expand our knowledge about the mysterious loon. As many loon experts have commented, the loon is a somewhat "strange" or even "weird" bird, and unraveling their secrets can be tricky business. However, the LPC has made many important loon discoveries, and while some of their work, including field operations, raft placements, loon rescues and the annual Loon Census, have been well-publicized, other aspects remain out of the public eye or less well-known. Here, we'll take a look at three key LPC operations and examine how they have added to our loon knowledge.

THE LPC LOONCAM

Now, at first glance, the LPC's annual LoonCam broadcasts may not seem to fit in this category of "out of the public eye" scientific activities. However, consider this—how many LoonCam viewers consider their livestream broadcasts a scientific tool rather than a form of entertainment? The LoonCam is actually both, and for LPC biologists, these cameras, rolling 24-7, offer a unique insight into loon behaviors. The original goal of LPC biologists and Bill Gassman was to develop a LoonCam system, the best in the business, and in the beginning, there were huge challenges to overcome.

Finding a suitable location was the priority, which was done on an island where a resident had internet service. At first, the bandwidth was limited, but the technical bugs were eventually worked out. After the first two years, an additional LoonCam was added. Power was generated by the aid of 200-watt solar panels, the cameras used being basically security cameras, the same you might see on a highway. They have a 30x zoom feature that offers great close-up shots of loons doing all sorts of things. The infrared lighting is what allows for the excellent nighttime viewing, while the microphones are wrapped in pillow foam and placed in waterproof PVC piping and embedded in the nesting raft. These microphones are so sensitive that you can hear the peeping and pecking sounds a chick makes as it emerges from the egg. This infrared capacity is a key to the whole operation. As Dr. Mark Pokras commented, "We don't know much about what loons are doing at night…. That's a big hole in our knowledge." The LoonCams have helped in this regard, as well as offering new perspectives on a variety of loon behaviors. For example, while it was known through anecdotal sources that predation by eagles was increasing, the LoonCam actually caught one of these events as it happened live for the first time. Other scientific observations include the following: eggs in the middle phase of incubation that have gone untended for 10 hours can remain viable in some situations; loons have a wider variety of nesting schedules between males and females than previously thought, as the LPC acknowledged, "As soon as we start predicting who will be on the nest at a certain time, the pair will call our bluff"; and loons have more ways of losing eggs than was previously thought. Many eggs are lost to predators (both by land and by air), boat wakes can wash them away, loons can accidentally knock them out of the nest and sometimes humans are even suspected of stealing them. However, the 2019 LoonCam captured an egg that was accidentally buried in the mud by one of the loon pair. As the LPC states, all these events "add to our knowledge base and reminds us that we don't know everything [about loons] and sometimes we don't even know what we think we know." For the viewer, the LoonCam opens a whole new world and gives us a glimpse into the environment of a territorial pair. We get to see and hear them up close and personal, observing their behaviors at all times of the day, whether it be calling to each other, the nest exchange, periodically turning their eggs or seeing their interactions with wildlife visitors to the nesting raft, including turtles, ducks, geese and even a heron. While all the camera footage is highly interesting, I particularly enjoy the nighttime view and accompanying sounds. Not only does this footage offer insight to the activities of loons at night, but it is also somewhat otherworldly

The LPC's LoonCam has captured some amazing images over the years, including visitors to the loon nesting rafts like this heron in the 2018 season. *Courtesy LPC.*

and oddly calming. Just how popular is the LoonCam? It had some 360,000 views worldwide in 2023, which makes our New Hampshire loons some of the most famous on the planet!

As to problems that the LoonCam has faced over the years, folks have hit the post it is mounted on with their boats, while others, once having discovered the camera, will "photobomb" the LoonCam—whether out of ignorance for the camera's purpose or a desire to gain a bit of internet fame isn't always clear. Luckily, the incidents seem to be few and far between. Which brings us to one of the most often-asked questions: "Where are the LoonCams located, on what lakes?" Well, that is information the LPC tries to keep secret, for obvious reasons. In some cases, the same site has been used for years, so some locals are in the know. But most folks respect the fact that it's best for the loons to keep the location secret. Gassman does an excellent job in monitoring the messaging chat on YouTube and keeping the chatters focused on loon-related talk. If you have not used the chat feature, consider giving it a try. Along with the chat feature on YouTube, viewers can also tune into the LPC's website to read the LoonCam blog posts authored by biologist Chris "Biff" Conrod. His posts offer both scientific and humorous insights into the behaviors that are occurring on camera, as well as some historic background. Between the YouTube chat and Conrod's posts, it's a great way to learn about the loon behaviors that are happening before your very eyes around the clock. As far as what to expect, Gassman comments that there is drama every year on the LoonCam, and if it's not earlier, it comes later. His hardest work, the "payoff" as he calls it, comes in the 48 hours immediately after a chick is hatched, when there is much action and the viewing audience is high. However, for both Gassman and LoonCam viewers, there can be difficult moments to watch, including seeing nests flooded or moments of sibling rivalry. Perhaps the worst came when a loon chick emerged from its egg, only to be predated immediately. This was a shock not just to viewers but Gassman too, who recalled that "within seconds it was over." Such incidents are a reminder that the LoonCam is a scientific observational tool, and from its live images, the LPC has learned much about loon nesting behaviors over the years.

BANDING OPERATIONS

Bird-banding operations have a long history worldwide that dates back far into antiquity. The first birds mentioned, the swallow around 218 BC and the pigeon by 44 BC, were banded by ancient Romans in order to use them as messengers. The first bandings used to identify a bird's owner, primarily falcons and hawks, and their place of origin, got their start in the 15th century, but the first bird known to have been banded and thus identified on its return for 10 years in a row was a bluebird, probably in the early 1600s. Here in America, the first informal bandings took place in 1803, conducted by John J. Audubon using a silver piece of thread. However, it wasn't until 1902 that systematic banding was begun. So, it's been a tried-and-true scientific method of gathering bird data for over 120 years. However, loons were not included in these efforts until very recently. This was for two reasons: early on, few people saw the need to band loons, and even after loon conservation efforts began, it was found that loons are difficult birds to catch and band. Dr. David Evers and his team performed the first loon banding work in New Hampshire. His work here started in 1992, first on several lakes in the central and southern part of the state and then primarily on Lake Umbagog in 1993 and later. From a public standpoint, these first loon-banding operations by Evers and his team got off to an interesting start, and many folks, especially LPC volunteers and lake-side residents, were opposed to the idea. They were concerned about the spotlights shining across their lakes and were unsure what was going on, and as former LPC director Jeff Fair recalled, "I received lots of phone calls and letters complaining of the late banding nights and telling me to leave the loons alone....People, good people, forget to communicate." On Lake Umbagog, one camp resident was so angered with this activity that he fired off several shotgun rounds to scare off the unknown searchlight-wielding intruders. However, the LPC quickly stepped in and solved these types of issues with public outreach to lake residents and volunteers wherever banding was to take place, as well as educating them about the value of this activity and that the loons were being handled carefully and respectfully. From this time forward, LPC biologists would be involved in New Hampshire loon banding efforts. Jeff Fair, after leaving the LPC, continued to work on loon conservation efforts in Maine and on Lake Umbagog. A "conservative" biologist who had rarely banded any birds, he "actually started going out with Dave's crew in order to judge how the loons were being treated. They were very carefully handled, and in cases of overheating, they were released back onto the lake, etc. I trusted them."

Since those early days over 30 years ago, 665 loons have been banded in New Hampshire as of the end of summer 2023, including 5 fitted with geolocators from the following lakes: Winnisquam (2012), Mirror Lake in Tuftonboro and Hatch Pond in Eaton (2013) and Massabesic Lake at Birch Island and Squam Lake at Moon Island (2014). So, how do the banding operations work, and what have they told us about New Hampshire's loons?

Banding operations always take place at night, usually just after sunset, though they can sometimes stretch far into the night. Loons are not banded during the day for one simple reason: they are impossible to catch. However, at night, the banding crew uses a variety of tools to get the job done. Even before the nighttime operations begin, the target loon, or loons, is identified, whether on a single-territory lake or a lake with multiple territories. Operations usually take place, except in the case of rescued birds, after the target territorial pairs chicks have hatched, usually beginning in early summer. The length of time these nightly operations takes really depends on how easily the loon can be caught. The team will shine spotlights on the water, hoping to catch a loon in the beam of light and cause it to freeze briefly in place. This light, combined with a recorded loon call, makes the loon think there might be another loon behind the light. The adult loon, trying to defend its chick or keep its family safe, may stay in place long enough to be captured, scooped up in a salmon net, or may dive. The trick is to keep the spotlight on the loon: if the light dips down and catches any part of the boat, the loon will be able to see the people trying to capture it and will make a speedy getaway. When this happens, the trick is to figure out where the escaping loon may resurface. Some people, like Jeff Fair, seem to have a knack for sensing where the loon may reappear, but at other times it can be a lengthy process. Once the loon is captured and brought aboard the boat, the banding process begins. Handling a loon in these operations can be a difficult task; their head is gently draped with a cloth covering so that their sharp bill cannot be used as a weapon, though sometimes the loons are successful in pecking their handlers. The other end of the loon can be challenging too, as the frightened bird will often defecate. Once the bird is firmly but gently in hand, a feather sample is taken; a blood sample is drawn from their leg; and key measurements are taken, such as weight, bill length and overall length. Bands are applied to both legs. On the right leg of an adult banded loon (on the left if a juvenile) is applied a silver metal Federal Bird Band, stamped with a unique eight- or nine-digit number, along with some contact information should the bird be found, dead or alive. Though the band itself is visible in the wild, the number is usually not unless a bird is recovered, usually not in good circumstances. Should you happen to recover a bird of any type with such a band, you can report the bird band at www.reportband.gov, though if it's a loon the LPC should also be contacted, and if deceased, the carcass should be held and turned over to the LPC if possible, for scientific study. On the left leg of the bird are applied color-coded bands of two or three different colors, these leg bands visible while the loon is in the wild and are an identifier when or if they are sighted. I had a chance to watch LPC biologist Caroline Hughes, with assistance from Maria Colby holding the bird and myself holding its legs still, perform a banding operation on land on a rescued loon prior to it being released into the ocean at Odiorne Point in Rye. The operation of drawing blood, banding and taking measurements was quick and painless for the loon, taking about 15 minutes, which is typical for operations out on the lake. The flat leg bones of the loon make banding them different than most birds, which have circular leg bones, and so crimping the bands requires a bit more work. Once all this work is done and the data recorded, the loon is released back into the water, where it will quickly dive away. Depending on difficulty of capture, time and distance traveled, several loons may be banded in a good night's work.

It should be noted that five loons from the state, as noted by senior biologist John Cooley Jr., have been "fitted with geolocators that record light-based geolocation (a modern, miniaturized digital sextant, basically) but do not transmit the data. You have to recapture the loon and retrieve the device to download the data. The light-based technique is also imprecise, within

50–300 km [31–186 miles] of actual location. So, we've retrieved two of them. One didn't work (the one from Hatch Pond in Eaton), and the other one, from Bow Lake, confirmed winter range in the Gulf of Maine, which was expected. The geolocator units are tiny and fit on the outside of the usual plastic leg bands. They are a fraction of the cost of the satellite/radio transmitter units used in the early 2000s," which were "implanted surgically."

So, what has been learned from these banded loons? First, it should be noted that feather and blood samples are not only archived but also tested for mercury and lead poisoning, with the latter condition able to be determined in quick time by field testing. The blood DNA is also important in that it can determine the area of origin of the loon, as well as provide definitive proof on the sex of the bird. However, one of the most interesting of the early findings was that by the resighting of these banded birds on a variety of lakes, it was determined that, contrary to popular belief, loons do not mate for life but instead may take another mate if they have poor reproductive success or because of territorial disputes that result in a pair member being displaced. The other interesting aspect of bandings is that of recovered or resighted loons while they are outside of New Hampshire after their winter migration. From this data, it was discovered that a loon banded on Lake Massabesic spends its winters in the waters of Narragansett Bay in Rhode Island, while another loon from a pond in western New Hampshire wintered in Rhode Island Sound. Meanwhile, a loon banded on Squam went eastward, spending its winters off the mid-Maine coast. Conversely, a deceased banded adult loon recovered in Kingston in June 2021 was found to have been originally banded on a lake in Minnesota in 1998 and was at least 26 years old. It is speculated that the loon was in poor health and, unable to migrate back to its home state that spring, "strayed" into New Hampshire.

This migration data is important not just for tracking movements, but the resighting of many of these loons, like the Sweat Meadows female on the Androscoggin River, year after year gives insight into the lifespan of the loon. While the Sweat Meadows female as of this writing is one of the oldest known loons anywhere, and the oldest in New England, this information could never have been known without banding. Too, the disappearance of a banded bird from its longtime home lake can be an indicator that it has become deceased or has possibly gone elsewhere. Loons, once they reach breeding age, will typically return to an area, called the "dispersal" range, within 3 or 4 miles of the lake where it was hatched, but there are cases where the dispersal range has been discovered by the use of banding data to be more far-ranging than was ever thought to be the case before. The first known occurrence of a wider dispersal range came in 2017, when a loon banded on Walker Pond in Boscawen in 1999 turned up on Tower Hill Pond in Auburn, some 25 miles away. This loon had originally stayed on Walker Pond through 2002 but then disappeared until showing up in Auburn 15 years later. Where this loon may have been during this time is unknown, though the LPC speculates that it may have been displaced from multiple territories over the years. Sadly, this far-ranging loon died on Tower Hill Pond as a result of lead poisoning after having hatched a chick. An even more unusual case of dispersal happened in 2019 with my favorite loon in Wolfeboro, whose cries I began hearing out my window that same year and whose story is told in the next chapter. As I've mentioned previously, in some cases, sick or injured banded loons have sometimes been recovered far away from what was thought to be their normal wintering range, including a bird that made its way down to Cape May, New Jersey, and the, so far, longest-known distant migrant, a banded loon from Pioneer Pond in Stoddard recovered off the North Carolina coast. While both loons met a sad end, even in death their banding increased our knowledge of the movement of New Hampshire loons.

Finally, one may wonder how many of the 655 loons that have been banded over the last 31 years are still alive. Cooley's explanation provides some insight: "Based on an approximate annual survival rate of 92–94 percent, perhaps as many as 400 or more of the totals that have been banded have died over time, through expected attrition. We resighted 141 this year [2022], out of perhaps as many as 160–200 that are likely to be extant/surviving and returning." Of the banded loons, through 2022, 146 have been reported as deceased: "The recoveries [are] based on reports where an observer found a dead banded loon and reported it to the central banding lab; often those come in from a beach walker in the winter."

LOON NECROPSIES

Ever since 1976, when the first loon ever confirmed to have died from lead poisoning, a bird from Squam Lake, was discovered, the LPC has been engaged in medically examining deceased loons. This procedure is used to determine the various causes of death for loons, in order to gain further knowledge in pursuit of their conservation efforts. This work is done through a process known as a necropsy, the animal equivalent of a human autopsy. Since the LPC has only recently gained the space and equipment to aid in the performance of necropsies, this work was first done on their behalf by veterinarian experts from outside New Hampshire. These included Dr. Mark Pokras and his veterinarian students at Tufts University, as well as, early on, the U.S. Fish and Wildlife Service. Today, necropsies are largely performed at the LPC's headquarters in Moultonborough by either staff biologists—primarily John Cooley Jr. and Caroline Hughes, as well as summer biology or veterinarian interns—or a visiting expert like Pokras. So, what exactly does a necropsy look like? These examinations take place largely during the winter season, when the LPC's field activities have wound down, there usually being a backlog of loon carcasses stored in the LPC's refrigerators. Each deceased loon brought to the LPC is tagged, with data surrounding either its finding or circumstances of its death if known. Prior to being necropsied, the loon carcasses are thawed before being brought to the LPC's wet laboratory for the procedure.

I had the privilege of witnessing two necropsies that took place at the LPC in January 2023, with a visiting Dr. Mark Pokras leading the efforts. Three birds were originally chosen to be necropsied, but the one from Lower Baker Pond in Orford, a chick that was all but certain to have died due to eagle predation, was eventually set aside for another day's work. The other two birds were a chick from Pool Pond in Rindge (humanely euthanized due to compound wing fractures in August 2022) and a juvenile (age undetermined) that was recovered from the ice on Partridge Pond in Littleton in early December 2022 and subsequently humanely euthanized because it was believed to have aspergillosis. Prior to being opened up for examination, each loon was weighed and measured, with Caroline Hughes in charge of the Pool Pond loon necropsy and Dr. Pokras leading the examination of the Littleton loon, assisted by Winnipesaukee field biologist and student Ashley Keenan, with John Cooley Jr. following both examinations. Hughes showed me the broken wing of the Rindge chick, multiple breaks that were inflicted by an intruder loon and injuries from which the bird could not recover and survive in the wild. Hughes speculated that an examination of the chick might show that it was underfed, as its mother was previously killed. As a result, the father was left to defend two chicks (one of which survived), leaving less time to feed them. However, on opening the bird, it was shown to be surprisingly well-fed, a testament to its embattled parent. Further examination of its gizzard, lungs and vital organs were also made, with blood taken, a primary feather saved and tissue samples harvested to be sent to Dr. Ellen Martinsen's lab in Vermont for avian malaria testing. In the end, there was no mystery here as to its cause of death, and it was hoped that the valiant father of this loon would return to Pool Pond in 2023.

The juvenile loon necropsied by Pokras and Keenan from Littleton was, as it would turn out, a highly interesting case. After being iced-in and subsequently captured, this loon was humanely euthanized because X-rays showed what was thought to be the presence of aspergillosis in the lungs and air sacs, this manifested as numerous white spots. Remember that aspergillosis cannot be cured and the respiratory effects cause the loon great suffering. Pokras pointed out these spots to all, a sight that LPC biologists are all too familiar with, as well as the remnants of a fishing hook in the loon's gizzard. It seemed an open-and-shut case, but nonetheless the necropsy was begun. While the bird was being measured, all present were amazed at the size and otherwise healthy appearance of the bird and could only speculate on its age. Whether it was a loon chick from elsewhere, perhaps Vermont, that had stopped on Partridge Pond during its first migration to the ocean or an older, second-year immature loon that had somehow made its way inland was unknown. It was also unknown, and remained so, why the loon was not compelled to leave Partridge Pond. Pokras, ever the teacher, opened the bird, with Keenan's assistance, pointing out different features of its anatomy and what to look for while doing so. I hadn't known what to expect but found the necropsy and Pokras's comments highly enlightening. In the approximately one-hour procedure, I learned more about loon physiology than from any book I'd read. I couldn't help but think of some of those TV crime dramas, like *CSI*, where the autopsies of the victims help reveal the cause of death and who the killer may have been. Little did I know that Pokras, the world's record holder for loon necropsies, also gives a PowerPoint presentation on loons titled "Loon CSI."

Once opened, it was clearly evident that the Littleton loon was well-fed. I was amazed at the rather small size of the bird's voice box—based on the loud and powerful calls a loon makes, I expected it to be bigger. The examination of the gizzard and its contents was also highly interesting. A count was made of the number of stones found there, used to help digest a loon's prey that is swallowed whole. Despite the fishhook that was clearly visible on the X-ray, no remnants of the hook could be found anywhere, which was a bit of a mystery. Pokras also pointed out the body cavity where the joints of the loon's legs are located, which provided a better understanding, visually, of why these birds are so ungainly on land. As with the other bird necropsied this day, tissue, feather and blood samples were also taken for future testing. However, the biggest surprises in this necropsy were the white spots around the bird's lungs and air sacs. Pokras spent some time examining these and made an unusual discovery. These spots were not aspergillosis but merely deposits of fat, an indicator that this immature loon was a well-fed bird indeed. This was baffling to all, including Pokras, who was quite surprised and stated that such a finding was a first for him. In effect, the Partridge Pond loon was a healthy bird. This highly unusual finding was somewhat of a blow to LPC biologists, as the decision to euthanize a loon is never taken lightly, but decisions are made in the field with the information on hand based on the best-known science. As a result of this new scientific finding, LPC field protocols for loons with suspected aspergillosis based on X-rays will be changed. And that, in a nutshell, is why necropsies on deceased loons are performed, so that the further mysteries of the loon may be unraveled, thereby increasing the knowledge of those working to conserve loons in New Hampshire and beyond.

PART III

NEW HAMPSHIRE LAKE ACCOUNTS

In this section, we take a closer look at the loons on several of New Hampshire's lakes and ponds, based on the personal experiences of resident observers. These are regular folks like myself, most LPC volunteers, with no wildlife expertise, who have a fascination with, and strong bond to, these treasured birds and hold their experiences dear as a part of the New Hampshire way of life. This small sampling is representative of what is happening all over the state. Even if your lake is not mentioned here, chances are, if it has loons, you'll recognize the same challenges, behaviors, triumphs and tragedies that follow. Though official LPC reports for 2023 were not yet compiled when this book went to press, I have included reports from observers on these lakes.

1

ADVENTURES WITH THE LOONS OF BARNSTEAD

My first close-up experiences with loons came on several lakes and ponds in Barnstead. During the summers, my wife and I rent a lake house somewhere in that town and invite our family from both far and wide to come and stay for an extended visit. Being the parents and caregivers of our beloved daughter Anna, who is disabled and requires around-the-clock care, we seldom get away from home, so our time at the lake is especially important. Terry enjoys a cup of coffee while gazing at the lake in the morning in quiet solitude. Me? I enjoy spending some time with whatever loons I can find in the early morning hours, a brief spell of wild solitude and wonder, combined with a bit of a kayak workout.

The summer of 2018 was our first on 149-acre Locke Lake. I took up kayaking this year, without any expectation of seeing any water birds beyond some mallards or geese. The shore of this lake is well-developed, and there is not much to explore, but being out on the open water was nonetheless enjoyable. And it was here, in the center of the lake, that I encountered my first loons close-up, a pair of them in their beautiful summer plumage. They were quite curious at my appearance on that late August day, the only watercraft on the lake at that time, and I was able to get a nice view while floating quietly. It is a memory that is seared in my brain. We coexisted there peacefully for about 20 minutes before they finally dove away. Several more times during the time I spent at Locke Lake, a single loon would make an appearance in my vicinity, almost always in the late afternoon, usually just floating lazily or performing preening activities. The following year,

2019, only a single loon was ever spotted at one time while I was out on the water, again usually out in the center of the lake toward the late afternoon. I would later learn that the loons on Locke Lake for both years were floaters, this body of water not recorded as having a territorial pair since the LPC began keeping records in 1975. This is not surprising, as the developed shoreline, combined with the fact that there are no islands for loon nests, makes it unsuitable. However, perhaps these loons were scouting out the lake for a potential home, for in 2020 a territorial pair nested on the lake but hatched no chicks. In 2021, no loons were recorded here, possibly due to water quality issues, including a cyanobacteria bloom. However, in 2022 a territorial pair nested, again without success. Whether Locke Lake can ever support a territorial pair is open to question, but the loons are trying.

In 2020, we stayed on Huntress Pond, a peaceful but smaller body of water, without any islands and, once again, with a well-developed shoreline. By now, while out kayaking, I hoped that I would encounter some loons, but my expectations this year were low. However, one morning I spotted a lone loon, busy preening and unconcerned by my presence at a respectable distance. I would see a single loon on one other day during my weeklong stay on Huntress Pond, and that was that. Once again, though surveyed over the years, Huntress Pond, a mere 49 acres in size, has not had a territorial pair of loons recorded since the LPC began keeping records.

In subsequent years, my wife and I moved our summer vacation stays to Lower Suncook Lake, a 295-acre body of water averaging about nine feet in depth. While it does have three small islands, the lakeshore is heavily developed. This lake is also connected by a narrow channel to Upper Suncook Lake, which is 402 acres in size and less developed, having some conservation lands on its eastern and northern shorelines. In 2021, during a weeklong stay on Lower Suncook, I noticed a pair of loons many times during the course of my kayak outings, most of the time on the northwestern part of the lake, but also on the eastern shoreline parallel to Ridge Road. This pair was active, and the first time I saw them was while I was out kayaking during a minor hurricane in the midmorning hours. I also several times observed a pair of loons foraging in the channel between Lower and Upper Suncook. The last time this occurred, just before the end of my stay, they were in proximity to a fishing boat, the angler manning it having no idea that loons were in the waters right behind and beside him.

That same year, 2021, I spent quite a bit of time among the pair of loons on Upper Suncook, always in the center of the lake, and always in the morning hours. Indeed, during my last morning before heading home, I floated in proximity to them for a half an hour, barely raising a paddle except to turn the kayak around, after they surfaced close to my position and floated rather contentedly nearby after a bout of feeding. At one point, I did drift too close to them, probably about 75 feet off, and the larger loon, probably the male, rose high out of the water and flapped his wings. I immediately got the message and moved farther away, a reminder that the LPC advises boaters to stay 150 feet away from loons at all times if possible.

Upper Suncook's loons have had an up-and-down history. From 1975 to 1988, the LPC recorded no loons on the lake at all. In 1989, there was a territorial pair, but no nesting occurred then, and there were no loons on the lake for another nine years. Ever since 1998, there has been a territorial pair on Upper Suncook. Successful nesting attempts were made in 1999, 2002–03, 2008 and 2010–14, resulting in 18 chicks being hatched and 15 surviving. However, since that time, including in 2023, the pairs have nested but failed to produce any chicks. What factors may be disrupting breeding there is unknown, but there are a number of potential stressors on that lake, including an increase in bald eagles, likely territorial intrusions, as well as the boating activity and at least one float-plane that operates there.

Finally, several of my encounters with the loons on Lower Suncook in August 2022 and 2023 were quite interesting. Prior to this time, none in our party had ever heard any loon sounds on any of the Barnstead lakes and ponds, primarily because our stays were always in the late summertime, when loons are less territorial. But not on a mid-August night in 2022— just around sunset, a few wails were heard and then things quieted down. They started up again about 9:00 p.m., immediately after someone began letting off loud fireworks, the wails getting louder and more intense until the fireworks stopped after about 8 minutes. Clearly, the loons were stressed out at this noisy disruption. All stayed quiet for almost an hour, but at 10:00 p.m., wails were again heard from across the lake, lasting about 10 minutes. Was this a call for a nighttime gathering of loons? Exactly an hour later, the wails started up yet again, but this time some tremolo calls and one yodel by a male were heard. It was clear that something was up, but after about 5 minutes, the calls subsided and all was peaceful for the remainder of the night.

The next morning, I went out kayaking a bit earlier than usual, before 6:30 a.m. While heading out on the lake, I noticed some loons flying overhead, approximately six to seven in number. I headed for the far western shore, where I had spotted a territorial pair in the days before. I saw no loons or any bird activity in that area, so I turned and headed back toward the center of the lake. As I approached closer to one of the islands, I began to hear a lone loon wailing but could not see it. I continued and soon encountered a group of six or seven loons all swimming together, looming out of the early morning fog. This social gathering was a remarkable sight, the first time I had seen more than two loons gathered together in one location. I stayed within a respectful distance of this group as they maneuvered around the lake, the loons occasionally stopping, peering into the water, circling about and making short dives. At one point, there was a minor escalation when one of the loons rose out of the water into a "vulture" posture, but things quickly quieted down. Shortly after this, I witnessed my first loon water landing when one hit the lake several hundred feet in front of me. I then heard a loud splash behind me, within 25 feet, only to see another loon that had also just landed and very quickly dove away. It seemed like everything was happening all at once, and shortly after this, both loons joined the other group I had been tracking. Periodically, throughout the 45 minutes I had been observing this growing group, now up to eight to nine loons, a single loon would wail, though I could never see the bird. I had seen a bald eagle perched on a tall tree on the island in question, and it is possible this was what was causing concern. Eventually, after I followed the loons for another 20 minutes, two of the loons dove and disappeared, never to be seen again, while yet another took off from the lake after a plaintive wail. Eventually, each of the remaining loons dove for one last time and disappeared out of sight. Left alone, I began to paddle home, when I saw a lone loon, circling in the water. The bird subsequently dipped its head in the water, and then, when at its most buoyant state and sitting high, hesitated as if checking the wind direction and then began paddling eastward across the water and flapping its wings furiously, taking to the air after about 150 feet. This was my first time witnessing a loon takeoff. As I paddled back home, I saw four loons flying silently back over the lake. The loon that had been wailing periodically somewhere in the vicinity of the island began wailing again but soon stopped, and a short time later I saw a single loon flying overhead in a rush to join its companions. As I approached our lake house, I spotted one more loon feeding close to the shoreline. By the time I arrived home at 8:00 a.m., my loon observations had lasted an hour and 40 minutes. It was a great start to the day observing this type of social gathering, which is typical in the late summer.

Where all these loons, which had no visible leg bands, had come from for their social gatherings is unknown. In 2022, two pairs certainly came from the Suncooks, while the others could have been floaters from other locales

A late season, early morning social gathering of loons on Lower Suncook Lake, Barnstead, August 2022. Note the aggressive behavior of the loon flapping its wings, as well as the loon second from left lying low in the water with his neck extended. *Author photo.*

in Barnstead since no other body of water in town has had any territorial pairs recorded. It is also possible they came from New Durham, where Chalk Pond has had a territorial pair since 2018 (3 chicks surviving out of 5 hatched from 2019 to 2021), or Merrymeeting Lake, which has had at least one territorial pair for every year since 1988, excepting 1989, 1990, 1997 and 2004. Sunrise Lake in Middleton, which has had a territorial pair every year but one since 1979 (fledging an incredible 32 chicks out of the 40 hatched during that time), is also a possibility, as is Wild Goose Pond in Pittsfield, which has had a territorial pair of loons for many years since 1981 hatching just 7 chicks, of which 5 survived. Too, Halfmoon Pond in Alton is also a possibility, it having a territorial pair since 2005, with 10 chicks hatched since 2016 (none in 2022), of which 7 successfully fledged.

However, the social gatherings I observed on both Suncooks for the 2023 season had an added twist. In August, several social gatherings were again observed, though only six loons were present this year. This year's gathering was accompanied by many more vocalizations, tremolos and wailing, possibly due to the close eagle presence, these predators more visible than in the prior year and a constant presence. However, as biologist John Cooley Jr. related to me, not only did both Upper and Lower Suncook each have their usual breeding pairs, but another pair established a third territory in the channel that links both lakes as well. This was a first ever since the LPC began its work in 1975 and accounts for the six loons I had frequently observed. While this Middle Suncook territorial pair nested near the Narrows Road bridge, their efforts were unsuccessful. It will be interesting to see if they try again in 2024 and beyond.

Lower Suncook Lake had no recorded loon activity from 1975 to 2005, but in 2006 a territorial pair was finally recorded. The lake has had a pair of loons ever since, and 5 chicks were hatched here in 2008–11, with 3 surviving. No chicks were hatched in 2012–14, but success was achieved again in 2015–18 and 2022–23. During this time, 10 chicks hatched (including 2 in 2023) but only 2 survived. While the exact cause for the chick loss on Lower Suncook in 2022 has not been documented, bald eagle predation quite likely played a part, as they nest on the protected lands of Upper Suncook Lake and have been observed flying over both lakes, which are their hunting grounds. In fact, while kayaking on Upper Suncook in August 2022, I noticed a close encounter between an adult bald eagle and one of the pair of loons on that body of water. The juvenile eagles could be heard in their eyrie in a pine tree along the edge of the lake while I spotted the adult flying low over one of the loons, probably the female, which I had been observing. This loon wailed for its mate, and the encounter was over

A loon parent (*left*) and its chick, Lower Suncook Lake, Barnstead, August 2023. *Author photo.*

in just a few seconds. In August 2023, for the first time in my observations on Lower Suncook, I spotted an adult pair with a loon chick, with eagles constantly overhead. While both parents were extremely vigilant and kept the chick close by, I fear for that chick's safety once the migration season begins. Such is the unique problem, as many observers know, when we become attached to the loons on our lakes. This pair actually hatched 2 chicks in 2023, but one of them was rescued by the LPC at the age of three weeks and, likely due to sibling rivalry, was "undernourished." The LPC attempted to foster it on Lake Winnipesaukee with the Mink Island territorial pair whose eggs had failed to hatch. The loons accepted the chick, but it died within a day due to its already weakened state.

No matter what the case, the circumstances of the loon population on these smaller bodies of water in Barnstead and surrounding towns are in many ways typical of what is happening throughout the state in terms of the continued challenges to sustaining their population. Some years are good, others are not and nothing can be taken for granted.

2

A LOON POND WHICH SHALL REMAIN NAMELESS

There is, in the western part of the state, a small 300-plus-acre pond where loons are defying all the odds, thriving in a place where, quite frankly, they have almost no business doing so. Almost. This pond is not being identified by name or specific location because of the sensitive nature of its loon nesting sites and due to the fact that more and more people are flocking to its waters every year; all this visitation increased after it was highlighted in a popular outdoors magazine. You may recognize it by its description, having already been there perhaps. If so, just don't tell anyone about it, don't "spread the word"—for one day, the loon bubble could burst. Loons like this pond because it has an undeveloped shoreline surrounded by conservation land, and it also has many small islands suitable for nesting sites. While thousands of kayakers, anglers and swimmers visit every summer, no fuel-powered boats are allowed. There is a small dam that controls the outflow of water, built in 1918 and upgraded in 1979. Water levels do fluctuate at certain times of the year, which can cause problems, and the pond is part of a larger watershed that flows into the Connecticut River, supplying water to one major New Hampshire town along the way. So, despite its small size and wilderness appearance, this pond is not as isolated from the outside world as one might think. And yet, loons are making a go of things here. You might even call them, oddly enough, "city" loons, for, so far, they have been tolerant of the influx of human visitors. Indeed, on a pond that would normally support just one territorial pair, it supports three territorial pairs, an unprecedented occurrence.

When this pond was first surveyed by the LPC in 1975, it had one territorial pair, later called the North territory, which is just about what one would expect given the size of the lake. However, in 1987, another pair established the South territory, now giving the pond two pairs of loons. In a way, perhaps, this is not surprising. Few ponds of this size in New Hampshire have a combination of a large number of islands *and* undeveloped shoreline, so loon nesting sites are plentiful, and there was enough space in between that chicks could be fledged in a protected environment. However, things got even more interesting in 2011, the first year that the third, Middle territory, was established on the pond by yet another pair of loons, "squeezing themselves in" to make a home. This event made this small pond an unusual outdoor laboratory of sorts. Just how close together can territorial pairs exist and thrive in proximity to one another, and can such a pond even provide enough in the way of food for this many loons to survive? So far, the results have been positive. Indeed, this pond has produced 115 loon chicks since 1975, of which 99 fledged—that is an incredible 86.08 percent survival rate, well above the figure needed for loon sustainability. This pond's reproductive success is further highlighted by these additional facts: full broods of chicks have survived in all territories where hatchings took place in all but seven years since 1975, and since 1975, there have been only two years, 1983 and 2023, when no chicks were successfully fledged on the pond.

However, these successes have not come without conflict and potentials for future decline. Rick Libbey and his wife, Libby, have been photographing the loons on this pond since 1995 and have well documented the many loon events that have taken place here. The North territory of the pond, which has been occupied since 1975, has had no chicks hatched since 2018, the pair there trying three different nesting spots in the years since where they had previously been successful. Regarding the current North territory loons, Libbey commented that they are a "lovely pair, a bit more secretive than the other pairs. In 2013, the resident male showed up with a pretty good break in the top of his bill, but he seems to do all right."

As to the Middle territory, Libbey noted that the original pair here were together for five years, but "then had a devastating murder of a chick by a rogue [male loon], disrupted the pair, no nesting in 2016, and a new marriage in 2017 that retained the male....Both chicks survived and it's a great example of how resilient loons can be." In 2022, the Middle territory hatched two chicks, one of which survived.

Finally, by 2012, the parents on the South territory were "in a lengthier than most marriage" but in 2015 had a mate change, the older male

Loon and chick on nest, an "unnamed" pond, 2014. The chick in this photo would fledge, but the egg that was being incubated would never hatch. This was the last time the male shown here was on this territory, he being displaced the following spring. *Courtesy MooseMan Nature Photography.*

"ousted by a bigger, younger male," the nest "moving a few feet from the previous one." In 2016, the loons here were "somewhat triumphant, parents nested early, were driven off by black flies, renested" and "successfully raised both. The territory had been a long established and productive territory but was quite unproductive from 1996 thru 2008, hatching some chicks, but also a high number of failures. Starting in 2009, the territory began [to be] VERY productive often raising two chicks each year. They had an eight-year run without losing a chick from 2009 to 2016."

Of this small pond in general, Libbey added that these "loons are unusual, the volume of kayaking is very high, some folks understand the fragility, others not, but at only 300 plus acres, the loons have had no choice but to 'swim with kayakers,' they are very used to people. Recently eagles have been a threat too, more so the last few years than ever." It has also seen changes that threaten the food supply. As professionals who have spent hours photographing loon parents feeding their chicks, the Libbeys have noticed "the lack of fish. Up until 5 years ago, a chick's diet was approx. 80–90% fish. We'd actually count how many out of 10 were fish

Loon parent bringing food to its chick, unnamed pond, 2020. The pair shown here formerly had two chicks, but the second was lost due to "siblicide," killed by the chick shown here just the day before. *Courtesy MooseMan Nature Photography.*

as opposed to crawdad. Now it is completely flipped the other way. Only 1 or 2 of every 10 are fish."

While it is true that the original North territory has declined in the total number of chicks hatched (three) and fledged (two) in the last five years, the other territories have held their own, and the pond's reproductive success rate has remained high. Whether or not this western New Hampshire pond can continue to support three territorial pairs, only time will tell, and it is being closely monitored. One can only hope, but the reports for 2023 are dismal. The Libbeys report that the North pair abandoned their nest due to flooding; the "Steady Eddies," the Middle Territory pair, "never showed any mating behavior"; while the South pair "laid two eggs, hatched one [chick], and it was attacked by a rogue [loon] on July 26 in the evening, survived the attack but succumbed during the night. Tough year."

3

THE LOONS OF UPPER AND LOWER BAKER PONDS

Out in the western part of New Hampshire, you will find two ponds, connected by a small stream. Upper Baker Pond lies entirely in the town of Orford, while Lower Baker Pond lies in the towns of Orford and Wentworth, the line split nearly down the center. Eight miles distant, living in the town of Orford, you will find the residence of Cathy Eastburn. Many local folks, no doubt, have seen the loons on these ponds, but make no mistake. These are Cathy's loons—she visits them daily, watches over them, protects them and has even helped rescue them. They are her babies, and she is the LPC's eyes on the water when it comes to the Bakers. Upper Baker Pond is 166 acres in size with an average depth of 10 feet, a good part of its shoreline abutting camps Moosilauke and Merriwood, while Lower Baker Pond is 120 acres in size with an average depth of 17 feet. Lower Baker is bounded by Camp Pemigewasset on its southern and western shorelines, while state Route 25A runs along its northeastern shore.

The history of loons on the Baker ponds is relatively recent; they returned after Eastburn's move to Orford, not far from her native town of Lyme, in 2004. Upper Baker, according to LPC records, was devoid of any loon activity until 2001, when one floater made it its home. No other loons were recorded in subsequent years until 2009, when a territorial pair arrived but did not nest. In 2010, Upper Baker was once again empty, but in 2011 and 2012 territorial pairs once again returned, and again no nesting occurred. From 2013 to 2016, no loons were on the pond, but a territorial pair reappeared in 2017 and then again from 2020 to 2022. During this time, nesting occurred only in 2022 but was seemingly doomed from the start. The first nest, a natural one with two eggs, was abandoned due to black fly infestation, while a second nest was built on a nesting raft placed by the LPC that year. One egg was laid, but no chick was ever hatched, incubation ending after 45 days, long after the time hatching should have occurred. It was at this time that the female on Upper Baker was banded, with Eastburn holding her in her lap. So, Upper Baker has been in flux, and though loons had returned, reproduction success had not yet been achieved. That would all change in 2023. As Eastburn reported,

> Upper Baker loons hatched one chick on June 24, the other egg did not hatch, the loons sat on it for two days after the first chick hatched. The LPC collected it after the loons left the nest. It is the first loon chick I have ever named. We call him Gary, after Gary Miller, who owned the girls camp on the pond. He was pro loons and built a nesting platform for both ponds after the natural nest failure on Lower Baker in 2020; he was very saddened for the loons. Gary Miller unexpectedly died two days after he put the platforms out. It just seemed like a nice tribute to him to name the first ever recorded loon chick on Upper Baker after him. Gary is huge, it's amazing how fast a single chick grows. He rarely has to beg for food; the parents feed him till he's stuffed. When he's full and refuses the food, the parents will just swim around for 30 minutes or so with a fish in their mouth waiting for him to want it.
>
> Gary at only a couple of weeks old was trying to make loon sounds.… He is going to be a big loon; he has inherited his father's extra-long neck. At nine weeks old he is just giant.

As for Lower Baker Pond, it's been a slightly different story. In the history of the LPC, one territorial pair was recorded here in 1983, but no nesting occurred. From that time to 2007, the pond was home to no territorial pairs, though single floaters occupied Lower Baker in 1995, 1999, 2001 and 2003, with three floaters recorded in 2004 and two in 2006. A territorial pair came here once again in 2007 but did not nest, and after that the same happened in 2010. Lower Baker was once again home to only floaters in 2013 and 2016, but in 2018 a territorial pair arrived and nested for the first time since the LPC began keeping records. The pair hatched no chicks that year, and despite nesting in 2019 and 2020, no chicks were hatched in those years either. However, 2021 saw a turnaround here, along with plenty of action, when two chicks were hatched, with both surviving into mid-August. This

Loon pair on Upper Baker Pond, Orford, May 2022. *Courtesy Cathy Eastburn.*

occurred again in 2022, so, for now, Lower Baker is back in the loon business. Cathy Eastburn is helping to keep it that way.

It's no wonder Eastburn keeps a close watch on her loons, anywhere from two to four times a day in-season, "to take a head-count and make sure everybody is still there," as loon success on the Bakers has been fleeting and fragile. As she noted, "The loon pair on Lower Baker are smart and they recognize me." Flooding has plagued Lower Baker Pond for over a decade, with 2019 a particularly bad year, when the territorial pair had three successive nest sites flooded. The first flooded while it was being built; a second nest was built in which two eggs were laid, but it was flooded and the eggs lost. A third nest was hastily constructed, and one egg was laid, but that nest, too, along with its egg, was flooded out. In 2020, a nest with two eggs, after having been incubated for 25 days, was flooded out on July 1; this was a heartbreaking loss, as the eggs were due to hatch in days. Because of these events, a nesting raft was placed in Lower Baker by the LPC in 2021 and resulted in the successful hatching of two chicks. However, one of these chicks, too, was threatened by a climate change event. After the adult loons left, their chicks were on their own. According to Eastburn, one flew off the pond to begin its first migratory journey before Thanksgiving, but the other chick lingered on the pond, and lingered, and lingered until it was too late. Though it tried to fly out, it could not do so because of the ice forming on the pond. Eastburn reached out to the LPC after Thanksgiving and sent them photos. She monitored the pond twice a day for three hours, and as she recalled, "It does give you anxiety." Finally, senior biologist and master rescuer John Cooley Jr. arrived on the scene on December 8, with the bird finally rescued on December 10. Eastburn, along with another local "loon stalker," Nancy Masterson, and Camp Pemigewasset caretaker Reed Harrington, helped in the efforts, which took hours with Cooley out on the ice and the loon diving from one hole in the open ice to another. Once rescued, the juvenile, which weighed 3.8 pounds, was found to be dehydrated but otherwise OK and was sent to Maria Colby for a brief stint before being released into the ocean at Odiorne Point. It is interesting to note that the female of the territorial pair on Lower Baker was banded on nearby Lake Armington in Piermont in 2015.

The year 2022 would prove to be an equally eventful one on Lower Baker Pond. Once again, the same territorial pair nested and hatched two chicks. While both survived according to LPC records (observations ending in mid-August), this, sadly, was not truly the case. Interestingly, Eastburn has closely watched the parenting style of these loons—in 2021,

LPC senior biologist John Cooley Jr. holding a juvenile loon he has just rescued from the ice on Lower Baker Pond, Orford/Wentworth, in December 2021. *Courtesy Cathy Eastburn.*

she described them as "very uptight and protective and the chicks listened to them." This was not the case in 2022, the chicks described as "very independent" and often off on their own, "doing what they wanted." One of these chicks flew off the lake after the male adult had departed in the fall of 2022, leaving the female and one of its chicks. On September 23, 2022, both female and chick were observed by Eastburn earlier in the day, as well as several full-sized adult eagles. The chick was 13 weeks old at the time and able to fly yet stayed on the pond with its mother. On another check later in the day, Eastburn spotted one of the bald eagles with the carcass of the loon chick in its grasp. She was able to recover the dead loon, though "there was not much left," and held the carcass for the LPC. To her it was a sad day, there being little doubt that the chick had been predated by an eagle; as she succinctly stated, "It's nature. There's no way to intervene, so I just hold my breath and pray they're OK. I'm done with eagles." Following this event, the female adult, according to Eastburn's observations, was despondent, "definitely mourning," and flew off the lake three days later.

Happily, this same female and her mate returned in 2023, and the results were much the same, a mixture of tragedy and, so far, a bit of hope. As Cathy Eastburn tells it,

It's been tough at Lower Baker this year. Two chicks hatched on June 20 and 21. They immediately started fighting only a few hours after the second chick was hatched. The first hatched chick was clearly dominant. On July 18, the smaller chick left the family (4 weeks old); the bigger chick was really beating up on it, pecking it relentlessly and holding its head under the water. The adults did not intervene. The chick was trying to feed itself, and once in a while an adult would go and feed it some. On July 23, 2023, John Cooley from LPC came out to try to band the adults on Lower Baker and capture the chick so they could weigh and check on its health. Unfortunately, we were unable to capture this chick or either of the adults; they kept evading us. We did, however, capture the bigger chick and were able to get measurements and weight (a little over three pounds). It was too small to band though. I held the chick in the boat, and it pooped and bit me....After the attempted capture...the adults started showing more of an interest in this lone chick. The chick was spending more than 50 percent of its time with the family, or one adult would be with one chick and the other adult with the other. The larger chick was not so aggressive because the younger one would lay flat and not challenge for the food. The younger chick did get wise though; it would wait for the bigger chick to get full, watch the parents with its head under the water and dive to follow them so when they popped up it could quickly get the food. If the other chick was too close to it, it would dive with the food. It was molting to juvenile feathers normally only a little behind the bigger chick. The eagle presence has been high on both ponds this year. They pond hop since they are only about ¼ mile away from each other. On August 16, 2023, I sadly had to witness the eagle kill the smaller chick and eat it. An adult was fairly close by, but the chick was too close to shore to dive to get away from the eagle when the adult gave the warning sound. I videotaped a lot of this horrific incident and then went to Camp Pemi where the eagle took the chick to collect its remains for the LPC. It was not a good day. The remaining juvenile will be 10 weeks old on August 29; it is doing well, and I expect it to start practicing flying any day now.

So, why does Cathy Eastburn do what she does year after year? She took up wildlife photography after her children were grown and said of loons and the Baker ponds, "They're cool birds, living for a long time. They make wonderful sounds and are wonderful parents. It's my Zen place, it's refreshing. I'm called the 'loon lady,' but they're not my pets. I love watching them." Through her caring efforts and watchful eye, Cathy Eastburn is helping to ensure that the loon recovery on the Bakers is a continued success.

4

THE BIG-CITY LOONS
OF LAKE MASSABESIC

No story of New Hampshire's loon population would be complete without an account of the loons on this large lake in southern New Hampshire. Now, admit it—when you think of loons, you think of the Lakes Region and all the beautiful bodies of water there, not the big city of Manchester. However, just four miles from Manchester City Hall, and less than two miles from busy I-93, there is a good-sized loon population on Massabesic. The 2,560-acre lake lies in Manchester and mostly the town of Auburn and is the public water supply for New Hampshire's largest city. Because of this, swimming is prohibited here. However, the lake is heavily recreated, popular with powerboats, kayakers, canoeists and sailboats, as well as anglers. Its average depth is 17 feet, though there are some spots that can reach depths of 50 feet. Today it is home to eight active loon locations, these designated as the Back Pond, Birch Island, Canfield Cove, Deer Neck, Grape Island, Ladies Island, Severance and Yacht Club territories. A ninth territory was also periodically recorded by the LPC from 1975 to 2017, but nesting occurred only in 2008, with no chicks hatched.

In a way, it's a miracle there are any loons on this lake. While much of its shoreline is undeveloped because of its status as a public water supply, it has many factors working against it. First and foremost is its southern location, where climate change, in the form of increasing summer temperatures, has possibly had an impact. Second, it is also because of its location in the heart of industrial New Hampshire that Lake Massabesic was a hot spot for mercury contamination in the state, not to mention other possible

Loon family on Lake Massabesic, Auburn, June 2016. *Courtesy John M. Rockwood.*

contaminants. Because of the mercury issue, many loons have been banded on Massabesic, so we know the level of mercury in their blood and eggs. Finally, the water fluctuations that occur here result in a higher level of loon nest failures from this cause than anywhere else in the state. Though the LPC works closely with the Manchester Waterworks, the fact of the matter is that 17 million gallons of water are pumped from the lake every day to accommodate some 160,000 users. Add to this the multiple years since 2016 when droughts have occurred in southern New Hampshire, with the lake at record low levels in 2020, and you have a prescription for failure. With all these factors, it's no surprise that Lake Massabesic's eight territories have hatched just 12 chicks since 2016, with 8 of them fledging successfully. With the heavy rainfall that New Hampshire experienced in 2023, it was a difficult year, and the struggle for loon survival continued. Overall, seven of Massabesic's territories were occupied, with three pairs nesting, but no chicks hatched. While this lack of reproductive success greatly threatens the loon population for the long term, the LPC continues its efforts here, and it's not unusual to spot 20 or more loons here at some points in the late summer before fall migration.

The LPC's eyes on this lake are many, but as LPC biologist Chris Conrod wrote, John Rockwood, a.k.a. The Loon Man, "is our go-to man on band readings and nesting dates," having been on Massabesic for over 30 years. Rockwood, a resident of Auburn, first started canoeing here with his wife when they moved here in 1984. As Rockwood recalled, "My most consistent interactions with the loons started in the spring of 2002," after he was laid off from his job the previous year and had more time on his hands in between night school and job interviews. As he stated, "Any day it was not raining I spent four to six hours kayaking on the lake taking photos of loons....Being there so often the loons being curious would come within a few feet of me and fish under my kayak. One female would answer when I whistled and bring her chicks for me to babysit while she and her various mates defended their territory." And from then on, Rockwood has become a loon expert in his own right, his photographs some of the most stunning to be found and something for which he has received national recognition. Indeed, Rockwood shares his experiences through his many Loon Man public speaking engagements, as well as through his 2009 book *Adventures with Grapenut*, which details his interactions with one particular loon chick and its parents. His most memorable experience during his years among Massabesic's loons has been that of "meeting and hanging out with a female loon for more than

Loon chick on Lake Massabesic, Auburn, July 2012. *Courtesy John M. Rockwood.*

12 years. Books claimed that males were owners of the territories on the lake. In June 2002, I watched a banded male hide when the Grape Island female flew in. The male showed the female a few nesting spots which she ignored. She came around the island that I was hiding behind so as not to interfere with choosing a nest site. She passed by me within two feet and found her nest site for that summer."

Over the years, Rockwood has seen the changes on the lake, including more eagles, which "are taking a few chicks each year," and fewer chicks surviving overall, lamenting that "we lose chicks to an increase in large snapping turtles, eagles and many more motorboats on the lake seven days a week sunrise to sunset." Despite these challenges, John Rockwood remains an optimist, succinctly stating, "I believe the lake will always have loons."

5

A CURIOUS CASE
ON WOLFEBORO'S BACK BAY

My family and I have lived in Wolfeboro, just several hundred yards from the head of Back Bay, for nearly 20 years now, and for most of those years, I've never heard a loon. That all changed in 2019, when, for the first time, I heard a loon call twice on Back Bay in the late evening hours in May. I was both thrilled and stunned—what was going on? As it turns out, local photographer and veteran Brooks Campbell helped provide the answer. While walking around Back Bay that spring, he photographed the loon there, catching foot waggle views of both legs, the bands on them clearly visible. Campbell sent this information on to LPC senior biologist John Cooley Jr., and it was soon discovered through banding data that this loon had previously been a resident elsewhere. No big deal, right? Wrong. The resighting of banded birds is a common occurrence, but this was a shocker. As it turns out, this loon had been banded by BRI biologists on the Policeman's Cove territory on Little Sebago Lake in Gray and Windham, Maine, way back in 2005. So, this was an older loon, probably around 20 years old by 2019, but that was not the most interesting thing about this loon, which I now refer to as the Back Bay loon. The most unique thing about this arrival was the fact that he was some 50 miles away from his home territory, a rare case of dispersal and one that was farther from home than any other previously known territorial loon in New Hampshire. Remember, loons typically stick within a few miles of their home lake. Just two years before, an "anomaly" was discovered on Tower Hill Pond in Auburn, that bird having dispersed some 25 miles from home. With the discovery of the

Back Bay loon, the known possible dispersal distance had doubled. It is not yet known what implications such dispersals may have over time, but it proved that there is still much to be learned about loons. Where this loon had spent his summers from 2005 to 2019 is a mystery, but he likely was a floater on the bodies of water located somewhere between Little Sebago and Wolfeboro. Interestingly, as I began speaking with Campbell about this loon, he looked through past photos he had taken and made another discovery—the Back Bay loon had actually arrived in Wolfeboro in 2017, his leg bands clearly evident in Campbell's dated photos. However, the old loon, which had hatched one chick in Maine in 2005, apparently has only nested once since his arrival in Wolfeboro, this being in 2019.

The Back Bay territory, a tenuous one at best since it gained this designation only with this loon's arrival, has never had much loon activity over the years, though locals have seen a floater in its waters from time to time. Despite its appearance today, it is not an ideal spot for loons and has not been for well over 100 years. The bay empties into Wolfeboro Bay via a channel that runs under Wolfeboro's Main Street, while the Smith River drops over Wolfeboro Falls at the head of Back Bay, this river connecting Crescent Lake and Lake Wentworth to Lake Winnipesaukee. The head of the bay was the site of some of the earliest industrial activity in Wolfeboro, and by the late 1800s there were three mills in the Back Bay area, as well as a shoe factory. The area between the bay and what is now Center Street, including where Foss Field is today, was once the town dump site for years, and though the area began to be developed, its use as a dump continued until about 1966. The town road closest to the southeast shore of Back Bay, Lehner Street, was once called Factory Street, with a shoe factory located here. For years after its demise, old leather shoe parts were sometimes fished out of Back Bay by local anglers. And of course, the railroad's entrance to downtown Wolfeboro rolled right along this shore, where the popular rail trail begins today. So, not an ideal spot for loons, and even today it is marginal at best. Not only is Back Bay heavily recreated, with a private marina and a ski-jump ramp located here in the summer months, but the shoreline, which is mostly undeveloped and some of it conservation lands, is rocky and not suitable for nesting sites.

Back Bay does have one marshy inlet that has the only potential loon nesting sites on Back Bay, but the surrounding area is heavily developed and flooding often occurs here. In fact, the only known loon nesting attempt was made here in 2019 by the Back Bay loon with his mate, but the egg never hatched after being washed out of the nest. It is unknown if heavy rains resulted in the nest being flooded or whether boat wakes were the problem.

This egg was subsequently recovered by Brooks Campbell and given to the LPC. The Back Bay loon has returned here in the years since as a floater, and while he has not succeeded in finding a mate, he seems to have made this place his home and many folks have enjoyed his presence. This intrepid loon, according to Campbell, seemed to have a habit of sticking around Wolfeboro well after Thanksgiving, and in the fall of 2022, I decided that I would try to track his movements. And so, beginning in late October, the Back Bay loon became "my loon." At that time, it was still unclear if this last loon in Wolfeboro for the season was the same bird banded in Maine, but soon enough I could see his leg bands to confirm his identity.

The first day I began my tracking, October 22, was a warm day, and it was interesting seeing him feeding in Back Bay within proximity of paddle-boarders. The loon typically feeds across the bay near the marina but occasionally will make his way over to the rail trail shoreline, which is where I usually started my day. All my observations were by land, walking along Back Bay, sometimes following him as he made his way down the channel by the docks by the train station and even under the Main Street Bridge into Wolfeboro Bay or near the town docks. One thing I learned firsthand pretty quickly—he can swim much faster than I can walk. Usually, though, most of my early observations were in Back Bay proper before the cold weather caused him to remain in Wolfeboro Bay. It was interesting seeing the loon undergo his winter molt, gradually changing from black and white plumage to gray and brown—it was as if he was aging before my very eyes, especially on his head, but he was still a fine-looking fellow. On November 5, I had a scare when he came under threat by a pontoon boat traveling at high speed. Luckily, the boat operator spotted the bird and slowed down in time to avoid him. Not all loons are so lucky. By the end of the first week of November, I was getting to know this loon's habits well and where he would likely be found, feeding in the morning, preening in the afternoon. Mostly he would stay in the center of the bay, although he would occasionally make his way toward the upper area, feeding near the boathouses there. During the summer months, I could sometimes see him from Front Bay Park on the opposite shore, but by now I could seldom do so. Often the Back Bay loon would drift down the channel, under the bridge and into Wolfeboro Bay, feeding near the buoy off the town docks area. I would see him in this location close-up and personal many times over the next month and a half. Usually, as sunset approached, this loon would make his way farther out in Wolfeboro Bay, where I believe he spent his nights in the open water before making his way back to Back Bay in the morning.

The Back Bay loon, Wolfeboro, December 2022. This banded bird is pictured here off the town docks just a few days before his migration to the ocean for the winter. *Author photo*.

November 18 was a thrilling day, as my loon spent his time close to the rail trail shore and I heard him vocalize for the first time, a small hoot before continuing his activities. Was he acknowledging my presence? The following day, he was again close to the shore in my presence during the morning hours and at one point cocked his head and stared in my direction for several minutes, not alarmed but seemingly curious as to who it was that had been keeping an eye on him. Later that same morning, he rose out of the water when several geese came in his vicinity. Much honking ensued, but after a few minutes, things calmed down. This would not be the last such encounter, and though loons do not typically defend a territory once the breeding season has ended, the Back Bay loon was clearly annoyed at their presence in his waters. On November 21, I once again encountered my loon close to the shore; he stopped within 15 feet of where I was standing and gave a small hoot. I decided, as crazy as it sounds, to respond with a soft hoot of my own. I was a bit embarrassed, but no one was around, so I figured, "What the heck?" The Back Bay loon responded back with two short hoots and after a minute or so went back to his normal activities. I will believe to my dying day that right there and then, my loon and I had made a connection, and subsequent interactions would confirm this. During later close encounters, he would almost always hoot at me, either when first arriving or just prior to diving and heading off elsewhere. Sometimes I responded with a hoot of my own, though I admit that when other people were around, I felt a bit embarrassed and refrained from doing so.

By November 23, Back Bay was starting to freeze up, and my loon subsequently was spending more time near the town docks in Wolfeboro Bay. This was a regular feeding spot for him in the early hours right around 7:30 a.m. With weather now turning even colder, I was beginning to get worried about my loon—when would he migrate to the ocean? November 27 turned out to be an eventful morning, for the Back Bay loon would gain some unwanted company. While feeding about 150 yards from the town docks, another loon appeared farther off in Wolfeboro Bay, coming in from out in the lake. I could hear some hoots exchanged between them, and then they drifted away, usually 50 to 100 yards distant from one another but always keeping a watchful eye out. After a time, the newcomer came close to the Back Bay loon, and together they stayed in close company, with some dives, for about 5 minutes. At this time, a third loon appeared on the scene, but it disappeared to the east just minutes later. Soon after, the Back Bay loon let out a tremolo call, and the newcomer quickly dove—was he attacking my loon underwater? For several minutes, there was a great deal of wing-flapping on the surface by my loon, it appearing as if his head was in the water, but then the other loon surfaced and quickly swam away to the east, where he hung out around a fishing boat before leaving for good. Once again, no one messes with my loon! After this episode, he made his way under the bridge and into the Back Bay channel, where three mallard ducks flew low over him and attempted to land in his vicinity. The Back Bay loon was in no mood to deal with these guys and, with much wing flapping, drove the ducks away. The Back Bay loon stayed in this area for about 20 minutes, mostly preening, before heading back out into Wolfeboro Bay. It was one memorable day for loon observations. By this time, the Back Bay loon was spending most of his time in Wolfeboro Bay, and the following day, November 28, he may have spotted another loon intruder. While I could see no other loon, he let out another tremolo call that morning, and I could see him briefly thrashing the water around him. I began to wonder if my loon might be considered an out-of-season cantankerous old man just seeking to hold on to his territory, much like that loon in Northwood.

With the arrival of December and wintertime fast approaching, there was an increasing amount of dockside construction and barge activity on the town docks, but this did not faze the Back Bay loon one bit. I was getting increasingly worried about my loon and his departure. Aware of the large rescue of Winnipesaukee loons early in the year, I did not want my loon to be in that same position. And yet he continued to stick around. Sometimes, as on December 2, it would seem like our schedules were perfectly synchronized. I knew about where and when he would make his appearance, and that day, as I drove to the town docks, he popped his head up out of the water close to shore within moments after I had gotten out of the car. Who knew whose schedule? From this time on, I would have many close encounters with my loon at the town docks, he often hooting and staring at me before continuing his feeding. This was an ideal time for observations, as I could clearly see him underwater for the first time at close range and could easily see his banded legs. From the bubbles that appeared on the surface, I could frequently predict where he would resurface.

December 4 proved to be another loon encounter day. When I arrived later than normal, I saw one loon fly overhead and out into Wolfeboro Bay. I did not see the loon land, but minutes later I did see, for the first time, my Back Bay loon in flight, landing several hundred yards offshore. Shortly after, I could see two other loons farther off near the Sewall Road shore. My Back Bay loon kept a distant watch over them, but after those loons, perhaps on their migration journey, departed, my loon, whose leg bands I caught sight of, made his way close to the entrance to Back Bay. The following day, I was greeted by my loon with a short hoot upon my arrival on the town docks, as if he was waiting for me, and the same thing happened the next day. Was I getting attached to my loon? You bet! Seeing him was always a great start to my day. The next four days it was the same; we greeted each other simultaneously at the town docks. Interestingly, on December 8, my observations were interrupted by a cellphone call. I watched my loon while talking, and he came close to the side of the dock, perhaps curious what my new activity was all about or maybe wondering why I wasn't giving him my full attention. He stuck around, patiently; we exchanged a few hoots; and despite some construction noise, he was still feeding on my departure. By this time, the Back Bay loon had largely abandoned Back Bay, spending his time in Wolfeboro Bay and beyond, as well as his usual morning visits to the town docks.

Sundays were becoming days of great activity during my observations, and December 11 was no exception. On this morning, I greeted my loon at the town docks as usual, but within a few minutes he looked away out into the bay, distracted, then hooted goodbye and dove away. I turned around to look out into the bay and spotted another loon about 75 yards distant. My loon disappeared for about 20 minutes, while the newcomer stayed offshore. Eventually, it dove and was not seen again. Whether my loon ever encountered him underwater I could not tell, but after this intruder departed, my loon was back in the town docks area feeding for an extended time in my vicinity. Our routine was largely the same for the week, though on December 14 I could not find him. However, the next day, I spotted him about 100 yards offshore when I arrived. Standing at the end of the dock, I could see what I assumed was my loon look directly at me. He immediately dove and in one swim made it to the dock close to my position and, on surfacing, gave me a hoot. Once again, there is no doubt in my mind that even from far off, my loon recognized my presence and came in to say hello and to get down to his feeding activities. It was our routine. On December 17, we got our first snow and I did not see my loon, thinking once again he had gotten the message to migrate, but he appeared in our normal meeting place the next day. This continued through December 22, and as the days were growing shorter, my anxiety was increasing—I was worried about my loon getting iced in. I did not spot him on December 23, it being a stormy day with heavy rain and strong winds. Luckily, the weather was in the 40s, but there was nonetheless much damage in this area from the storm. When I failed to see my loon on December 24, I was convinced he was gone but still made a check on the early morning hours of Christmas Day before we headed off to our son's house to celebrate. On approaching the town docks, I saw not one loon, but two. One was undoubtedly my loon, but he made no close approach to the docks, primarily because of the other loon and the large amount of floating debris in the water. Luckily, while the skirting of the docks was iced up, there were no ice chunks in the water.

The next morning, I did my loon check, and sure enough, there he was at the town docks doing his thing. It was cold and sunny, and though I greeted him as usual, I also told him (in my mind), "It's time for you to get gone." And this, as it would turn out, he did, heading off to the ocean on either December 26 or the next day. I continued my observations through the remainder of the year and, thankfully, saw neither him nor any other loon. I would make periodic observations in January and was a bit worried in February after I learned that the LPC had rescued some loons from the ice in Tuftonboro. Though one of these loons was probably drowned under the ice, the others that were rescued proved not to be my loon. So, I awaited his return for 2023.

The Back Bay loon in winter plumage, during his final stay in Wolfeboro Bay before heading off to the ocean, December 2022. *Author photo.*

Would he even return? Sure, he seemed to like Wolfeboro, but he also had had no breeding success here. With the calendar turning to April 2023 and the weather slowly improving, I again began my loon watch. There was some reporting of the sighting of a loon on Back Bay on April 7, but either he was hiding from me or folks were mistaking the common mergansers there for loons. However, on April 9 I did spot my first loons, far out into Wolfeboro Bay, one of them wailing in the early morning hours. I spotted loons on several other days far off into the bay but on April 17, 2023, spotted my first loons on Back Bay, a pair of them sticking close together.

Loon on Back Bay, Wolfeboro, April 2023, soon after making its arrival from the ocean. *Author photo.*

Was one of them my loon? I would gain no visual confirmation in the form of his leg bands as this book goes to press. This loon fiercely guarded what was clearly his Back Bay territory, making tremolo calls and chasing away geese and cormorants in his area. My sense, based on his observed movements and activities, is that this is my friend. His potential mate was clearly unbanded, but in the end they separated and no nesting occurred in 2023 on the shores of Back Bay. With the heavy rains and resultant flooding, the docks on Back Bay were underwater for a time, and some locals believe the lake level was higher than they had seen in years. The only area suitable for loon nesting was also inundated during this crucial time—climate change at work yet again. Still, what I believe to be this same lone loon continues to hang out in Wolfeboro, splitting his time between Back Bay and Wolfeboro Bay. However, despite all the threats that loons face, and the failed breeding success of my Back Bay friend, I remain hopeful. That's because the LPC has made me a believer in the loon's future here, and like so many others on numerous New Hampshire lakes, I will be watching over my loon for as long as he makes Wolfeboro his home.

6

A LITTLE GEM
IN THE MONADNOCK REGION

Way down in the southwestern corner of New Hampshire, there are many small ponds and lakes. Unlike other regions in New Hampshire, there are no truly big lakes here in the Monadnock Region, but that doesn't mean there aren't plenty of loon habitats to be had. It's also been a region that, historically, has had difficult loon challenges to face for over 100 years now. If you will recall, it was in southern New Hampshire that loons had all but disappeared by the 1920s, and even after the LPC came into existence, it would take time to make a difference. Not only is climate change one of southern New Hampshire's constant challenges, but so too was the Monadnock Region a hot spot for mercury contaminants, coming from not just coal-fired plants in New Hampshire but also from the area of western Massachusetts. However, the region has made a loon comeback. New Hampshire Audubon's Willard Pond has long been a loon success, and many other lakes and ponds are also seeing the return of loons, much to the pleasant surprise of area residents. One of those who had an interest in loons was Brian J. Reilly of Keene, a retired family physician and native of Antrim. He has served for 10 years as a trustee on the LPC's board, but how did he get to that point? As he relates, he had always enjoyed photography from childhood and in the early 2000s got his start as a wildlife photography enthusiast by taking a "real" photography class and bought his first digital SLR camera in 2006. "During the winter of 2006–07 I saw a photo of a loon family of four in a magazine I was browsing. I decided then that I'd love to be able to take a similar photo. That next Spring, I discovered a nearby pond with a pair of nesting loons and began to spend more and more time there observing and photographing that loon family. Upon returning the following year and observing more loon behaviors that I didn't understand, I began to search for additional information. In that process a Google search uncovered the Loon Preservation Committee in Moultonborough....I arranged a meeting with their Executive Director, Harry Vogel, and Senior Biologist, John Cooley. We had a great first meeting at which I learned much about loon behavior and the organization as well. I became an active member and volunteer, assisting with observations within the Monadnock Region in subsequent years. A few years later I was invited to join their board of trustees and did so from 2011–2020, serving also as board chair from 2016–2019. Before that Summer of 2007 I had done very little nature photography. While my initial focus was to photograph loons, I became much more aware of the diversity of animal and plant life on and around the pond. Since then, my nature photography has broadened substantially. Without that initial curiosity and desire to photograph loons, I'm not sure if my path would have crossed with LPC."

Reilly would frequent several habitats within a half an hour's drive from his home, including Willard Pond, Meetinghouse Pond in Marlborough

This loon was part of a territorial pair on Cold Spring Pond, Stoddard, in 2013. It is here wing rowing its way across the pond in response to the arrival of a floater loon. After 15 minutes, the floater departed, not willing to engage this fit and feisty bird. *Courtesy Brian J. Reilly.*

and Bolster Pond in Sullivan. However, one of his favorite locations is Cold Spring Pond, located in the northwest part of Stoddard. The pond is small but 31 acres in size with an average depth of 10 feet. It has only one seasonal residence on its shore, and there is no boat launch. Swimming is not allowed, but kayaking and canoeists frequent the pond. The pond is stocked yearly with trout but, according to Reilly, is not very popular with anglers. For decades, the pond was also not popular for loons, with the LPC recording no loon activity here from 1975 (and probably for many years before) until single floaters showed up in 2002 and 2003. After that, the pond was loon-less until 2008, when they rediscovered Cold Spring Pond and a territorial pair claimed it as their home, successfully hatching and fledging a single chick. Since that time, Cold Spring has been a consistent loon pond, hatching 21 chicks and successfully fledging 12 of them. The years 2017 and 2019 saw no nesting, but the last three years have been productive. That's an excellent record for such a small body of water, but it's not occurred without drama, and Brian Reilly has experienced much of it. With the aid of field notes he has kept over the years, Reilly related some of the interesting events on the pond:

> *I first learned of CSP [Cold Spring Pond] by word of mouth early in 2009 and made my first visit on June 23, 2009. I was not disappointed as I was greeted by a loon family of two adults and two chicks on that first visit. During a return visit later in August one of the adults took to flight while I watched and photographed. I was pleased to see that this loon was banded but disturbed to see fishing line and tackle trailing from its bill. Upon matching the bands with records kept by LPC, it turned out that this was a female that had been banded as a nesting adult on Long Pond in Lempster in 1998. As it would have likely been a minimum of 6 years old at that point, it would now be at least 17. Although I did not see that bird again that fall, I was delighted to see it return to breed again the following spring, having managed to free itself of the fishing tackle along the way. History repeated itself in 2011, 2012 and 2013 as that female returned yearly to nest and raise chicks. Sadly, catastrophe hit in mid-August of 2013 when that female was found dead on the shore of Long Pond, just 6 miles due north of CSP. Upon necropsy the cause of death was a puncture through the breastbone directly into the sac around the heart….It appears that the CSP female had flown to Long Pond to feed but, in the process, had appeared as a threat to those resident loons….*

Over those preceding 5 years that CSP female had essentially become "my loon." It was hard to say goodbye given how successful she had been at returning and breeding all those years. She was at least 21 years old when she died and could potentially have lived and bred for another 10 years or so. More recently a situation occurred that demonstrates the normal turnover of adults on a loon territory. This process will seem a little extreme and heartless to us, but it's a demonstration of "survival of the fittest" and just a normal part of the loon's life cycle. In mid-June of 2016, I discovered two adult loons with their two chicks peacefully foraging the pond for food and acting like a normal family. I reported this to the field staff at LPC after which they decided to band these adults for ongoing identification. The team from LPC successfully banded the adults the evening of July 1st . All was well until I received a call on July 6th from the land manager at CSP with news that both an adult loon and a chick had been found dead on the shore of the pond that morning. Indeed, the dead adult was the male of the pair that had just been banded 6 days before. The chick, although not banded, was certainly one of his chicks. The second chick could

A territorial pair on Cold Spring Pond, Stoddard, in 2015 responding to a territorial invader. These loons are lying low in the water, having compressed the air from their feathers, reducing their buoyancy, in order to "hide" from a rival loon. *Courtesy Brian J. Reilly.*

not be found and was presumed to also be dead. On occasion for the next few weeks observers noted the presence of two adult loons but no one was able to determine if either of those loons was banded. The following spring, I was delighted to see that two loons had returned to the pond, and one was the female of the original pair banded in 2016. The second loon was also banded and was identified as a male loon that had been banded on Granite Lake in Nelson in 2009, just 5½ miles south of CSP. This "new" pair nested on CSP in 2017 and now continues to return to CSP yearly to nest and raise chicks. That Granite Lake male had likely been evicted from Granite Lake sometime between 2010 and 2015 and was eager to reestablish itself in a territory which it obviously did successfully in 2016. So continues the story that adult loons work hard to secure and then retain successful breeding territories.

The story on Cold Spring Pond and the others told herein are ones that are repeated on numerous other lakes throughout New Hampshire. Residents often share in these triumphs and tragedies, and so too does the LPC. But even more, the LPC continues to gather vital scientific data and is continually refining its loon conservation efforts. With their staff's work and that of countless volunteers and loon enthusiasts of all ages, the mission to maintain and grow New Hampshire's loons' presence continues. However, the mission is not yet complete, and much remains to be done to save this Granite State treasure. It is an effort whose ultimate success depends on everyone who cherishes the New Hampshire experience.

ABOUT THE ORGANIZATION

*T*he Loon Preservation Committee exists to restore and maintain a healthy population of loons throughout New Hampshire; to monitor the health and productivity of loon populations as sentinels of environmental quality; and to promote a greater understanding of loons and the natural world.

YOU can make a difference for loons by supporting the research, management and outreach efforts of the Loon Preservation Committee. Explore your charitable donation options at www.loon.org.

Loon Preservation Committee
PO Box 604
Moultonborough, NH 03254
603-476-5666

www.loon.org

BIBLIOGRAPHY
AND FURTHER READING

Aldrich, George. *Walpole: As It Was and As It Is*. Claremont, NH: Claremont Manufacturing, 1880.

Audubon, John James. *Birds of America*. Vol. 7. New York: J.J. Audubon, 1844.

Barber, Joel. *Wild Fowl Decoys*. New York: Dover Publications, 1954 (1934).

Belknap, Jeremy. *The History of New Hampshire*. Vol. 3. Boston: Belknap and Young, 1792.

Brewster, William. "The Birds of the Lake Umbagog Region of Maine." *Bulletin of the Museum of Comparative Zoology at Harvard College* 66, part 1 (June 1924).

———. "Journals of William Brewster, 1871–1919." Biodiversity Heritage Library. https://www.biodiversitylibrary.org.

Brooks, David. "NH Loon Preservation Gets 800K Settlement 18 Years after Oil Spill." *Concord Monitor*, June 18, 2021.

Browne, George Waldo. *The History of Hillsborough, New Hampshire*. Manchester, NH: John B. Clarke, 1921.

Centers for Disease Control (CDC). "Raccoon Rabies Epizootic—United States, 1993." https://www.cdc.gov.

Colby, Henry B. "Among the Islands—A Sketch of Lake Winnipesaukee." *Granite State Monthly* 19, no. 2 (August 1895).

Colio, Quintina. *American Decoys*. Self-published, 1972.

Dearborn, Ned, and Clarence M. Weed. "Birds in Their Economic Relation to Man." *Granite State Monthly* 31, no. 3 (September 1901).

Dixit, Sushil S., Jody N. Connor and Stephen C. Landry. "Paleolimnological Study of Willard and Russell Ponds in New Hampshire." *Lake and Reservoir Management* 17, no. 3 (2001). https://www.tandfonline.com.

Eastman, John R., and George E. Emery. *History of the Town of Andover, New Hampshire*. Concord, NH: Rumford Printing, 1910.

Fair, Jeff. "Field Notes from a Backcountry Biologist." Biodiversity Research Institute. https://briwildlife.org/jeff-fair/jeff-fair-archive/.

Forbush, Edward H. *Birds of Massachusetts and Other New England States*. Norwood, MA: Berwick and Smith, 1925.

———. *A History of the Game Birds, Wild-Fowl, and Shore Birds of Massachusetts and Adjacent States*. Boston: Massachusetts State Board of Agriculture, 1912.

Foss, Carol R., ed. *Atlas of Breeding Birds of New Hampshire*. Dover, NH: Arcadia Publishing for New Hampshire Audubon, 1994.

Franson, J. Christian, Scott P. Hansen, Mark A. Pokras and Rose Miconi. "Size Characteristics of Stones Ingested by Common Loons." *The Condor* 103, no. 1 (February 2001).

Gage, George N. *History of Washington, New Hampshire*. Claremont, NH: Claremont Manufacturing Company, 1886.

Grade, Tiffany, and Harry Vogel. "Contaminants in Loon Eggs in New Hampshire." Loon Preservation Committee. https://loon.org.

Gurrier, Jeff. "Dwight Crow." Pawtuckaway Lake Improvement Association. https://pawtuckawaylake.com/dwight-crow/.

Hammond, David E., and Rawson L. Wood. *New Hampshire and the Disappearing Loon*. Meredith, NH: LPC, 1977.

Haseltine, Susan D., Jeffrey S. Fair, Scott A. Sutcliffe and Douglas M. Swineford. "Trends in Organochlorine and Mercury Residues in Common Loon Eggs from New Hampshire." *Transactions of the Northeast Fish and Wildlife Conference* 40 (1983).

Hayward, Silvanus. *History of the Town of Gilsum, New Hampshire*. Manchester, NH: John B. Clarke, 1881.

Higgins, Amanda, Meghan A. Hartwick and Mark A. Pokras. "Sternal Punctures in Common Loons (*Gavia immer*): Gender and Territorial Aggression." *Waterbirds* 45, no. 1 (November 2022).

Hoffmann, Ralph. *A Guide to the Birds of New England and Eastern New York*. Boston: Houghton Mifflin, 1923.

Hurd, D. Hamilton, ed. *History of Merrimack and Belknap Counties, New Hampshire*. Philadelphia: J.W. Lewis, 1885.

Jackson, C.F. "Troubled Oil on Water." *Bulletin of the Audubon Society of New Hampshire* (October 1952).

Jackson, Derrick Z. "Tropical Death in the North Woods." *Boston Globe*, April 6, 2016. https://www.bostonglobe.com.

Jackson, James R., ed. *History of Littleton, New Hampshire*. Vol. 2. Cambridge, MA: University Press, 1905.

Josselyn, John. "New England's Rarities." *Transactions and Collections of the American Antiquarian Society* 4 (1860). https://www.biodiversitylibrary.org.

Kenow, Kevin P., David Adams, Nina Schoch, David C. Evers, William Hanson, Dave Yates, Lucas Savoy, Timothy J. Fox, Andrew Major, Robert Kratt and John Ozard. "Migration Patterns and Wintering Range of Common Loons Breeding in the Northeastern United States." *Waterbirds* 32, no. 2 (2009).

Kirshner, Ralph. *The Common Loon on Lake Winnipesaukee*. Center Harbor, NH: Lake Winnipesaukee Association and the LPC, 1976.

Laine, Kristen. "Call of the Wild." *Yankee Magazine* (June 2011).

Lancaster, Daniel. *The History of Gilmanton*. Gilmanton, NH: Alfred Prescott, 1845.

Leland, Charles. *The Algonquian Legends of New England*. Boston: Houghton Mifflin, 1885.

Leonard, Levi W., and Josiah L. Seward. *The History of Dublin, N.H.* Dublin, NH: Town of Dublin, 1920.

Loon Preservation Committee. *Loon Preservation Committee Newsletter*. 2006–2022. https://loon.org.

The Loon Project. "A Revelation from Loon Capture: Small Lakes Are Ecological Traps." https://loonproject.org.

Lyford, James O. *History of Concord, New Hampshire*. Vol. 1. Concord, NH: Rumford Press, 1903.

Martinsen, Ellen, Nina Schoch and Mark Pokras. "Malaria and Other Blood Parasites of Common Loons from the Northeastern U.S." https://sites.tufts.edu.

McIntyre, Judith W. "The Common Loon Cries for Help." *National Geographic* 175, no. 4 (April 1989).

———. *The Common Loon, Spirit of Northern Lakes*. Minneapolis: University of Minnesota Press, 1988.

McIntyre, J.W., and D.C. Evers, eds. *Loons: Old History and New Findings. Proceedings of a Symposium from the 1977 Meeting, American Ornithologists Union*. Holderness, NH: North American Loon Fund, 2000.

Meyer, Elizabeth. "Notes from William Brewster: The Evolving Field of Zoology." *Biodiversity Heritage Library Blog*. https://blog.biodiversitylibrary.org.

Mishler, Craig. "Diving Down: Ritual Healing in the Tale of the Blind Man and the Loon." *Arctic Anthropology* 40, no. 2 (2003).

Mullens, W.H. "Robert Sibbald and His Prodromus." *British Birds* 6 (1912–13): 5. https://www.biodiversitylibrary.org.

New Hampshire Audubon Society. *Bulletin of the Audubon Society of New Hampshire* 10, no. 4 (1931).

———. "New Hampshire Bird Records, 1982–2020." https://nhbirdrecords.org.

Noon, Jack. *Rambles Through New Hampshire Early & Late*. East Sutton, NH: Moose Country Press, 2022.

———. *The Squam Lakes and Their Loons*. Meredith, NH: LPC, 1990.

Paruk, James D. *Loon Lessons: Uncommon Adventures with the Great Northern Diver*. Minneapolis: University of Minnesota Press, 2021.

Paruk, J.D., D.C. Evers, J.W. McIntyre, J.F. Barr, J. Mager and W.H. Piper. "Common Loon (*Gavia immer*)." Version 2.0. *Birds of the World*. Cornell Lab of Ornithology, Ithaca, NY, 2021. https://doi.org/10.2173/bow.comloo.02.

Pistorius, Alan. "Feathering the Loon's Nest." *Country Journal* (May 1979).

Potter, Claire. "Report Finds Contaminants in Loon Eggs." *Concord Monitor*, November 26, 2021.

Read, Benjamin. *The History of Swanzey, New Hampshire*. Salem, MA: Salem Press, 1892.

Rice, Arthur F. "Woodcraft." *Field and Stream Magazine* (August 1913).

Richards, Tudor. "New Hampshire Bird News." *Audubon Society of New Hampshire* 7 (October 1954).

———. "New Hampshire Bird News." *Audubon Society of New Hampshire* 8 (1955).

———. "New Hampshire Bird News." *Audubon Society of New Hampshire* 11 (1958).

———. "New Hampshire Bird News." *Audubon Society of New Hampshire* 14 (1960).

Ridgely, Beverly S., Robert Ridgely and Kenneth H. Klapper. *Birds of the Squam Lakes Region*. Holderness, NH: Squam Lakes Natural Science Center, 2022.

Ridgely, Robert. "The Common Loon on Squam Lake." *New Hampshire Audubon Quarterly* 28, no. 2 (1975).

Rock, Autumn. "Adirondack Loons Were Once Hunted." *Adirondack Almanac*, August 28, 2017. https://www.adirondackalmanack.com.

Samuels, Edward A. *Birds of New England*. Boston: Noyes, Holms, & Co., 1875.

Sidor, Inga F., Mark A. Pokras, Andrew R. Major, Robert H. Poppenga, Kate M. Taylor et al. "Mortality of Common Loons in New England, 1987–2000." *Journal of Wildlife Diseases* 39, no. 2 (2003).

Silver, Helenette. *A History of New Hampshire Game and Furbearers*. Concord: New Hampshire Fish and Game Department, 1957.

Stearns, Ezra S. *History of the Town of Rindge, New Hampshire*. Boston: George H. Ellis, 1875.

Thomas, Matthew. *History of Fremont, New Hampshire—Old Poplin*. Fremont, NH: Matthew Thomas, 1998.

Triolo, Rosalie. "Wintering with the Loons." *The Laker*. https://thelaker.com.

Wallace, Vera H. *New Hampshire Bird News* 6, no. 4 (October 1953).

Waters, Hannah. "Bird CSI: A Loon, a Swollen Spleen, and a Mysterious Disease." Audubon. https://www.audubon.org.

Wood, Harold B. "The History of Bird Banding." *Auk Magazine* (1945). https://sora.unm.edu.

Wood, William. *New England's Prospect*. London: Tho. Cotes, 1634. https://www.gutenberg.org.

ABOUT THE AUTHOR

Historian and author Glenn A. Knoblock has written over 20 books, 9 with Arcadia and The History Press, including *Hidden History of Lake Winnipesaukee*, *New Hampshire's Kancamagus Highway* and *Women of Granite*. He resides in Wolfeboro Falls, New Hampshire, where he tries to keep track of the local loons.